PRAISE FOR
HORSE BARBIE

"Like Geena Rocero herself, *Horse Barbie* is vivid, hilarious, exhilarating, and loving—both dazzlingly confident and thrillingly perceptive and honest. There's plenty of glitz and inspiration and triumph to be found within its pages, but Rocero never pulls away from the absurd, the embarrassing, the unglamorous, the sharply sad. Her journey toward womanhood, which begins in the alleyways of Manila and takes her to the billboards of Times Square, is a story of truth in transformation and performance and community that will captivate so many people, as it did me." —JIA TOLENTINO, author of *Trick Mirror*

"Powerfully introspective and wildly entertaining, *Horse Barbie* is a celebration of truth, transformation, and self-acceptance. I laughed, I cried, and I fell deeply in love with Rocero and her story."
—BOWEN YANG, actor and comedian

"Packed with grit, ferocity, and grace, Geena Rocero's story proves that embracing who you are—in all your complexity and in a world that often seems to think you're simply not allowed—is a truly revolutionary act. There's magic in these pages of the very best kind: the everyday magic kindled when courage meets love. Reading *Horse Barbie* feels like staying up way too late with your most interesting friend, drinking a little too much wine, and laughing (and crying) until the sun comes up."

—GABRIELLE UNION-WADE, actor, producer,
and author of *We're Going to Need More Wine*

"*Horse Barbie* is everything Geena Rocero is. It's a groundbreaking book befitting a groundbreaking icon in the Filipino community and beyond. In these chaotic, uncaring, incoherent times, this memoir shines as a beacon of courage and empathy. You can't not be inspired by Rocero's journey to self-acceptance and self-love, and the kindness of her family and friends along the way."

—JOSE ANTONIO VARGAS, Pulitzer Prize–winning journalist and author of *Dear America: Notes of an Undocumented Citizen*

"Geena Rocero's story is inherently American: an ambitious young immigrant works to make her dreams come true while compelling her new home to become a more accepting and humane place. I deeply admire her dedication to fostering safety and freedom for the transgender community. Rocero's enthralling, redemptive, and heartfelt journey forces me to see the world through newly bright and hopeful eyes."

—AMERICA FERRERA, Emmy-winning actor and producer, and author of *American Like Me*

"Geena Rocero's *Horse Barbie* is as electric as she is: a propulsive read, animated by the author's honesty, wit, and indomitable spirit of self-acceptance."

—RONAN FARROW, journalist and author of the Pulitzer Prize–winning *Catch and Kill*

"Witty, heartbreaking, and vivid, *Horse Barbie* is a must-read for anyone looking to know more about self-acceptance in the face of profound struggle, what it means to be trans, and Rocero's outstanding impact as a groundbreaking advocate, model, writer, and inspiring woman."

—SARAH KATE ELLIS, president and CEO of GLAAD

"Rocero's tender recollections . . . exemplify the creative loopholes that trans people always find to live our lives. We find them because we've always had to find them. . . . But persistently, Rocero nurtures sisterhood and solidarity to create not only safety but love and care. . . . *Horse Barbie* joins a constellation of recent stories told by queer people and especially trans women navigating the world with vigor and style."

—*Datebook*

"[Geena Rocero tells] the story of one woman's life with enough heart and candor to make it accessible to all . . . paying homage to the trans women in fashion who came before her, and more. . . . a moving chronicle of trans resilience and joy."
                                                                    —*Vogue*

"Groundbreaking . . . *Horse Barbie* [is] an exploration of some of the most universal themes of womanhood: belonging, confidence, and love. . . . *Horse Barbie*'s publication was a balm as a years-long wave of anti-LGBTQ legislation crested in 2023. More than 500 pieces of legislation have been introduced at the state level in the U.S., many targeting trans people and youth, specifically. There have been attacks on everything from health care access and drag performance to adults simply affirming queer and trans youth. Given the stakes, it's no wonder that Rocero's memoir has been received with such enthusiasm. She quite literally models what triumph can look like."
                                          —*Glamour* (Women of the Year)

"Geena Rocero's *Horse Barbie* has possibly one of the most iconic opening lines in the history of queer literature: 'I learned how to be trans in the Catholic church.' . . . Ultimately, *Horse Barbie* is as much about transness as it is about Filipino colorism, American xenophobia, the inner-workings of the pageant and modeling worlds, and the universal power of telling your story on your own terms. With vivid descriptions and vulnerable narration, it's an instant classic. (And for those who'd rather listen, the audiobook—narrated by Rocero herself—is a deliciously cinematic experience.)"
                —SARAH BURKE, *them*'s "Our Favorite LGBTQ+ Books of 2023"

"Geena Rocero is an absolutely delightful human being who has lived a fascinating life, which is enough to make any memoir worth reading. But she also tells her stories with love, humor, and insight, taking readers into her life from being a trans pageant queen in Manila during the '90s to immigrating to the U.S. in order to change her gender marker legally on documents, to coming out publicly as transgender during a TED Talk. While the memoir is filled with all the emotions, by far the biggest one I felt while reading it was joy—especially with the audiobook narrated by Rocero."
                —JAMIE CANAVES, *Book Riot*'s "Best Books of 2023"

"Rocero forged a path for herself where one hadn't previously existed and in *Horse Barbie* gives us such a warm and relatable story of strength and spirit."
—*Elle*

"Candid . . . Ms. Rocero [is] no longer hiding. Her memoir does not shy away from topics like colorism, gender disclosure, sex work and the nuts and bolts of medical transition."
—*The New York Times*

"Rocero realizes that to come into her power, she has to live her truth—this memoir is such a beautiful testimony of her journey and the history she's made."
—*USA Today*

"[Rocero's] voice rings warm with a hard-won edge. . . . This book is another milestone for Rocero, and a must-read for all."
—*Esquire*

"Rocero writes with openness and humor."
—*Vanity Fair*

"Interspersed with vivid, captivating, and often hilarious behind-the-scenes stories about the pursuit of fame—on music-video sets, gaining entry into exclusive clubs and parties—*Horse Barbie* recounts Rocero's painful decision to hide her trans identity as she pursued a modeling career in New York, and her empowering journey toward reclaiming her true self."
—*Vulture*

"[Rocero's] story is a reminder of the importance of living authentically and being true to oneself, despite the obstacles that may arise. Her memoir is sure to inspire readers to embrace their unique identities and stand up for what they believe in, no matter the cost."
—*Galore*

"Rocero's life story is a completely engrossing whirlwind. Readers don't need to have previous knowledge of the colonialist history of the Philippines, gender-affirming care for transgender people or the modeling industry to enjoy *Horse Barbie*. She explains everything in accessible language, imparted like a trusted friend. . . . *Horse Barbie* is an emotionally engaging read. Rocero's pride in her success as both a fashion model and a highly visible trans woman of color is hard won, and having the chance to read about it feels like a privilege."
—*BookPage* (starred review)

"Vivid, swift prose about a thrilling, brave life."   —*Bustle*

"An achievement, expertly crafted, well written, at once highly specific and easily translatable . . . Belongs to that rich tradition of American immigrant stories, stories that remind us what determination, self-actualization, and a dream can drive us to accomplish."
                                                        —*Provincetown Magazine*

"How transgender culture in the Philippines shaped one model's life . . . In *Horse Barbie*, Geena Rocero explores her journey from trans beauty pageant queen to closeted American model to outspoken activist."
                                                        —*The Washington Post*

"Humorous, zesty . . . a jaunty and inspiring memoir of an eventful life with many acts left to unfold."   —*Kirkus Reviews*

"Intimate and vulnerable . . . it is also overflowing with trans joy, which makes it a pleasure to read."   —*Book Riot*

"Poignant and powerful . . . Her narration is full of life—sometimes buoyantly joyous, sometimes breathless with tension, sometimes playful and tinged with laughter. . . . outstanding."
                                                        —*AudioFile*

HORSE
BARBIE

HORSE BARBIE

A MEMOIR OF RECLAMATION

GEENA ROCERO

THE DIAL PRESS

New York

2024 Dial Press Trade Paperback Edition

Copyright © 2023 by Geena Rocero

Book club guide copyright © 2024 by Penguin Random House LLC

Published in the United States by The Dial Press, an imprint of Random House, a division of Penguin Random House LLC, New York.

THE DIAL PRESS is a registered trademark and the colophon is a trademark of Penguin Random House LLC.

RANDOM HOUSE BOOK CLUB and colophon are trademarks of Penguin Random House LLC.

Originally published in hardcover in the United States by The Dial Press, an imprint of Random House, a division of Penguin Random House LLC, in 2023.

Grateful acknowledgment to *Harper's Bazaar* for permission to reprint the interview with Geena Rocero in the book club guide.

Library of Congress Cataloging-in-Publication Data
Names: Rocero, Geena, author.
Title: Horse Barbie: a memoir / Geena Rocero.
Description: New York: The Dial Press, [2023]
Identifiers: LCCN 2023001802 (print) | LCCN 2023001803 (ebook) | ISBN 9780593445907 (paperback) | ISBN 9780593445891 (ebook)
Subjects: LCSH: Rocero, Geena | Beauty contestants—Biography. | Transgender women—Biography. | Beauty contests—Philippines. | Beauty contests—United States.
Classification: LCC HQ77.8.R65 A3 2023 (print) | LCC HQ77.8.R65 (ebook) | DDC 306.76/8092 [B]—dc23/eng/20230117
LC record available at https://lccn.loc.gov/2023001802
LC ebook record available at https://lccn.loc.gov/2023001803

Printed in the United States of America on acid-free paper

randomhousebooks.com
randomhousebookclub.com

1st Printing

To my Nature Boy, my love
To Mama, for her unwavering support and love
To Papa, I'll always be your Bojojoy
To Tigerlily, for showing me the magic onstage

They were significant not only because they crossed male and female gender lines. To the Spanish, they were astonishing, even threatening, as they were respected leaders and figures of authority. To their native communities they were *babaylan* or *catalonan:* religious functionaries and shamans, intermediaries between the visible and invisible worlds to whom even the local ruler (*datu*) deferred. They placated angry spirits, foretold the future, healed infirmities, and even reconciled warring couples and tribes.

—J. Neil C. Garcia, "Male Homosexuality
in the Philippines: A Short History,"
*International Institute for
Asian Studies,* 2004

CONTENTS

NOW WHO IS SHE?

I had just turned twenty-one when I got the call that I had been cast in a John Legend music video. It was 2005, almost a decade before *Time* magazine announced the "Transgender Tipping Point," and no one—not John, not even my agent—knew my history. They couldn't know. The modeling world was no place for an out trans woman. Not yet anyway. But I said yes, knowing I would have to hide—again.

Back in the Philippines, where I was born and raised, it would have been impossible for me to keep a low profile. On the other side of the Pacific, I was a celebrity—the most famous transgender beauty queen in a country of over 75 million people. I started performing when I was fifteen, frequently competing on nationally televised pageants, earning the top prize again and again.

Just five years before I got the call from John Legend's team—and only months before I moved to the United States—I had won the Miss Gay Universe crown, a prestigious prize in the Philippines trans pageant scene.

In New York, I kept my pageant past a secret from everyone I worked with. I wanted to be successful without getting outed, which felt like driving right up to the edge of a cliff before slamming on the brakes. In 2005 I was rising through the modeling ranks, but no one had dug into my past yet, and I wanted to keep it that way. I might have been out and proud in Asia, but here in America, I had to be in the closet.

You might think it would have been the other way around. The Philippines has a reputation for being a conservative Catholic country—and it is. We have centuries of Spanish rule to thank for that. But as journalist Carmen Guerrero Nakpil famously said, the Philippines spent "300 years in the convent and 50 years in Hollywood." We embrace spectacle and theatricality with open arms. When I was growing up, Catholicism and trans beauty pageants inspired equal fanaticism. Families would go straight from mass to watching the Super Sireyna trans pageants on TV back at home. No one really saw this as a paradox; it was just part of our unique cultural blend.

If social media had been big back in 2005, I would have been screwed. Someone from the Philippines could have posted a clip of me to YouTube or shared a pageant photo on Instagram, and then everyone would have found out who I was. But in the time before Facebook or Twitter, I could live a dual existence, famous overseas and a nobody in New York.

Well, not exactly a nobody. My profile was rising. I was on the cover of magazines, appearing widely in lingerie and fashion advertising. A commercial I had shot the year before for Emerson Radio that was playing in Times Square, and an ad I'd appeared in for Rimmel a few months earlier, as risky as they were, were both lifelong fantasies come true.

When I was dominating pageants in the Philippines, my mentor once showed me newspaper clippings of an international model named Caroline Cossey, better known as Tula, who had appeared in prestigious magazines like *Harper's Bazaar* and been photographed for *Playboy*. Tula was transgender, but no one knew it—not at first anyway. She managed to keep her secret all throughout the 1970s. Her story was a legend in our community, passed down from generation to generation.

It was my dream to be like her one day. I wanted to be on billboards and in magazines. Tula's face on that crinkled newspaper was proof that I could do it. Maybe I wanted to show that being trans couldn't hold me back. Maybe I was vain—what aspiring model isn't? But I think more than anything, I wanted to be seen.

Years later, with my face showing up in newsstands and fashion publications, I was more visible than ever. My successes should've made me happy. But the bigger my modeling job, the more crushing my anxiety became. Every camera lens felt as threatening as a loaded revolver. I was betting my livelihood on a roulette spin every time I accepted a high-profile assignment.

But a music video? And not just any video, but a music video for John Legend's "Number One," a hit song on a debut album that was getting Grammy buzz? That could get me *real* exposure, catapulting my career at a critical moment. As much as I was terrified of being found out, I couldn't resist vying for that next level of prestige. I had already reached the pinnacle in one country—why not try for two? Breaking through in the United States would be hugely validating, not just of my looks but of everything I had sacrificed to get to this point: I had left my celebrity standing in the Philippines and my family and friends in California all to make it as a model in New York.

As I prepared for the shoot, I thought about all the women who had made names for themselves by starring in sexy music videos. I mean, *everyone* remembers the iconic trio of Naomi Campbell, Christy Turlington, and Linda Evangelista in George Michael's video for "Freedom." Helena Christensen's role in the sensual black-and-white video for Chris Isaak's "Wicked Game" sent her career into the stratosphere.

I wanted to follow in these women's footsteps. They had cemented their place in pop culture by appearing as themselves. And yet I couldn't be seen. Not fully. Not for who I am.

In 1981 Tula was publicly outed in a British tabloid under the headline JAMES BOND GIRL WAS A BOY. The ensuing uproar—outrage, disgust, contempt—drove her to the brink of suicide. I should have seen Tula's story as a warning. Instead, with all the boldness of youth, I think I took it as a challenge, I wanted to go even further than she had, then—though my vision for this was blurry at best—come out on my own terms.

But of course, the media of 2005 was no kinder to trans women than the media of 1981. If I valued my career, my safety, and my family's privacy, I had to avoid Tula's fate.

Ironically, I ended up dancing behind a curtain in the John Legend video. My body was on full display, but I was a silhouette. A shadow in lingerie. During takes, my moves were slow and deliberate. I tried to dance as sensually as I could, but each hair flip lengthened my neck, threatening to expose my Adam's apple. What if the director zoomed in on it? Adrenaline surged through my body. My breathing sped up. It didn't help that the smoke-filled set was frigid, despite the space heaters around us.

Between takes, a production assistant would rush over with a warm coat, but in truth, I was shaking because I was nervous. Still, I used the temperature as an excuse when the director asked how I was doing. He was friendly and chatty, but my survival instinct kicked in: Instantly, I feminized myself, doing my trans version of what Mystique does in the X-Men movies, restructuring my whole being in a split second.

"Hey, Davy, how's it going?" I said, shifting my voice into a high femme register. "What's our next shot?"

I didn't want to end up like the trans models before me who had been outed and lost everything. Once the public found out, their careers vanished. They were dehumanized in the tabloids, their reputations thrown in the trash just as quickly as yesterday's paper.

In a literal flash, I could be reduced from a sexy woman in lingerie to a headline: NEW YORK FASHION MODEL REALLY A MAN. Everything I'd achieved would be gone—*poof*—whisked away into the ether.

That nightmare scenario played out in my mind anytime I talked to people during jobs. Maybe some of them would have been allies, but I couldn't trust anyone. Fashion and modeling might seem like creative and open-minded fields, but at its core, the industry wanted to propel only what it believed was trendy, cool, and beautiful, which usually meant white people and *always* meant cisgender people.

In 2005 a transgender Filipina immigrant was the last person the industry would want to put front and center. The decision makers could make my rags-to-riches dream a reality with a snap of their fingers, but they could take it away just as fast.

After a few more takes on the John Legend video, the on-set stylist pulled me aside—"Geena, can you come with me, please?"—and led me toward an RV parked outside on the cobblestone streets of the Meatpacking District. The huge production lights made me feel like I was walking into an interrogation.

Do they know? Did the camera catch something? My mind was full of negative fantasy, always expecting the reckoning to come at any moment.

But when we got into the trailer, the stylist just wanted me to try on different-color lingerie. I could breathe again. The adrenaline left my body all at once, draining me. *Oof.*

I wanted to go home. We had started shooting at nine P.M., and it was already three A.M. But if I wanted my big break, I had to return to the lion's den.

I convinced myself that if I was always careful, if I remained hypervigilant, I wouldn't get clocked on the job. *I can do this,* I told myself as I pulled on the new lingerie, trying to be my own best friend, hyping myself up. But I felt so alone.

Back on set, I flicked my hands delicately, swaying my hips as I danced to the sensual R&B beat. The backlit shot made me look even more mysterious. And I was a mystery—to myself as much as to anyone else. I wanted to be seen for who I was, but that was not an option. And because I couldn't let anyone else truly know me, I barely knew who I was anymore.

Sometimes I second-guessed my modeling dreams. Still, I found affirmation in the fullness of my feminine expression, where I felt my power. So many voices in society had told me to act a certain way, dress a certain way, think a certain way, *be* a certain way. Modeling was my way of trying to define my own womanhood—to free myself from those cages. The work was sometimes rote; posing for department store catalogs did little for my soul. But when I did shoots that felt more personal, that allowed me to say something with my body that could be captured for eternity, there was no substitute for the high I felt.

I might have been thousands of miles from the little alley in Manila where I grew up, but inside I was still that little femme boy who dreamed that one day she could express her girlhood. I had chosen to hide in plain sight. I was paranoid, like a spy behind enemy lines, constantly on high alert. But amid that pain, there were still flashes of freedom.

By the time I got home from the music video shoot, it was seven A.M. I crawled into bed, exhausted—a bone-deep fatigue that had nothing to do with the all-night shoot and everything to do with the stress I'd been living with for years, with no end in sight.

Before I fell asleep, I imagined the celebratory phone calls I would get when the video premiered. And I knew that every single time my phone rang, I wouldn't be smiling at the thought of a proud friend on the other end of the line. Instead, I would be bracing myself for my agent's voice, indignant, bordering on irate: *"Geena . . . are you really a boy?"*

Now, when I watch that music video on YouTube, where it has over six million views, it looks like the R&B gods were playing a trick on me. For the money shot, at the fifty-five-second mark, I part the curtain I've been dancing behind and gesture for John to get closer. *Come hither,* my whole body is saying. I had never felt more naked, physically and spiritually, than I did in that moment.

As the camera pans up to my face, bathed in sensual golden light, John sings, "Now who is she? What's her name? You don't need to know about everything."

For a long time, that's what I believed, too. Until that belief no longer felt true enough to live by.

Who am I? What's my name?

It's a long story. But I'm finally ready to tell it all.

PART I

MAKATI

1

SUN KID

I LEARNED HOW TO BE TRANS IN THE CATHOLIC CHURCH.

When I was ten years old, before I ever entered pageants, I was in the children's choir at Our Lady of Guadalupe Parish Church in Makati. As we stood on a three-tier set of wooden choral risers, crammed up against the wall, our voices reverberated, bouncing off the marble floors, reaching every crevice of the gently arched ceiling sixty feet over our heads, filling the space with sound.

Still, when I knelt with my eyes shut to make the sign of the cross, I could hear the motorized tricycles whizzing by outside, and the distinct sizzle of ripe *saba* bananas, coated in brown sugar, deep-frying at vendor stands, their caramelized aroma wafting in through the open door.

The lives of everyone in our neighborhood revolved around the church. Good kids participated in the services. Trustworthy kids got to collect donations, holding out red-velvet baskets as they walked among the pews. The altar boys displayed an almost otherworldly level of devotion; they didn't walk, they *floated* alongside the priest, their floor-length white dresses brushing against the floor, steady little hands clutching bronze communion cups and tapered candles.

The position I aimed for in that hierarchy of holiness was the choir. People who sang in church were special, and I wanted to be special. At first the choir director tried to keep me out because he didn't think my voice was good enough. But most of my friends were in choir, so I showed up to practice anyway, week after week. Eventually, the director felt bad for me, and so I earned my spot on the risers.

Well, on the *bottom corner* of the risers. Everyone's got to start somewhere, right?

One Sunday, the director picked me to "hand interpret" the opening song mere minutes before the four P.M. mass was scheduled to start.

Traditionally, a child would stand in front of the altar, gesturing in sync with the lyrics, interpreting them to add another layer of pageantry to the proceedings, performing for hundreds of churchgoers as they filed to their seats. Usually children from rosary study group were selected for this honor, most often girls, very rarely boys.

I wanted to make the most of my big moment. As I slowly walked toward the front of the altar, I looked out at the incoming *titas*, the kids held tight by their mamas, and at all the *lolos* and *lolas* minding their own pace but still laser-focused on securing their seats. They played it cool, but God help anyone who tried to take their pew.

As I took my place on the second marble step in the center aisle, I felt each sensation acutely: The crispness of my pale pink short-sleeve shirt, freshly ironed, brushing against my skin. The scratchy fabric of my high-waisted navy cotton pants, reminding me to stand up straight. As I looked out over the congregation, their faces shrouded by the *abaniko* hand fans they were waving to keep cool, I felt dizzy. They looked like they were animated in stop-motion, my anxiety blurring their faces together.

But as I heard the first notes of the opening song and began to interpret them, I started to feel more at home. The gentle movements were familiar. At home, I liked to mimic the powerfully feminine hand gestures my mother made whenever she conducted the national anthem at my school, where she worked as a teacher. Now I was imitating her in front of an entire congregation. As I swept my hands in front of me, I sang, "*Santo, Santo, Santo, Diyos makapangyarihan. Puspos ng luwalhati Ang langit at lupa.*"

The choir behind me swelled at the Hosanna chorus, "*Osana, Osana. Sa kaitaasan.*"

As we sang those three words, I spread my arms, mirroring the body of Christ on the crucifix behind me. I felt like His power was flowing through me.

But the way I flicked my fingers, slowly unfurling each of them in turn as I stretched my arms out to their full extension—the gentleness of that gesture was all me. My motions were soft but regal, almost grandiose and yet filled with the innocence of a child honoring the Lord. My hands met in prayer. The choir sang again, "*Osana, Osana.*"

As they repeated their supplication, the words seemed to me, for the first time, to mean something else, too, their reverence for Christ expanding to an affirmation of my own budding identity: *I am a child, I am Catholic, and I am femme.*

Walking out of Our Lady of Guadalupe that day, my friends and I inhaled the sweet, tropical jasmine scent wafting from the fresh sampaguita and ylang-ylang flower vendors right outside. The vendors sold necklaces made from the blossoms, dipping them in colorful buckets of water so that they would still be fresh when we offered them to our statues at home. Holding hands together in a row, the other kids and I spanned the width of the street, following the smell of delicious, freshly baked *pan de coco* with creamy shredded coconut filling.

The church might have been my sanctuary, the place where I strived to be holy and pure. But these Makati streets were home.

I was born and raised in an *eskinita*, a six-foot-wide alleyway connecting two parallel thoroughfares. To the north was Dapitan Street, named after the remote missionary town on Mindanao Island where Filipino national hero José Rizal was exiled for four years, from 1892 to 1896.

While imprisoned on Dapitan for publishing books criticizing our Spanish colonizers, Rizal wrote poetry. In my own Dapitan, I learned how to *kembot*, a feminine way of walking in which you sway your hips while you move. I was fantastic at it—but practicing it put a mark on my back.

"Oh, that boy who *kembot*," people would taunt me as I walked down the street, my hips swinging side to side.

To the south was Kalayaan Avenue, which means "freedom." On Kalayaan, you could catch a jeepney to buy groceries in the *palengke* near the EDSA, a congested highway that was also the site of our revolution in 1986, which toppled the brutal dictatorship of President Ferdinand Marcos.

And there, sandwiched between Dapitan and Kalayaan, between heroism and freedom, was my little *eskinita*. "The shortcut," my neighbors called it, because unless you lived there, you spent less than a minute walking through it, eyes pointed straight ahead. But for me and the other kids, it was an entire universe. We filled our days playing Chinese garter and a Filipino version of tag—Langit, Lupa, Impyerno, or Heaven, Earth, Hell. Even our games were Catholic. I was known as the one who always played outside: *batang araw*, the "sun kid"—a reference to my dark, tanned skin from all the time I spent playing outside.

The fun didn't stop when it rained. Showers at my house meant dipping a *tabo* into a *timba* and rinsing off one pour at a time. So during the frequent storms between May and October, the neighbor kids and I loved to run under the gushing outflow from a leaky gutter in the alleyway and pretend like we were in a luxurious waterfall shower at a five-star hotel. For a moment, our *eskinita* could have been the Ritz-Carlton. We'd all line up to wait our turn for a shower. But nobody wanted to stand under the water too early, because it would still have dried-up cat shit in it. I learned *that* lesson the hard way.

Picture the sublevel house in the movie *Parasite*, a step down from street level with a cement floor; that was my home. When I walked in through the bright blue front door, my feet would often splash into a puddle before I'd catch a big whiff of diluted Clorox oozing from the linoleum, soon to be overtaken by the aroma of garlic fried rice cooking on the stove.

It was usually Papa making food, pushing back his tousled shaggy black hair as he minded the stove. He had a dark brown complexion and a commanding stare, bordering on cocky, that always made it seem like he knew something you didn't.

Papa was a complicated man. During the day, while Mama worked, he took care of us with the utmost tenderness, cleaning the house and handwashing our clothes. There was a rhythm to his homemaking. The sound of soapy bubbles escaping the friction between fabric and fist was our soothing afternoon soundtrack. But once night fell, he would drink rum—sometimes alone, sometimes with his buddies—and become a towering, rageful presence. His shouting rang out into the night; we tried our best to sleep through it.

What seemed contradictory, like Jekyll turning into Hyde, was the predictable result of wounded masculinity. Even at a young age, I could tell his ego was bruised a little more with every reminder he wasn't the breadwinner, every time he had to ask Mama for money to buy groceries.

At five P.M. most days, he and I would take a father-and-femme-son trip to our famous *palengke,* the Guadalupe Public Market. He held my tiny hand a little tighter as we walked between the wet stalls; I hated when the smell of seafood got in my flip-flops. When I met the gaze of stacked-up fish and squid glistening in my eyeline, I'd squeal my little femme squeal and turn the other way. By seven we were back home, and the smell of Papa's pork *paksiw* or savory beef *kare-kare* would be wafting out the window, filling our alley with the scent of home-cooked deliciousness. When he made coconut fish *tambakol*—a special treat—he always set aside the head for our hard-working mama because it was her favorite. She loved to suck on the eyeballs.

In all, there were six of us—my mother, my father, my two sisters, my brother, and me—living in what was effectively a nine-by-twelve-foot room separated from our neighbors by a flimsy plywood wall. Whenever it rained too hard, the house would flood, and we would have to use wooden dining chairs to elevate our beds. We also had to keep a watchful eye for the crafty jumping rats who liked to steal pieces of our marinated pork *tocino* or slices of Spam that had been left on the table, ferrying them back to places unknown as they squeaked with the delight of their pillage.

My *ate* or sister, Rhomalyn, two years older than me, wasn't afraid to shoo the rats away. She was a brave little tomboy who preferred toy trucks to dolls. Kuya Mhel, my brother and the oldest sibling, would join in with low grunts, using his deepening voice to send the rats scurrying. Glenda, my other *ate,* and I would squeal in terror as we climbed into the very middle of the bed, as far away from those nasty rodents as we could possibly get.

It was cramped, but we were lucky that we had a small family, relatively speaking. Our next-door neighbors had ten kids in a space the same size. They played human Tetris just to move around.

In such close quarters, life happened in every direction simultaneously. Mama's younger sister Tita Bebe lived in the apartment over ours, and we could hear her family's footsteps at all hours. Sometimes while lying in our lofted beds, waiting for the floodwater to subside, my siblings and I played a game: "Who's walking above us now?"

There was a sense of community in our alley. We could show up at a neighbor's house and take a cup of rice if we needed some for dinner, knowing that they'd come knocking a week later, ready for the favor to be returned.

On the street in the summertime, I sold *kalamay*, a sticky-sweet delicacy made from coconut milk, brown sugar, and ground glutinous rice. I would walk for miles carrying double-stacked twelve-by-fifteen-inch wooden trays, chanting *"Kalamay, kalamay!"* as I passed through the neighborhoods, letting my regular buyers know that I'd arrived.

I could sell a lot of *kalamay* at the small private pool nearby, but there was a fifty-cent charge to get in, so I collected and sold metal scraps with my friends to afford the entry fee. Conveniently, the pool was near the junkyard and right around the corner from our local parish church. I was always outside, always moving.

But there were parts of our neighborhood that I avoided. Places where the moment I called out *"Kalamay!"* a voice out of nowhere would boom *"Kinakamay ng Patay!"*

Oh, I knew I was in trouble then. Translated, it meant "The dead will be eating your *kalamay*." Suddenly rocks would be sailing toward me, thudding against the sidewalk as I dodged them.

"Bakla, bakla!" the kids would shout as they hurled more rocks, shaming me for my feminine sway.

My fingers would instinctively wrap tight around my *kalamay* trays as I shifted their weight from shoulder to hip, and I would run away as fast as I could—but still in my *kembot* sway.

. . .

At school, I was shielded from the bullies because of Mama. A be-
loved teacher at Guadalupe Elementary School for over twenty-three
years, she was known as "Ma'am Rocero." Everyone liked her. Even
better, they respected her. During our morning flag ceremony, she
would stand in front of the whole school and conduct the national
anthem.

"*Bayang magiliw perlas ng silanganan, alab ng puso sa dibdib mo'y
buhay,*" we'd sing, mesmerized by the distinctive way she waved the
¼ time signature with both hands, as if she were pulling invisible cotton candy out of thin air.

Behind her, our flag would be hoisted up the pole, the golden sun
emblem rising into the morning sky, but my eyes would always stay
fixed on Mama. Her hands looked so feminine and elegant as they
glided through the air, just like mine when I did the hand interpretation at church. Her favorite forest-green pencil-cut skirt and matching shoulder-padded suit jacket were the pinnacle of understated
elegance. I wanted to be just like her—a gorgeous femme no one
could take their eyes from, her body moving with a graceful quality
that felt close to magic.

Her reputation acted like a force field around me. After class, I
liked to hang out with my friends at the playground outside the
school gate. We'd snack on green mango with shrimp paste or *saba*
bananas with caramelized sugar in ice, taking turns on the swing between bites. We'd giggle on the seesaw and chase one another around
playing endless games of tag.

One afternoon when I was taking my turn on the swing, pumping
my legs until I was flying as high as I could get, I heard a kid complaining below me.

"*Bumaba ka na, ako na,*" he grunted, interrupting my euphoria at
its apex.

I ignored him at first. Everyone had to wait their turn, after all.
But then he grabbed one of the metal chains connected to the seat,

stopping me suddenly, and I tumbled onto the ground. Miraculously, I managed to keep hold of the seat. I looked up at him and saw the anger in his face, as if he were no longer a child but a demon determined to hurt me.

"Di ba sabi ko sayo ako na!" he yelled—his final warning for me to give up the swing.

Still, I didn't budge. We tugged on the wooden seat until finally he yanked it away from me. But instead of sitting down in it, he pulled it backward, getting ready to push it toward me, clearly gunning for my face. And then, with all the drama of God stopping Abraham from sacrificing Isaac, my friend cried out, telling him whose child I was.

"Anak sya ni Ma'am Rocero!!!"

His face transformed into a mask of surprise and something else—reverence—and he dropped the seat as if it had burned him. I was spared.

But Ma'am Rocero's influence could only extend so far. Most days, I left for school later than Mama because she had to be there early. Sometimes Ate Rhomalyn and I would walk together. But some days I had to walk alone. In total, it was thirty minutes of zigzagging between alleyways, chicken *sopas* breakfast stalls, and bakeries making fresh *pandesal,* always watching where my feet landed because there was dog shit everywhere. In the Philippines, they say that it's actually good luck if you step in it, but it never felt lucky when I had to go back home to hose down my rubber shoes and arrive to class late.

Besides dodging dog shit, I was also trying to avoid men on the street. Whenever I heard a motorized tricycle driver get close, I tensed up. The *kembot* sway of my hips made me a constant target. The revving got louder, and I would pray, *Lord, please, don't let it happen today.*

But then I'd hear the shouts, as predictable as they were degrading:*"Baaakla! Baaakla!"*

A grown man hurling slurs at a child in an elementary school uniform—you'd think he'd be ashamed of himself. But whenever I made the mistake of looking back at a driver who yelled at me, he'd grin widely, as if it were his big accomplishment for the day, and then he would whisk straight by, wind blowing through his hair, not a care in the world. That sight would send a chill down my spine.

I prayed it would never happen when I was around my family. I'd feel too ashamed of myself—and for them—if they heard what people called me.

On the days Mama walked me to school, I'd grab her hand tight and walk even closer when I heard a tricycle coming close. She'd look down at me and ask, *"OK ka lang, anak?"* Her tone was assuring and affirming. She held my hand even tighter. But she didn't know I was afraid of the drivers. I was pretending that I only wanted to be next to her—that I was squeezing her hand only because I wanted more of her attention.

As scary as it was to get yelled at by men on the street, it was the bullying from the other children that hurt me the most.

Even at that young age, I could tell there was a gentleness in my soul that somehow put a target on my back. Like a bull charging at a red cape, the other kids couldn't resist chasing me down. But then their anger would subside, the emotion passing through them with childlike speed.

Soon enough, we would start up another innocent round of tag, running around, squealing with joy. I learned early how to tamp down my hurt. How to not let anyone else around me see the pain I was feeling inside. Risking mistreatment was better than being left out.

There were times when I thought I could end that cycle of teasing and forgetting. The neighborhood boys who bullied me liked to play TEKS, a street game in which players tossed small cards up in the air with a finger flick and bet on which side would come out on top. I thought if I got good at it, they would respect me; instead I got *too* good at it, winning stacks and stacks of TEKS that I stored in shoeboxes. Turned out, the boys didn't like being beaten at their own game, and their taunting only got worse.

Whenever the mistreatment grew too much for me, I ran back home to rinse off my sweat and wash away their judgment. One day as I got ready to take one of these sad shame-filled showers, I walked over to our vintage *apparador* with its dark-finished wood. I stared in the middle of the mirror, the painted white jasmine pattern around the border crowning my face as if it knew I, too, yearned to bloom one day.

But only a sad child looked back at me. Why was my femininity such a threat? It felt so innocent for me to express it, yet it seemed to enrage the other kids, puncturing our childhoods with violence and fear.

But I saw something else in my reflection, too. The face of someone who could save me.

Standing there in front of the mirror, I started to take off my T-shirt, which had a print of one of the animated robots from the show *Voltes V,* so I could step into the shower. But right before I was about to slip out of it, while the collar was still around the top of my head, I paused and looked at my bare face. There was a presence in it. It was speaking to me out of nothingness. The oversize shirt had flattened the top of my hair, the fabric draping behind me like a veil all the way to the floor below. As I swayed gently from side to side, my shirt moved like actual real long hair would, brushing against my shoulders in a powerful moment of recognition.

"It *is* my long hair," I whispered to myself. "I'm a girl."

2

ASSUNTA DE ROSSI

MAMA'S LOVE WAS AS STEADY AS THE SUNSHINE, AND I WAS HER shadow. To me, she was the kind of woman I wanted to become—one who understood that femininity and boldness belonged together. She always called me her *maswerteng bata,* "lucky kid," but the truth was that Mama made her own luck.

To make ends meet, she had multiple side hustles on top of her teaching job, working twice as hard because Papa wasn't working at all by the time I was in the fifth grade. I would tag along with her as she sold Kikkoman soy sauce she had gotten from her contacts at the Manila Harbor Port to the Japanese restaurants on Makati Avenue. She'd go in and negotiate with the manager while I waited in a double-parked taxi, gallons of soy sauce weighing down the trunk. Even when she didn't close the deal, she'd give them a sample bottle anyway.

"Maybe not tonight, but after they use that sample bottle, they'll want more," she'd tell me, always hopeful.

My femininity was obvious to her, and her approval, though tacit at first, made my family life so much more accepting than it might otherwise have been.

When we had parties at Tita Bebe's house, I would cinch and tuck my T-shirt to make it look like a bra, and tie a yellow sarong around my waist, completing my transformation from ten-year-old femme into full-on island goddess. Then Mama would watch me with a blissful look on her face as I performed hula dances for the whole family, balancing on the elevated garden ledge, gently swaying my hips, and letting my body follow my hand gestures from side to side.

I vividly remember watching Mama's face as I danced to the classic Hawaiian song "Pearly Shells," my family singing in unison: "My heart tells me that I love you."

She smiled up at me, humming along to the music, absolutely radiant. Entranced by the song, buoyed by my mother's gaze, I felt totally loved for who I was.

My siblings more or less accepted my budding transness, too. Ate Rhomalyn would let me steal her Barbie collection. Those blond, brunette, and redheaded dolls were my early glimpse into a fantasy world. I would go to our neighbor's tailor shop and collect scraps of throwaway fabric to craft outfits for them. By the time I was done tying, wrapping, and pinning up their fashionable attire, they looked like Miss Universe candidates. And that's exactly how I treated them, guiding their legs as though they were strutting across a stage, and imagining a crowd applauding in the background. In truth, I was imagining myself on that stage. I wanted to be one of my Barbies. But then I'd remember they weren't *my* Barbies; they were Rhomalyn's. And I could only use them as long as I let her borrow my fire trucks. We had an unspoken understanding, both defying early gender norms in a way that only brought us closer. I looked up to her, and she let me be. She let me dream.

Kuya Mhel was confused by the duality he saw in me. On one hand, I was his baby brother who he'd take to SM Megamall to buy Nintendo games. He was the first to show me how to get one hundred lives in *Super Mario Brothers* World 3-1 by stomping on the turtle next to the flight of steps at the end of the level. Basically invincible, we'd play into the wee hours of the night.

On the other hand, Mhel would knuckle me on the head every time he saw me try on my sister's dress. *"Huy mahiya ka nga, lalaki ka,"* he'd say self-righteously, telling me to "man up."

Ate Glenda was too busy playing peacekeeper to care how I dressed. The most level-headed of all of us, she was tasked with making sure Ate Rhomalyn and I took our afternoon naps during the hottest part of the day.

For his part, Papa knew I was femme—a loud *bakla* at school, and a sharp contrast to the way he carried himself. He had never said a word about my flamboyant ways, so I could only guess how he felt about it. Optimistically, I chose to take his silence for approval, hoping he was cool with me.

But my family's love could not protect me from the policing and taunting I came to expect in the world outside our home. Still, when Mama was around, I was her good luck charm, and she was my protector.

But I lost that protection when Mama left for America in October 1995, just before I turned twelve. Her uncle had been granted citizenship through service in the U.S. Army in the 1960s, which gave him benefits to petition on behalf of family members who wanted to emigrate. My grandma, grandpa, and aunties had followed him to California in the 1980s, and Mama longed to be with her family. I could tell she wanted to be away from Papa's unpredictability and nightly rages, too. Going to the States would be a way for her to end the marriage without really ending it.

Papa had been Mama's first boyfriend. She had been so smitten with him and his soft, handsome eyes that she agreed to elope right before she finished her coursework at the National Teachers College, bypassing any roadblocks that her religious parents might have placed in their path. They wanted her to finish her studies and find steady employment before she got married, but love had other plans.

What a difference it was, years down the line, that Mama's three jobs were not enough to sustain our family. Money became the root cause of so much late-night screaming. Papa's drinking only fueled their fighting.

When Papa didn't show up for dinner, for example, we knew where to find him. Mama would grab Ate Rhomalyn and me, taking us in a jeepney to our *palengke*. The Guadalupe market had a Mercury Drugs pharmacy, movie theaters, street food vendors, and a Jollibee all lumped together in a row, but Papa was always at the strip club. Holding our hands, Mama would stand in front of the blinking purple sign, which had the word HONEY printed on it above a bikini-clad woman in silhouette.

Every time a patron came out of the tufted swinging gold-and-black-leather doors, we'd get a peek of seminude women slowly spinning around stripper poles to the delight of ogling customers. Mama ignored them; she was too busy scanning for Papa. When she spotted his face, she'd tell us to stay put, then rush inside with fire and brimstone in her steps. A few minutes later she'd reemerge with Papa in tow, followed by a cloud of cigarette smoke and the odor of alcohol. Back on the street, Mama would give him a menacing stare, thrusting her index finger mere inches away from his eyes. He would act scared of her—but the fear he caused was worse.

Papa could be angry, sometimes violent, his tempestuous moods hanging over our home like storm clouds. One night when I was eight years old, I woke up at two o'clock to the sound of his yelling, *"Putang Ina mo Elsie!"* By this time, Tita Bebe on the floor above us had moved away, and we had moved up a story. Still half-asleep, my vision blurry, I rubbed my eyes and saw Papa holding a big machete knife, running toward Mama. Before my brain even knew what my limbs were doing, I was scurrying to the other side of our house and huddling in the corner. Kuya Mhel tried in vain to deescalate the situation, squeezing himself into a doorframe between my parents, midchase.

"*Papa tama na poh!*" was his guttural plea.

But despite his son begging and crying for all of it to stop, my drunken papa pushed right past Mhel, determined to get to Mama.

"*Tumigil ka dyan!*" he roared. You better stop that.

My sister Glenda must have grabbed me and Rhomalyn because my next memory is of standing in the alley, staring up at the second-story bedroom window. There was Mama in her green floral *daster*, her face gaunt with fear, on the brink of falling twelve feet to the street. From deeper inside the house, we could still hear Kuya Mhel pleading, "*Papa tama na! Papa tama na!*" and Papa shouting back, "*Tumigil ka dyan!*" their awful call-and-response echoing through-out the *eskinita*.

Mama was going to jump. It was the only way to escape.

Thank God for the man who lived next door who came outside to investigate the commotion. He stood below Mama and helped her down.

Papa appeared in the window moments later, furious that Mhel had stopped him from getting to Mama before she got out.

Mama scooped up the rest of us, hurrying off to the neighbor's house, where we were offered a room for the night. Though we were safe at last, her face was twisted in shock, her eyes still panicked even after her body stopped shaking.

We clung tight to Mama, the three of us like a blanket for her, the only comfort available to her. Four chaotic years later, I understood: In order to find peace, let alone survive, she would have to leave us behind.

The day I said goodbye to her at the airport with Papa and my sister Rhomalyn, my chest hurt from crying. When the three of us got back home, the dipping of the afternoon sun underscoring our sadness, we lay in bed and hugged one another.

Papa cried as if he knew Mama was not coming back to him. Before she left, we'd all casually talked about some hypothetical future day when we'd all move to America. But somehow, even as a child, I could sense my mother's calculated restraint whenever she spoke about that future. I didn't feel any enthusiasm at the thought of Papa being part of that vision. A veil of denial always lingered in the air, all of us afraid to name it, to speak it into reality.

The rhythms and sounds of our busy alley didn't stop, but without Mama at home, they were overpowered by a loud, crushing emptiness. We breathed in, we breathed out. She was gone. She was really gone.

"*Anak, gusto ko yakapin mo ito* whenever you miss me," Mama had instructed Ate Rhomalyn and me the night before she left, holding back tears as she gave us our "hot dog huggy pillows"—stuffed toys we could cling to if we ever felt too alone. Rhomalyn's hot-dog-shaped pillow was red; mine was green, printed with the face of a Teenage Mutant Ninja Turtle. It didn't take long for mine to be soaked with tears.

I didn't leave that bed the day Mama left. I must have cried myself to sleep. I woke up the next morning to the smell of Papa cooking a meal. "*Kain na anak,*" he said, trying to coax me to eat something.

But I just stayed there, my *hagulgol* crying echoing onto the streets.

Soon afterward Kuya Mhel, eighteen years old by this time, moved out of the house, and I saw him less and less. Glenda had already left by then, too, which left me, Rhomalyn, and Papa at home, our family of six now divided in half.

When she got to Vallejo, California, Mama started working at a kitchenware factory and rekindled her love of education, taking on assistant teaching jobs at the local middle school.

Back in the Philippines, I only started presenting more femme. A friend of mine took me to Mercury Drugs one day after school, after I asked him about the growing boobs that were beginning to poke out from beneath his white uniform shirt. For fifty cents at the pharmacy, he told me, I could get three weeks' worth of over-the-counter birth control pills. Because of the estrogen in the pills, I started growing boobs of my own within a month.

Soon I would no longer look like the young man Mama might have expected me to become, with growing facial hair and a deepening voice. Instead, my face softened, and my perky hormone boobs showed through my shirt.

One afternoon when I was fifteen, a friend invited me to meet the Manila Girls after school. I was floored. These were real-life legends of the pageant world. When I'd watched Super Sireyna with my family, I could only dream of being like the beautiful queens I saw on my TV screen. Now I was going to be in the same room with them, breathing the same air.

When I arrived at my friend's house, the first person I saw was Tigerlily, a slender femme in her early twenties with pouty protruding lips and long lustrous hair who'd made a name for herself as the Beauty Queen Maker. She carried herself like royalty, surrounded by her entourage: Ruel, Poca, Jojo, and Sabel. Tigerlily immediately sized me up, always on the lookout for the next big star.

"*Ay Sariwa! Ay Banat!*" she proclaimed.

In queer Tagalog lingo: I had fresh, youthful skin. She began tugging at my clothes, then stepped back and pointed a finger at me. "Take that off, and put on this bikini!"

Was she serious? Tigerlily's compliment had become a challenge so quickly, but there was a gentleness in the way she said it—an invitation in the form of an order. Suddenly I was holding a tiny neon-pink bikini that fit easily in the palm of my hand. But would *I* fit into *it*? Turns out I did, but barely. I wriggled my way into the swimsuit and stood there, awaiting further instructions.

"Walk for me," Tigerlily commanded.

For a moment, I hesitated, adjusting the bikini uncertainly. Sensing my anxiety, Tigerlily extended her arm in a graceful, sweeping motion across the floor to show me where I should perform.

"*Doon oh,*" she said, her pouty lips protruding in the same direction as her hand—our classic Filipino cue to follow where your mouth is pointing.

I wanted to be a legend like Tigerlily—what young trans girl wouldn't?—but I didn't feel like one. I had a bare face and a short boy's haircut. The tiny pink bikini top stretched on my chest with every nervous breath.

But as I looked down at my friend's living room floor, something suddenly clicked. The narrow space between the velvety couches on either side of me seemed to open wide, like the Red Sea parting for Moses, but for a femme boy who dreamed of more. Slowly, I lifted my bare heels off the ground, finding balance on my toes. I felt the power rise in my calves, my hamstrings holding me upright.

With an almost audible snap, my upper body synced with my core, like a lightning strike that makes your hair stand up straight. I was in a different realm now, only three inches higher off the ground than I was standing flat-footed, but miles away from the anxious child I had been a moment ago. In my mind, I was already a professional beauty queen.

I stepped forward, my imaginary heels making me feel elegant and polished. Each stride was a glide toward a spotlight made just for me. I was accessing the divine inside me.

When I looked up after my performance, I found the corner of

Tigerlily's mouth turned up in a smile. She wasn't looking for technical expertise; she was looking for *that*. That electricity. That spark. Her half smile was a sign I had star potential.

And just like that, she became not only my manager but also my trans mother, my mentor, and my friend.

My first pageant was three days later: Miss Gay Evangelista 1999. I rode there squeezed tight in a taxicab between Tigerlily, piles of garment bags, and the rest of Tigerlily's—now *our*—entourage.

The air conditioner was no match for our sweaty bodies, so we rolled the windows down, freeing a cloud of cigarette smoke and Aqua Net hairspray into the night. Colorful *banderitas* crackled in the air where they hung between electric poles. The distant beat of Janet Jackson's "Together Again" grew louder with each intersection we passed. But it was the smell of sweet smoky barbecued *isaw* and pork cooked right there on the street that told us we were getting close.

Miss Gay Evangelista, hosted by the city council every January, was the much-anticipated marquee event at the end of a multiday celebration honoring the Catholic patron saint of San Ildefonso. I was having fun with my friends, but this was serious business, too.

In the Philippines, transgender pageants are a national sport. We watch them the same way Americans watch football on Sundays, which makes sense if you know our history. Before colonization, we honored gender-fluid identities. Then the Spanish instituted dozens of festivals for Catholic saints. Beauty pageant culture was imported via American colonization in the early 1900s. Put all those influences together, and you've got our vibrant trans beauty pageants—a cultural amalgamation built through centuries of war and conquest.

In short, Miss Gay Evangelista wasn't just a pageant; it was a testament to our national spirit.

The cab stopped at a street corner, and six of us stumbled out on cramped legs. There, at the end of a street that had been blocked off to vehicle traffic, was the stage, looking like a floating jewel beneath dancing pink and purple spotlights. On either side, enormous loudspeakers blasted the pageant host's voice, greeting the politicians, celebrities, and local queer personalities as they waded through the crowd to their reserved seats up front.

Papas held children aloft so they could see the stage, while smaller children wriggled in their mamas' arms. Some parents carried plastic stools, searching for a place to sit down, while teenagers climbed atop parked jeepneys for a better view of the action. *Kabataan* flirted with their crushes as a steady stream of San Miguel beer, crispy *lumpia,* and sizzling pork *sisig* flowed into the crowd from the food carts along the edges. It was a street party, but it was so packed, you couldn't even see the street anymore.

The dressing room backstage wasn't much roomier. Every spot was taken. My five-person team and I would have to improvise. Standing there trying to make sense of the chaos, I was brushing shoulders with contestants whom I had just watched on the latest Super Sireyna. This was a dream—a beautiful, bizarre dream. These trans women, decked out in sparkly regalia, were icons in our community.

I tried to breathe and let the scene sink in. I couldn't believe this was really happening. Only a few hours before, I had still been in my high school uniform in San Pedro, Laguna, a rural province just outside the capital city. But now I was in the big leagues. All the great beauty queens had traveled from far and wide to be here. Their names were the stuff of whispered myths, their presence evoked fear, and yet they emanated the aura of goddesses, graceful and serene. If you wanted to make a name for yourself, this was the place to be.

. . .

The two-hundred-square-foot, tarp-walled dressing area was bursting at the seams with garments, gowns, and mirror-toting divas. The humidity inside was sweltering, smog and cigarette smoke forming a thick yellow haze in the air beneath the unflattering light of a single exposed bulb. All the queens and their entourages were packed tighter than a can of sardines. I was overwhelmed, my nerves quivering as veteran queens shot judgmental stares my way. They were wary of young upstarts like me. This was their domain—and they acted like it.

My hands were sweating, but the rest of my body felt cold, despite the heat. Then I felt Tigerlily's hands on my shoulders, and she whispered, "I found a spot just for us."

Once we escaped the suffocating atmosphere inside the tent, Tigerlily pointed across the street to a 7-Eleven with a truck parked behind it that we could use as a barricade: a makeshift dressing room away from the madness. A few minutes later, after a pep talk from Tigerlily, I took a deep breath and stepped back into the street. I was wearing a fuchsia peplum dress with long matching pink gloves, so I looked like a life-size Barbie doll, lit on one side by the fluorescent reds and oranges of the 7-Eleven sign and on the other by the purples of the stage.

Prying kids trailed behind me as I made my way back to the action. "What's your name? What's your name?" they yelled at me.

In our trans pageant world, new candidates typically choose a celebrity name to use as an onstage persona.

"What's your name?" they called out again.

I took a beat. Another breath. And then—

"Assunta de Rossi," I said, my voice clear and steady.

It felt good to say it out loud. Assunta de Rossi, star of the hit sketch show *Bubble Gang,* was the freshest young actress in the Philippines. Assuming her confidence in that moment was invigorating on a spiritual level. In that moment, I wasn't just announcing my name, but coronating myself with my new identity—the rare new candidate in Tigerlily's exclusive group making her debut.

I turned to face the kids, flipping the long hair of my wig over my shoulder. Their faces shone up at me like little sunsets in the red, orange, and purple lights. "My name is Assunta de Rossi," I said again.

Moments before the pageant started, "Spice Up Your Life" by the Spice Girls blasted through the speakers. From backstage I could hear the crowd pounding the front of the stage with their hands, echoing, accentuating, and underscoring the bass in the music.

And then it was official: Miss Gay Evangelista was under way! The crowd roared in anticipation of the first phase, during which each contestant would strut toward center stage and take a turn at the microphone to greet the audience. The introductions followed a specific format:

First, we'd say where we were from.

Next, we'd invent a college degree.

Third, we'd announce our stage names.

Last, we'd finish with an Oprah-esque saying or a campy Filipino joke.

One by one, all forty-five contestants took the stage. I listened for their closing lines. "If a diamond is polished by friction, then a man is perfected by trials," some would say, with all the authority of Eckhart Tolle.

Some chose a more comedic route, with a classic closing line like *"Batu-bato sa langit ang pangit wag magagalit!"* which they called out through fits of laughter, as if they had just drunk one too many Red Horse beers with their friends. Translated, it meant that you shouldn't be mad if a stone that got thrown in heaven ended up hitting your head; it would just mean you were not too blessed in the looks department—a bit of Filipino shade with a queer Catholic bent.

Finally, it was my turn.

I stepped onstage, the lights brighter than I expected, to standard claps and cheers—no one here knew me. Not yet. I took a deep breath, reminded myself that Tigerlily had rolled the dice on me, and strutted as confidently as I could to the mic.

"Good evening, ladies and gentlemen," I announced, my feminine voice projecting through the loudspeakers. "Standing in front of you is a fifteen-year-old stunner from San Pedro Laguna. Taking up a bachelor's degree in mass communication, I am your one and only sweet *Bubble Gang* girl . . . Assunta de Rossi!"

And then my final flourish, delivered like I was imparting serious wisdom on a grateful crowd: "I believe in the saying, 'A man without a principle is like a man without a soul.'"

I exited the stage to scattered applause, mostly from my entourage and the kids who had followed me across the street.

After the last contestant introduced herself, my team and I went back to our makeshift dressing area behind the 7-Eleven, spreading out purple tie-dye sarongs like wings for a scrap of privacy. I quickly changed into the same neon-pink bikini I'd worn when I'd first met Tigerlily mere days ago, except this time I had learned a new magic trick—or a clever bit of tradecraft, depending on how you saw it. With surprising strength, Tigerlily rolled beige-colored duct tape into a V-shape around the highest part of my waist, the adhesive giving off a loud *crack* as she pulled it super tight to give me some hips. I was cinched.

Off to the side of the stage, near the 7-Eleven, the other candidates and I waltzed around in our swimsuits as we waited our turn, some smoking cigarettes, others taking shots of beer, many of us stealing bites of *pulutan* fish balls and barbecued chicken. We were a rainbow-colored orchestra in motion—and we drew *lots* of looks.

Our barely there attire was a magnet for men. They circled around us, clamoring for attention. Some just wanted to flirt for a few min-

utes, but the real go-getters asked for our cellphone numbers straightaway. The little kids who had trailed behind me watched in awe as a
bevy of young men fought for my time.

The guy I picked—the local *kuya,* tall, dark, and manly—carried
himself like a village leader. He instantly took on the role of private
security guard, clearing my way to the stage when my turn came, fanning my face and flirting the entire time.

When the swimsuit round began, I glided across the stage with
my brand-new curves, strutting like a pro. Walking with the tape felt
different. My hips moved of their own volition. I felt like I was getting
the hang of this: Pageants were part confidence, part craftiness, and
part that star quality Tigerlily was searching for. Did I have it?

After that round, all the candidates were brought back onstage so
that Best in Swimsuit—the first award of the night—could be announced.

The host's voice soon called out over the loudspeaker: "Best in
Swimsuit goes to . . . Assunta de Rossi!"

I screamed, doubling over from shock and excitement.

But I also felt a twinge of doubt, wondering: *Why me and not the
more veteran candidates? Do I really deserve this?* Call it Catholic
guilt—Lord knew I still had enough of that.

As the Best in Swimsuit sash was slipped over my shoulders, I
looked over at the grinning faces of Tigerlily and my entourage just
to the right of the stage. Even some of the veteran queens greeted me
with enthusiasm as I walked back to my place. But one beautiful candidate named Chandra shoulder-butted me as we passed each other.
I was shocked—she was one of the most iconic queens in our trans
pageant world and one of my favorites—but apparently, she was a
total bitch.

I glided past her, holding my head high, deciding I didn't have to
feel bad upstaging the pros after all.

The next event was the evening gown competition. In our make-

shift dressing area behind the 7-Eleven, my stylist Ruel produced a
mermaid-cut iridescent orange dress with an intricately beaded rainbow corset that shimmered in the light like fish scales. Ever intuitive,
Tigerlily sensed that I was getting nervous again, so she suggested we
pray together. Closing our eyes and bowing our heads as the jeepneys
roared by, we made the sign of the cross.

"In the name of the Father, the Son, and the Holy Spirit," she
opened, then prayed, "Lord, Jesus, please guide us as we continue this
pageant. We leave it up to you, in whatever way you want this pageant to go. We thank you, Jesus. Amen."

I felt better—calmer—after that, knowing it was all in God's
hands. Let the Chandras of the world shoulder-butt me all they
wanted. He would decide in the end.

The tight gown made it hard for me to walk; I tottered back to the
stage like a newborn duckling. I focused hard on each step as I performed for the judges, trying to cover up my discomfort with precise
movements. When I was backstage again, Tigerlily told me I had
glided mechanically, "like a robot Barbie," and I wondered for a moment whether she meant it as a compliment. But I didn't have much
time to consider the point, because the next moment the host announced over the loudspeaker that I was the winner of Best in Long
Gown, too!

What?!

Ecstasy raced through my body like wildfire. I was on a roll now.

My winning both the swimsuit and the evening gown portions as
a newcomer provoked some *chismis*. Whispers circulated among the
crowd, but especially backstage. The malevolent gossip grew louder,
and the insidious stares icier, every time I walked by the other candidates. The longtime queens didn't even care if I heard them, chatter-
ing away like demons on my shoulder.

"Who is this bitch?"

"Do you know who she is?"

"I don't think she's that pretty."

"How did she beat Chandra and the others?"

Although it shouldn't have been that surprising, given that I had won two rounds, I was still floored when I was selected as one of fifteen candidates to advance to the final round.

This time, though, the challenge was different: We all had to answer a series of questions from the judges. I knew how to walk—and I could wear the hell out of that bikini—but I wasn't sure how to sound smart, especially off the cuff. I waited my turn, listening to the other candidates give perfectly poised and polished answers, feeling certain that absolute nonsense would spill out of my mouth once I opened it.

At last, it was my turn. My teeth chattered as I stood onstage. The bass coming off the speakers sounded like thunderclaps. The crowd looked on expectantly. I was petrified. But I forced myself to breathe in, hold it, then exhale. If I could control my voice—and stop my trembling—the judges wouldn't know how fearful I was.

"What is your greatest contribution to society?" the host asked me.

I took the mic. *Don't shake*, I told myself.

"I believe, um—" I started, briefly losing my train of thought. But then the words came tumbling out, and to my shock they were coherent: "I believe that being gay in this society does not diminish our humanity. But our purpose in living is to contribute. To love, and to be loved."

I barely knew what I'd said, but I had delivered it with confidence, my voice smooth and even. I hoped it was good enough. But when I walked backstage, I found Tigerlily scratching her head.

Turned out, my answer was actually someone else's: I was so nervous that I had inadvertently used one of the other pageant candidates' introductions, nearly verbatim. It must have left an impression on me! Worse, Ibona—the girl from whom I had accidentally cribbed my answer—was one of the most famous pageant veterans out there, so there was no doubt that the judges and other candidates noticed. That would earn me bad marks for sure.

But in a funny way, my mistake helped me relax for the rest of the pageant. There was no way I could win now; instead, I could just enjoy the rest of the evening. I had already gotten so much further than I expected.

At the end of the night, all fifteen finalists stood in a line in our evening gowns as the host welcomed last year's winner to the stage to bestow her crown on her successor.

Lucy Pereira appeared like a vision, gliding across the stage, waving to the crowd with all the regality of Queen Elizabeth. Her long shiny black hair was perfectly laid around her shoulders. She wore barely any eye shadow, drawing even more attention to her punchy red lipstick and green-velvet tube corset gown. I was in awe not just of her beauty but of her ambition. This would be her last appearance in the pageant scene before migrating to San Francisco. She was showing me what I could have one day, laying out a path for me as she walked to her mark.

I waited as the winners were announced. And then a bolt of lightning struck me in the heart. They were crowning the second runner-up and I heard—yes, it was *my name*.

"Assunta de Rossi!"

I was shell-shocked, not even aware of my movements as I walked to the front of the stage to receive my crown, sash, and a bouquet of gorgeous purple flowers. Tigerlily was screaming in delight somewhere behind me, the entourage going wild.

I felt as giddy as Sally Field on Oscar night. The judges must've liked me! *Really* liked me! More than enough to overlook my botched Q&A.

The rest of the candidates looked as stunned as I felt, but out of jealous disbelief rather than excitement. I didn't care about them anymore; I was the runner-up, not them. Let Chandra *chismis* about me all she wanted. I was going places now.

The pageant finally finished around three A.M., the crowd slowly trickling back home, teenagers climbing down from the jeepneys. I had won a total of 3,600 pesos—or around seventy-five dollars—which was about half the average monthly wage in the Philippines at the time. You can see why it was so tempting to become a trans beauty queen: It could be both gender-affirming and moneymaking.

Afterward, our entourage went back to Tigerlily's house and shared a celebratory meal of *goto*, a garlic rice porridge with pork *chicharron* and crispy soy tofu bought from Aling Baby's food store, a twenty-four-hour food stall next door. There was no catty whispering about me among this crew; instead Ruel, Poca, Jojo, and Sabel all shared how proud they were to have discovered me. They were welcoming me into Tigerlily's group—into their sisterhood. I couldn't imagine ever feeling happier than I did in that moment, surrounded by a group of people who not only accepted me for who I was without question but also saw me as special—a pageant prodigy in the making.

At around five A.M., Tigerlily took me to the bus station. I politely asked her if I could bring the sash, crown, and flowers back home with me.

"Of course," she said.

It was daylight by the time I got home, where I took a shower and got ready for school. I didn't have time to sleep, but with all the adrenaline coursing through me, it would have been impossible anyway.

I walked into my classroom proudly wearing my sash, bouquet, and crown in place of my usual butterfly barrettes. As I was the first in our class to join a beauty pageant, my classmates and teachers were endlessly curious and let me tell stories all day. I regaled them with tales of my pageant adventures, talking about the people I'd met in Manila just a few hours earlier as if they were already old friends. I was beaming with excitement and jittery with adrenaline.

The kids at school were more fascinated than they were accepting. Even though they all saw the trans pageant on TV—everyone did—having a femme classmate who had actually competed in them was a different story. Even at that age, I could tell that to them, I was more like a circus performer than an object of envy. But I didn't care much about their ambivalence. I was still riding the high of my victory.

For the first time in my life, I felt fully affirmed, totally aligned with my feminine expression. I hadn't just—almost—won a pageant, I had unlocked something essential, something spiritual, inside me, too: I was a performer. It felt like a calling from above.

New possibilities had opened for me literally overnight. I was set to graduate from high school in a few months, but now, instead of going to college, I pictured myself joining pageants. I figured that I could have fun, express myself, make money, travel, and hang out with my friends all at once. What would be *not* to like? Best of all, I could keep learning from my pageant mentor.

When I got home from school that day, Tigerlily called.

"You are the talk of the pageant world," she told me. "My phone has not stopped ringing with people wanting to *chismis* and know more about you! I just reply, very simply, that there's a new girl in town."

Word traveled fast in the trans pageant scene—and I would have to travel, too.

"So when are you coming back to Manila?" Tigerlily asked me. "We have pageants lined up for you!"

I was like a fish that bit down hard on the bait.

I was hooked on pageants and I wouldn't let go.

. . .

All this, though, I hid from Mama. As much as she loved me, I worried she'd be unsettled by the drastic changes to my appearance and my body. I was afraid that she'd feel I disrespected her by my not becoming the boy she thought she had had. She accepted my femininity, but could she accept that her little boy was now a beauty queen?

One day Ate Rhomalyn called for me from the neighbor's house, "Mama's on the phone!"

It was an overseas call, so I had to hurry—every minute cost a fortune. On the other end of the line, Mama sounded so excited, her tone sweet as she lovingly said, *"Dalaga na ang Bojojoy ko ha. Ang Ganda Ganda mo anak."* She was teasing, complimenting, and affirming me at the same time: "Hey, my little baby is now a lady. You look so beautiful." She had seen the photos.

Unbeknownst to me, Ate Rhomalyn had mailed Mama some photos of me from one of my pageants. In my orange-and-yellow gown, midstrut and smiling, I looked like a grown-up woman—in stark contrast to the little boy Mama had said goodbye to at the airport.

I didn't need to come out to her. I never said those declarative words—and I didn't even know them at the time. Vocabulary like *trans* would come much later in my life. All I needed was to hear the pride in Mama's voice as she called me beautiful.

Sometimes the things that go unsaid are more powerful than anything that can be uttered aloud: emotions that pierce your soul, moments of connection that mean so much more than binary answers and direct responses.

My eyes welled up as I said thank you into the phone—*"Salamat po ma"*—but I felt as though she were next to me, not halfway across the globe.

As I listened to Mama tell me about life in Vallejo, I thought back to when I was five years old, prancing around our living room with my T-shirt wrapped around my head. She had asked me once, "Why do you always wear the shirt like that?" and I said, "Mama, this is my hair! I'm a girl!" echoing the conclusion I had come to in front of the mirror.

Mama had smiled back at me. Where would I be now if she hadn't?

3

GARCIA

AFTER I INTRODUCED MYSELF AS ASSUNTA DE ROSSI AT MISS GAY
Evangelista 1999, my trajectory shot straight up. I won early and
often and became the top queen on the scene, a vibrant new flower
that bloomed out of nowhere. I won dozens of pageants in rapid suc-
cession. My name was on everybody's lips. The money was good, too,
allowing me to make large contributions to my family's budget. With
high school behind me and college out of the picture, my sole focus
in life now was to become the best transgender beauty queen in the
country. There were no distractions: Mama had been in the United
States for three full years by then, and Rhomalyn was taking care of
Papa, who'd experienced some health issues recently, back home as I
toured.

The kind of meteoric rise I had was almost unheard of in pageant
circles, which meant it was only a matter of time before I shot back
down. After a few months of victories, I ended the year on a losing
streak.

My winnings dwindled to the point that we didn't even have
enough money for the entrance fees. But desperate times call for des-

perate measures, and Tigerlily pawned her mom's wedding ring for cash—a secret we would keep for fifteen years. I still remember the night she looked me in the eye as we sat on her bed, fanning the cash from the pawnshop between us.

"This is all we got," she told me—only 2,000 pesos.

I felt tremendous pressure—but it was also one of the first times anyone had truly trusted me. It was one of those moments in life when I can remember a clear distinction between Before and After. It was as if Tigerlily knew I was standing on the precipice of an ethereal door, with boundless possibilities waiting for me on the other side, and all I had to do was take one more uncertain step. My biological family loved me, but my pageant mentor acted as if she could see my future.

Tigerlily and I had a trans mother-daughter bond forged in heaven, and she wanted to bet everything on us. If I had lost that first pageant, there might not be a pageant queen writing this book. But I trusted myself as Tigerlily trusted me, and after that it was all winning streaks for us.

It was among warplanes and bikinis that I cemented my place in pageant history.

The stage at Miss Gay Villamor 2000 was the only light in the vast dark expanse of the airfield. As my entourage and I arrived, murmurs bounced through the crowd like radio waves. If you listened closely, you could hear the *chismis: "Oy Andito na si Assunta."*

They were saying my name. I was on the rise again, having won a half-dozen pageants since the night Tigerlily pawned her mom's wedding ring for me. That night I wanted more than the crown. I wanted to become a legend—and this pageant was the place to do it. All the famous queens joined this one, and everyone remembered the winner.

Tigerlily and our entourage formed a protective shield around me as we waded through the crowd. I guarded the ends of my long black human hair wig, which was set in curlers. The atmosphere might have been pure Catholic fiesta, but the ground was dense with history. The Villamor Air Base in Pasay City had been built by the Americans in 1919, when the Philippines were still a colony. It was later renamed after Colonel Jesus Villamor, a Filipino pilot who fought the Japanese during World War II. It ultimately became the headquarters of the Philippine Air Force. That night it was the venue for an annual celebration of Saint Thérèse of the Child Jesus—and we queens were the main event.

Behind the stage, the silver-painted hulls of World War II Tora-Tora planes reflected the light of the stage, their proud display a reminder of struggles past. They were symbols of resistance and beauty, the perfect backdrop for a trans beauty pageant. This night was a culmination of intertwined histories, vibrant and rich. Our people are survivors, and we carry our culture with us through conflict and colonization, repurposing, reclaiming, and remaking traditions along the way. Which was how a bunch of trans girls ended up at an air base, ready to strut our stuff for thousands of fans.

After pushing through the crowd, my entourage and I reached the backstage area, which felt like a glamorous Filipino backyard party. There were no private changing rooms, only a dressing area filled with cigarette smoke, our sequined gowns sparkling like diamonds through the nicotine fog. Multicolored plastic stools were being used as barricades between teams, but Red Horse beers still got passed over them, the clinking of bottles sounding from every corner.

Before finding a spot in the dressing area, we took a moment to look up at those hulking planes, all bearing hyphenated names—Boeing PT-13D, T-28 Trojan, P-51 Mustang. I was just a young trans queen staring down everything that had come before her.

In 1908, during the American period, the Philippines' first-ever beauty pageant was held at the Manila Carnival in Luneta Park to celebrate the nation's friendship with the United States. The event was world famous, attracting visitors from all over the world. The winner, dubbed the Carnival Queen, would reign for a whole year, touring and promoting the event.

In the 1970s, the early iterations of Miss Gay pageants were born. Well-to-do families in the Tondo district of Manila would host *pasayaw mujeran* dance parties, blocking off the streets with coconut palm leaves. The *baklas* would line up for the occasion in full regalia, sashaying as if they were performing in the Miss Universe pageant. At the end of the night, the hosts, usually a dynastic political family, would pick a winner, giving out small prizes. Aspiring queens always had to impress not only the judges but one member of this family: the Hermana Mayor, the wealthy and powerful woman who had organized the entire evening. Every year these parties got bigger, and the prizes more substantial, until trans pageants became the highlight of Catholic fiestas all around the country—even on air force bases.

But there would be time for reflection later. For now, we had work to do. My entourage sprang into motion, each member fulfilling their assigned role. Tigerlily went to find the organizers so we could register and get the run of show. Bing, my trans auntie and wardrobe assistant, looked for the best spot for us to dock. Once we were set up, Eena, our hair and makeup guru, went to work on my face, applying vibrant sky-blue eye shadow and then standing by for last-minute touch-ups.

Finally, there was Yayamae, my trans grandma, a local salon owner who was our grounding force backstage, calming and centering us. But this grandma still had all her teeth: The second she smelled cheating or manipulation tactics from the judges—or heard about any backroom deals between candidates and organizers—she would leap to my defense, loudly and brashly, in front of the whole pageant.

"*Saglit, Saglit!*" she would protest, waving both hands and stomping her feet in front of the judges. "There's been a mistake!"

When that happened, getting in Yayamae's way was like standing between a mama bear and her cub. She was unrelenting and ferocious.

This was my team—and they were also my friends. Pageant life for us was both work and fun. Backstage, we settled into a familiar rhythm, bouncing between glamour and sisterhood, between *baklaan* and *landian* laced with shade, our loud *chikahan* chatter covering every topic from the guys we were seeing to the hairdos we wanted to try.

Tigerlily rushed back from registration that night with troubling news: "*Tang ina,* it's bridal wear for the introductions!"

We had brought only cocktail wear—the typical outfit for the opening portion of a pageant. Looking around, we realized the other candidates were all unpacking bridal wear. Why had everyone except us known about the change? It was more than a little suspicious.

This was where Tigerlily's pageant acumen came in handy. She had spent years in the scene, first as a fan, then as an assistant, before establishing her own pageant clan: the Garcias. She had started out with three petite queens—Corrine, Nathalie, and Paulene Garcia—all of whom had become mentors to me soon after Miss Gay Evangelista the previous year.

The other, more established clans had lofty names that sounded elegant as they rolled off your tongue: the Montecarlos, the Artadis, the Sytangcos, the Hilarios, and the Brunei Beauties. They all aimed to impress in their own way. The Montecarlos and Artadis had ghost-white skin, expensive clothes, and snob appeal. Sytangcos were known for their ornate gowns, rivaling the best haute couture. The Hilarios began in the 1980s, making them one of the oldest clans. The Brunei Beauties mostly consisted of girls who had returned to the Philippines from Japan, hoping to use the skills they had learned abroad to dominate the local pageant scene. They were known as the super femme clan Vavaihan.

And then there was our upstart crew with the humble-sounding name Garcia. Tigerlily borrowed it from the up-and-coming actress Cheska Garcia, who had a breakout role in the popular teen TV drama *Gimik*. That choice was a wild, cosmic coincidence: During my senior year of high school, before I even met Tigerlily and soon after I started taking hormone pills, I had named myself Gina after another character from that show. All the more reason for me to believe this powerful little clan was my destiny.

And a bridal category curveball stood no chance against destiny—and our scrappy little team.

At first, we looked around in a panic as the other candidates put on their intricate bridal wear, puffs of chiffon rustling gently as their gowns were tightened, each of their satin trains seemingly longer than the last. That's when Tigerlily leaped into action. She pointed at Bing—my trans auntie and pageant assistant—to start *halukay* within our garment bags, hoping for a miracle.

"*Eto pwede na yan*," Bing reported back, holding up a white floor-length sleeveless silk jersey gown. The light beading on top gave it a minimalist, almost Chanel-esque aura. This gown was only supposed to be backup eveningwear. I sometimes wore it during talent portions, too. But Bing was right: *Pwede na yan*. We could make it work.

Tigerlily found matching long white gloves, which we normally paired with another silver gown. Even with that touch, though, a look this pared down wasn't going to cut it.

But desperation breeds craftiness. Tigerlily produced a roll of toilet paper and directed Eena to incorporate it into my hairstyle. At first, the idea seemed totally wild. But as I sat on the chair, my scalp getting pricked with pins, I heard my team's skepticism become excitement in real time. When Eena handed me the mirror, I saw delicate layers of soft, flowing veils draped elegantly over my shoulders.

The white gown gave off Chanel, but my veil was the precise bit of couture polish the look needed. And when it was time for introductions, I made the most of it, gliding across the stage, letting my veil dance like ribbons in the gentle breeze. I owned the crowd, generating applause on command like a general calling this whole goddamn airbase to attention. I won Best in Bridal with a bunch of toilet paper on my head.

We were more prepared for the swimsuit portion, one of two categories, along with the evening gown contest, that typically decided who advanced to the semifinals. I hadn't debuted a new swimwear look since the tiny neon bikini I squeezed into when I first auditioned for Tigerlily, and tonight I was excited to introduce a newly bought black-and-white-striped bikini. Everyone wanted to be the one to beat in this crucial category—to be the subject of those envious whispers: "*Uy* Best in Swimsuit Girl *yan*." This change was going to make an impression, good or bad. People would notice.

But I was secure in the knowledge that this look had been vetted by my Garcia family. Their opinions were the only ones I trusted.

Earlier that week I'd tried on the striped bikini for the first time at Tigerlily's small riverside house in the city, which she shared with her mom, brother, and nieces. Her home was a world filled with possibility, and they shared it with the entire Garcia clan—a dorm for a bunch of transsexuals. Two of the four bedrooms were reserved for us. I split my time between Tigerlily's place during pageant season and home when I wasn't working.

The living room at Tigerlily's was part dining space, part runway, and part group therapy room. It was there that I first fitted the bikini, gliding along the floor on tiptoe in my invisible heels to test out the way it hugged my body. The Garcia clan was almost militaristic in their appraisal of the new garment, acting like I was presenting in my dress blues for uniform inspection. They scrutinized every angle with precision, meticulously noting how it looked from each side.

The suit was Sogo brand, bought for thirty dollars at the Robinsons Mall, and it looked like it was worth every penny. The black and white stripes drew perfectly flattering lines up and down my body, the elastic cinching in all the right places. The bra's underwire pushed up my growing hormone boobs. The classic round shape of the cups made my breasts look voluptuous, even jiggling from certain angles. The bikini bottom's vertical stripes made my long legs appear even longer as I walked up and down the room.

The suit was fabulous, but the family was split between whether I should wear it below the hip or ultrahigh cut. This new look couldn't be just any bikini strut; the clan was preparing me to enter a gladiator arena. There couldn't be any chinks in my armor. We had a decision to make.

Of course, we were no strangers to high-stakes conflict. I mean, when you put a bunch of feisty, horny, ego-driven, hormone-filled Garcias in close quarters, day in and day out, you've got a recipe for chaos. The living room was a place for us to have it out. Whether we were dealing with bubbling jealousy from one of the girls flirting with another girl's man, or with a joke someone told while drunk that was taken way too seriously, we put it all on the floor.

Tigerlily would let us bicker for only so long, though, before she brought an end to it. *"Ayusin nyo yan, mga bakla kayo!"* That command to "zip it" brought order back to the room in an instant.

Sometimes she would summon us to have our version of a "Meeting de Avance"—an old election season ritual usually held at a closing rally when a politician makes a final plea that is peppered with soon-to-be-broken promises. For us, it simply meant gathering everyone to address an important topic with an open heart. We'd hold one before taking in a young trans girl who had been kicked out of her home, and Tigerlily would remind us to be especially sensitive to her needs. When someone from the group wanted to hash out their feelings, we'd do a Meeting de Avance—usually followed by rounds of Red Horse beer.

"*Ok lang yan teh,*" we'd say. Let it out, girl!

On the surface, we were usually jolly, but we all knew what everyone else had been through. Everyone in that house teetered on a delicate edge between trauma and joy. When Pauline told us about being rejected by her mom for being who she was, we cried with her. When Corrine said she had been shamed by her father because of her femininity, we all knew how it felt. Everyone noticed when Nats stayed at the riverside house more than the others; it meant she was hiding from her family. She couldn't be seen as she was back home.

Tigerlily's house, like her heart, seemed to have infinite room. We slept like lined-up spring rolls, all six of us cramming into a six-by-eight-foot space. Three people in a twin bed? No problem! No wonder we'd wake up at seven dripping with sweat. Two people sleeping on the floor was the standard.

We got used to feeling the sudden pressure of something hard against our necks, meaning someone had opened the door to pee in the middle of the night, whispering "*Usog, usog.*"

"*Aray, aray, aray,*" the floor sleepers would say. It hurts, it hurts.

The lucky Shan, the most petite in the bunch, got the bedroom windowsill all to herself. It was where we kept our pageant trophies. All night long, surrounded by the golden sheen of our awards, the breeze caressed her voluminous hair until the morning sun kissed her awake. Whoever slept on the floor usually woke up wanting to slap her.

The room next to us was our costume department. Really, it was just an equally small space lined with garment bags full of all types of gowns and "national costumes" with feathers, glitter, and beads piled up high like a shag carpet. Bing conveniently turned it into her private bedroom. But whenever she wasn't there, the other girls used it for secret sexcapades. They'd all steal moments in that dark room for phone sex or to hook up with a *booking*—a guy they met on the street. While everyone else slept, the room would become its own private stage.

It was there in the costume department that Bing kept my bikini until it was time for its grand debut at Villamor. And for the record, that afternoon in Tigerlily's living room, we determined the ultra-high cut was best.

The clan had chosen; the rest was up to me.

At Villamor, we waited for the big moment that would determine my bikini's fate. If everything went well, it could become my signature suit.

As Tigerlily and Bing assisted in taping up my hips, the crackling echoed into the open expanse of the airfield behind us. But right in front of us were the huge lined-up World War II planes, their yellow glow giving me just enough light to tuck.

It was dark backstage, but when the candidates came out into the open to do our finishing touches, all the prying kids, the curious men, and the food vendors with their fish balls and barbecue circled around us, the yellow bulbs from street carts giving us more light. Once we were ready, we took turns nibbling on snacks.

Then it was my turn. There was no doubt in my mind about what the judges were looking for and whether I could deliver it: a girl who was fierce, a girl who was glamorous, a girl who was unforgettable. Standing just offstage, I already knew exactly where and how the spotlights would hit my legs and my face, catching the sparkles on my skin, hypnotizing the judges into picking me. So once I stepped onstage, no one else had a chance. I had wowed the judges with my makeshift toilet paper bridal look, but my perfectly executed bikini walk—with that ultrahigh-cut styling—made me untouchable.

I won the crown that night at Miss Gay Villamor. There was no other possible outcome. We took our winnings that night to the Tapsilugan by Tigerlily's house, a twenty-four-hour joint that serves the classic Filipino trio of garlic fried rice, eggs, and marinated beef, all dipped in garlic chili vinegar. This meal was our Holy Trinity.

By six A.M., our stomachs full of fried rice and victory, we drifted off to sleep in peace knowing that tomorrow we'd win all over again.

4

BOJOJOY

OVER TIME, TO MY SURPRISE, MY MACHO PAPA ONLY GREW MORE accepting of his trans daughter. In fact, even before I started joining pageants, he had shown me that I didn't have to apologize to anyone for being femme.

When he visited my high school for a parent-teacher conference in 1999, a few months before Miss Gay Evangelista, I was overcome with fear. His silence about my flamboyance at home didn't necessarily mean he'd react well to being seen next to me at school, where I typically dressed femme. That day I was wearing a brown-striped turtleneck that clung to my perky hormone boobs and tight beige pants that hugged my rounded hips. Butterfly barrettes glittered like jewels in my hair, and the Mary Jane Esprit shoes I had stolen from my sister completed my outfit. I looked like I belonged in *Clueless*.

I knew the stakes were higher here. This wasn't our *eskinita*; this was a formal event in front of all my peers. I was afraid Papa would feel like my appearance was a threat to his persona, with all his swagger and bravado.

Papa looked like a cop—and carried himself like one. His protruding belly hung out over his belted pants. He carried his five feet nine inches like he was about to interrogate anyone and everyone who crossed him. With dark brown eyes and messy black hair cut just below his ears, he had that precise mixture of authority and mystery that so many men wish they possessed. He liked to take long drags off his Hope Luxury cigarettes and shoot off a steely stare that said, *I've got you all figured out.*

That was the energy he carried with him when he walked into my school that day, taking long authoritative strides down the hallway of Colegio de San Pedro. We couldn't have been a sharper contrast. He was wearing a simple red collared shirt with jeans. I led him toward my classroom but hesitated, shuffling my feet and looking at the floor. Shouldn't someone as masculine as he was tell me to take the barrettes out of my hair? Why wasn't he berating me for how I was dressed or staring me down with that withering gaze of his? He couldn't possibly be okay with this, could he?

Papa must have noticed my downward gaze.

I felt a warm hand on my shoulder. "*Anak,* look at me," he said. "Look at me."

I met his unblinking gaze. His voice when he spoke was steady. Only a father can offer such calming assurance in so few words.

"There is nothing wrong with you," he said. "Chin up, *anak.*"

And with that he nudged me back toward the classroom, his touch as gentle as his heart as he guided us down the hall.

The following year my pageant career took me all around the country, requiring me to spend most of my nights on the road. After taking the crown at Miss Gay Villamor, I kept winning wherever I went. At a pageant in Manila, I had just stepped offstage after the evening gown category when I heard my little Nokia phone chirp. It was a text message from my sister Rhomalyn.

Papa is in the hospital.

I knew immediately it was another stroke. A year ago he'd had a mild stroke that paralyzed the left side of his face for a month, but I knew it wasn't good for him to have a second one so soon. Thank God my pageant that night was only an hour away. I told Tigerlily I had to withdraw from the pageant, then changed out of my evening gown and rushed home to see Papa.

When I arrived in the ICU of Evangelista Hospital in San Pedro, Laguna, I found Papa surrounded by tubes and machines, buzzing and pulsing and beeping as they performed their mysterious functions. I was sixteen years old, Ate Rhomalyn was eighteen, and we were scared. This time was so much worse than the first stroke, which he recovered from quickly with only a brief hospital stay.

We looked at him, then at each other, silently confirming the gravity of our predicament. *We have to be strong for each other,* we were saying, wordlessly.

Mama could only do so much over the phone. She offered words of motherly comfort, sensing even from San Francisco that my sister and I were teetering on the edge of despair. But as a factory worker, she couldn't fly back to the Philippines at a moment's notice without risking her job. We had to decide whether the situation was urgent enough for her to fly out, and ultimately we chose to wait until we knew more about Papa's prognosis.

Eventually he stabilized, and after two weeks in the hospital, he was sent home to recover under our care. I scaled back my pageants so I could spend more time at home with him and Rhomalyn, joining only about one a month.

Papa was bedridden at first. The left side of his body was paralyzed.

His behavior was loopy for the first month. Some nights we heard screaming from his bedroom, as if he had been possessed by an evil spirit. Once, I opened the door to find him punching the window screen with his right hand, pointing furiously at the hole he had made, and screaming, *"May sawa, may malaking sawa, patayin mo yung sawa!"* He was terrified, warding off a giant reticulated python that wasn't there, acting as if he could kill it with the sheer volume of his voice. The doctor told us the hallucinations were the result of brain trauma suffered during the stroke.

Soon, we got used to his screaming. When it woke me at night, I'd go into his room, lay a reassuring hand on his back, and sit beside him until he calmed down.

"Pa, magiging maayos rin po ang lahat," I would tell him. Everything will be fine.

It was my turn to reassure him.

Papa grew softer after that second stroke. It was as if being humbled physically had opened him spiritually. He stopped drinking. His moods were calmer. And a few months into his recovery, he became a born-again Christian after being converted by a pamphleteering neighbor.

He spent most of his time sitting in front of our house in his favorite chair—a yellow plastic stool. The other families started calling him "Kapitan" like he was the leader of our neighborhood watch, a *"ma* PR," because he was the public relations expert for everyone on the block. He talked to everyone who passed, collecting *chismis* like tolls.

After a few months, he started walking again, dragging his left foot behind him with every step. He could shower himself, too. But his cooking wasn't the same anymore. His new passion was talking about Jesus. There were times when he'd come home from Bible study crying. He would set his cane down and tell us what he had learned, usually ending on a note of regret, apologizing for his manic ways.

But no matter how religious he became—and oh, he got preachy—he never stopped loving me, transness and all. He liked to tell me, tears in his eyes, *"Anak, kahit anong sabihin ng iba, walang mali sayo, maging mabuti ka lang na tao."* Translated: My kid, no matter what people say, there's nothing wrong with you. Just be a good person.

As I saw Papa enter what seemed like a new chapter in his life, I came to understand that his softness had always been there.

Sure, Papa got angry with us as kids, especially when Rhomalyn and I fought. My sister and I would get into endless tussles, pulling each other's hair, kicking each other in the stomach, screaming and squealing as we ran up and down the alley. When we finally came home, Papa would be waiting for us with a leather belt. Or if he was feeling sadistic, he'd make us kneel on *munggo* beans for an hour with a Bible held in our outstretched hands.

But Papa had always been more than his temper.

When I was a kid, some nights, he would come wake me up around two in the morning, gently tugging on my hand as he called out my childhood nickname, "Bojojoy . . . Bojojoy . . . Bojojoy . . ."

I'd open my bleary eyes, annoyed but full of love for Papa. He would turn on the light and sit me down in front of our karaoke stereo, my Ninja Turtle pajamas wrinkled from sleep. Shirtless, wearing his favorite jeans, he sat cross-legged next to the stereo, as if it were a loyal companion, and started to sing along to his favorite John Lennon cassette, lapsing at times into drunken humming.

"You may saaaaay I'm a dreamer," he sang, his eyes welling up.

Afterward he would lecture me in a whisper about all the little ways I had disobeyed him. He reminded me to stop running straight to bed for afternoon naps without showering first because I was sweaty from playing under the sun, speaking with a solemnity as if he were imparting valuable instruction that he wanted me to remember after he was gone.

"*Opo pa,*" I'd grunt, barely awake.

Then he'd tell me his story about being an "overseas Filipino worker" in Saudi Arabia back in 1976. "*Alam mo anak,*" he'd begin, his voice thick with emotion, as he launched into a tale I knew almost by heart. Seven years before I was born, he was a forklift operator in a Saudi port, under contract for two straight years without any time off, even for Christmas—a holiday that's a joy-filled family bonanza in the Philippines more than anywhere else on earth.

After only six months of working overseas, being homesick took its toll on Papa, and he broke the contract so he could come back to his family. It was at this point in the story that tears would gush out of him, as if he were apologizing to me, a sleepy child, for not being the provider he thought he could be, begging me to understand that his love for us came first, his face a weeping mask of quiet pain and tender emotion.

After more singing, usually a duet of "Eternal Flame" by the Bangles, he'd get serious again. "*Alam mo anak,* I love you all very much," he'd tell me. "I love your mama even though she always gets mad at me when she comes home from work. Remember to be nice to Ate Rhomalyn. You are my Bojojoy."

After a few more minutes, I would hear him lie down, belly up, facing the ceiling. His snoring was my cue. Midnight karaoke was over.

I later realized those late-night sessions were his desperate attempt to be heard. Maybe he accepted my transness because he knew what it was like to have deep-seated emotions that he felt like he couldn't express. Maybe he saw a gentleness in me that he wished he could embrace in himself. Maybe his hypermasculinity felt like a weight on his back—one he needed to release when it became too heavy to carry.

I think we were both dreamers in our own way.

. . .

I saw Papa less frequently as his condition improved and I started doing more pageants again, traveling to far-off provinces to win all the crowns. I would come back bearing towering trophies that crowded our living room. But one day I got home, and my entire collection was gone.

I rushed to my sister Rhomalyn. "Where's my trophies?!" I shrieked.

"Look for Papa," she told me. "I saw him giving them to someone earlier."

I was flabbergasted; I thought Papa supported my pageant career. Why was he suddenly liquidating my trophy collection?

I went back out front and found his yellow plastic stool empty. In the distance, though, I heard a whistling and roaring crowd. I followed the noise to a nearby basketball court where hundreds of people were gathered to watch a game. I pushed through the crowd, toward the court, and saw Papa sitting on the sideline. Beside him, atop a folding table, were all my beauty pageant trophies glistening in the late afternoon sun.

He had donated them to the neighborhood basketball championship, replacing the plaques to suit the occasion. Even the figurines had been unscrewed, the golden tiara-wearing pageant queens swapped out for basketball players in that iconic mid-dunk Michael Jordan pose.

Papa was smiling wide as he cheered on the teams, filled with pride. For a second, I was upset. Papa, eager to impress the community, had clearly decided to repurpose my trophies to curry favor with the crowd. But then I saw him beaming at me from across the court, tilting his head with a playful smirk, and I knew that *I* was his champion. He just wanted to contribute something. Besides, I'd win more trophies.

It became a tradition for Papa to give me blessings before I left for pageants. He would place his hand on my head, close his eyes, and pray, his voice gentle and hushed.

"Lord, please keep Gina safe with all her travels, that she will come home safe. Give her all your blessings. Amen."

That blessing is still with me today, a cherished memory guiding my way.

5

HORSE BARBIE

MY WIG WAS MYSTICAL. I NEEDED SOME WAY TO EXPLAIN TO MY-self how quickly I rose through the pageant scene, and I chose to believe the secret was my hair.

Lush and long, it swayed like the tail of a prize pony as I strutted across stage after stage, my lustrous black tresses sparkling under the spotlight. It looked like the dark strands came from another, more spiritual realm—and in a way that was true. Some of the hair had come from an overcrowded Manila cemetery.

If a family couldn't keep paying for a plot five years after a loved one was buried, the cemetery would exhume the remains to make more space. The skeletons were transferred into tombs, but the fully intact hair was too valuable to be locked away. Usually the cemetery sold the hair—and Manang Sally was there to buy it.

A petite woman in her fifties with shiny black hair reaching down to her knees, Manang Sally was a famed wigmaker, shrouded in myth, her connections plentiful and closely guarded. In our trans pageant world, everyone wanted a Manang Sally wig. If she saw fit to sell to you, you were a chosen one.

Tigerlily had taken me to visit Manang Sally early in my pageant career. After I won my first official title inside our largest mall—the six-million-square-foot SM North EDSA—Tigerlily reserved a portion of the 20,000-peso prize for a wig of my own. She didn't just want to win more pageants; she wanted to build a legacy, and for that she would need legendary materials. What better way to turn a fifteen-year-old with a short boy's haircut into an overnight sensation than a magical wig?

We didn't know where Manang Sally lived, but a trans auntie from the Brunei Beauties took us to her home. We found her standing in a tiny alley in Caloocan City, surrounded by crawling plants that framed her door. She was wearing a loose black dress, the smoke from her cigarette only adding to her mysterious fortune-teller aesthetic. She looked at Tigerlily and me as if she had known we were coming—and knew where we were going, a trans mother and daughter galloping off to greatness.

When I arrived barefaced at pageants with my *banat* skin, I looked like your average high-school-age femme child. Dressed down in a loose shirt, jeans, and a pair of Converse, I was a nobody, totally unrecognizable to my fans. I liked that anonymity. Invisibility was my ally as I walked through the crowd, overhearing the *chismis*.

"Where's Assunta?" one pageant fan would say, on the lookout for my arrival.

"Che! Hindi maganda si Assunta," an assistant to another queen would snipe about my appearance.

Little did they know I was lurking among them, grinning to myself. I was a threat—the one to beat—but they couldn't recognize me when I was right in front of them.

And then I would transform. Whenever possible, my entourage and I would get ready away from everyone else, preparing my first look of the evening in privacy. When it was almost my turn to introduce myself, I would suddenly show up backstage in a breathtaking outfit. One of my favorites was a sequined midnight-blue dress with a long matching veil flowing behind me. I wanted to seem like an apparition who had come out of nowhere. With my bare face fully made up and my long wig securely clipped in, I was no longer the anonymous femme child, but a mythical Horse Barbie, part equine and all fashion.

The name was a reclamation. When I first started joining pageants, I wasn't really considered beautiful. With my extra-long neck and lips that protruded in profile, fans and jealous entourages liked to tease me by saying, "She looks like a horse."

It hurt.

The pretty light-skinned girls, by contrast, were celebrated. They achieved a ghostlike appearance with bleaching creams, soaps, lotions, powders, and all sorts of concoctions. Almost everyone belonged to the "whitening cult," believing that the promise of a happy light-skinned life was just a lotion away. If you had dark skin, people thought you were poor—that you were working the fields and you should be ashamed of it.

Colorism is deeply embedded in Filipino culture. People will ask, "Why are you so dark?" just as casually as they'd ask, "How are you?" The stigma in the Philippines is overt in film, TV, and advertising, but it comes in subtler forms, too. Watching any celebrity over time, I could follow their journey from a darker complexion to a lighter one, their skin color changing with each billboard.

It's a painfully ironic beauty norm for a country so close to the equator. You can hardly avoid the sun, and yet being exposed for too long made you seem almost sinful.

In our pageant world, those who subscribed to the whitening madness thought light skin made them look soft, femme, rich, and ethereal. *"Babae . . . Dyosa oh!"* onlookers would whisper in awe, gawking at light-skinned girls as if they were spirits floating past them.

Everyone wanted that, cisgender and trans. *I* wanted it, too.

At the beginning of my pageant career, I bleached my skin with Etta's bleaching powder almost every day. But after months of suffering the burning sensation on my skin, of standing upright for hours at a time wrapped in itchy whitening cake, I gave up. I realized that if I wanted to craft my own unique identity in a sea of sameness, I would have to embrace my difference.

I decided to embody their cruel name for me, flipping the insult on its head. Little by little, I became the dark horse, literally and figuratively. And once I was on top, "horse" wasn't an insult anymore.

Even our Garcia clan had equine roots. We loved the campy 1989 Filipino queer classic *Petrang Kabayo*, a film in which a horse goddess has the power to cast and reverse curses, punishing people who are unkind to their steeds and rewarding others for their courage. Tigerlily was our own horse goddess. She gave me the name Horse Barbie after identifying that special aura I emanated while gliding onstage, a mythical spirit possessed only by me. There were so many ways in which I looked like Barbie, that enduring American symbol of beauty, from my long legs to my statuesque physique, but I also celebrated my obvious differences, like my dark hair and protruding lips. The name Horse Barbie held all of that; if anything, its inherent internal tension made me feel even more iconic. I hadn't just grown up to be one of my sister's dolls; I was something *more*—a unique hybrid being who could straddle multiple worlds, unclassifiable and unique.

Fittingly, we were also fond of the Tikbalang, a half-human, half-horse creature in Philippine mythology. According to our legends, Tikbalangs live in the forest and play tricks on travelers, leading them astray. Is it any surprise that our ragtag group of queens embraced their mischievous energy? Our clan's whole identity was wrapped up in queer horsey magic.

When, at seventeen, I joined Miss Gay Jungle Town 2000 in the province of Pangasinan, I was at the peak of my horse powers.

That night, as we carried our costumes and luggage through the small provincial village, we were escorted to the home of the Hermana Mayor, the matriarch who had organized the town's fiesta. The Hermana Mayor's family opened up their home for us to get settled before the pageant began, complete with a bountiful Filipino Fiesta feast.

At every pageant in the province, Tigerlily reminded me to always get on the good side of the Hermana Mayor because she typically has the power to affect the results. I mean, they literally fund the trans pageants, so it's easy to see how they tip the scales.

The stage was on a basketball court surrounded by lush towering trees and by our traditional stilts, *bahay kubo*. In our dressing room, which was actually a repurposed classroom in the nearby elementary school, Tigerlily brushed and caressed my luscious human hair wig into waves as I undressed to put on my red halter gown for the evening gown round. After gently swinging my hair from one shoulder to the other, I shook it with a firm, powerful rustle, as if I were arriving at the racetrack, neighing with pride.

Huhummmm.

I was the prized thoroughbred of the Garcia clan, ready to bring glory to our name. As Tigerlily was putting the finishing touches on my style, we heard an award get called out over the loudspeaker: "Best in Beautiful Hair goes to . . . Assunta de Rossi!"

The other candidates, all of whom had real, long natural hair, shot me piercing stares, whispering their *chismis* to one another. They were right: How could I have won an award with *a wig*? Manang Sally's magic must have given me the edge.

That night's pageant was a marathon. It was in May, peak Catholic fiesta season, and it just so happened to coincide with an election, so politicians came onstage during each break to trumpet their platforms.

By the time I grabbed the mic for my final question onstage, early-morning sunlight was spreading through the surrounding woods, illuminating a shimmering layer of mist rising off the ground. The whole scene looked like a postcard from a rural getaway. If only my makeup weren't cracking from the heat and humidity.

After delivering my last answer, I placed the mic on my hip with conviction. It had been a long battle, but I was the sure winner. Then suddenly there was screaming in front of the stage. The judges looked confused by the uproar; meanwhile the remaining finalists and I were just exhausted, our feet swollen from sashaying since eight o'clock the night before. Amid the commotion, I heard Tigerlily's voice demanding a recount. As was her custom, my mentor had been stealthily standing behind the judges to make sure nothing fishy was going on.

This night she had noticed one of the tabulators doctoring the name of the local queen as the winner even though I had more votes.

"They are manipulating the results!" she yelled.

Her words were echoed by the crowd, or at least what was left of the crowd, which was now mostly made up of backpack-wearing kids holding their mamas' hands on the way to school. They had to wait until the pageant was over to get their classrooms back.

Finally, after fifteen minutes of deliberation, I was wearing the crown, with sweat dripping down my face. I was tired, but the Tikbalangs in the trees were smiling on me.

I helped Tigerlily grow the Garcia clan the same way a moneymaking thoroughbred allows owners to add more horses to their stables. As I won more pageants, she adopted more and more contestants, some of them debutantes like I had been, others defecting from their own clans to come to ours. Even Chandra, the girl who had shoulder-butted me at Miss Gay Evangelista 1999, became a Garcia. As our clan grew, I became more aware of budding jealousy or unfounded *chismis* in our group, usually instigated by our fans. Our young frag-ile egos were always ready to snap, so I realized at a young age that it was better to only compete with myself.

At our peak, throughout the year 2000, seven of us were joining every pageant. And I promise I'm not bragging—okay, maybe a little—when I say I almost always won, title after title, championship after championship, from one provincial town to the next. One May I made 120,000 pesos in a month, which was over fifteen times the average monthly wage in the Philippines at the time. Twenty percent of that money went to Tigerlily, 10 percent went to hair and makeup, 10 percent went to wardrobe assistants, and 5 percent covered food and travel, which left the remaining 55 percent all for me. Tigerlily kept track of our winnings in a dog-eared notebook, which she kept locked in her precious *baul,* and she would show me how much I brought in. I even made history as the only trans queen to win two crowns in one night, hurrying across town after a pageant held in a chapel to win an open-air street pageant, too.

"*Bakla naman,* you guys just won the title," the other clans com-plained to Tigerlily that night. "Why did you even join here? So greedy!"

But better than all the money I earned was the prize of getting to sleep in the middle of the twin bed in the room we all shared at Tiger-lily's house. The prime spot was reserved for the winner, the other girls swapping in and out depending on where they had placed in that night's pageant. Let's be honest: The bed might as well have been mine.

In hindsight, I think I was so successful in part because I was tak-ing the hurt of being teased and turning it into a performance, embracing every part of the animal my haters once called me. If they thought horses were ugly, I was going to prove how beautiful they could be. If you've ever seen the 2015 Triple Crown winner American Pharoah parading around a racetrack, that's how I walked during the swimsuit competition, standing with conviction and pride, my perfectly shined wig glistening as I whipped it across my body. I was always a shoo-in for Best in Swimsuit. I perfected my gait, stamping my feet to draw out my hip muscles into a perfect pose, my dark toned legs framing my curves.

Huhummmm.

That black-and-white swimsuit, with its vertical stripes, perfectly accentuated my dark skin, with the high-cut bikini pulled up to the highest part of my waist, gripping my hips like a saddle. The other candidates rubbed body foundation all over themselves to appear whiter, but I competed with my bare skin, a drop of mocha in an ocean of milk.

Wherever I went, I was a powerful dark horse. No words could stop me. All the little comments about my dark knees or my bikini line bounced straight off me. Every time I paused my gait onstage, I stared directly at the judges with the kind of intent that breeds results. Was I casting spells? Maybe.

Or maybe my stare really was that powerful, capable of creating an unbreakable intimacy with the audience, whether I was performing in a fifteen-thousand-seat coliseum or a neighborhood street pageant. When I was in my element, I was possessed—whether by our ancestral Tikbalang or by one of the spirits from those Manila graves, I'm not sure.

A superstition says that whenever there's a sun shower, a Tikbalang is getting married. *When it rains, it horse,* I used to think—a play on "When it rains, it pours," that I remembered whenever a pageant took place during bad weather. Much like my namesake, I didn't mind getting a little dirty.

Once we were competing on a stage by a large rice paddy in Porac, Pampanga, a town near Mount Pinatubo, the site of the second-largest volcanic eruption of the twentieth century. Right before the evening gown portion, rain started pouring, and the Lahar mud remnants from the eruption created a mud flow that slowly surrounded us. But given that we had traveled for hours to join this pageant, I wasn't going to let some flood get between me and the crown.

I saw the worried faces of the other candidates, all of them trying to figure out how they could do their planned routines under these conditions. But I decided to do something only the legendary Horse Barbie would do—something certain to capture the judges' attention.

My signature hairstyle, perfectly crafted by Eena, was the *palong*—teased-out hair in front, then combed to create a one-sided arch that framed my face as though it were a painting in a museum. Like blinders for a horse, my hair kept me focused on my goal, my vision set only on what lay ahead.

I walked out in my red evening gown, but instead of trying to avoid all the rain and mud, I embraced the messiness instead, flinging the trail of my gown to the judges' delight as I walked back and forth in front of the stage. The audience applauded my ingenuity. Never had they seen a performance that was so down to earth—literally!

When I got back onstage, the bottom of my gown was dripping, covered in mud. I was absolutely filthy. But I still won Best in Evening Gown that night—and the pageant title along with it.

Sometimes I could even upend the pageant results. No matter how the pageant had gone, I always knew the final walk—the last time the judges saw us before making their decision—was my moment to shine. This was when I felt my magic the most.

In some pageants, like one in San Jose, Nueva Ecija, I flubbed the

Q&A, causing confusion and head scratching among the crowd. But in that final moment, I stepped out with confidence in my iconic red halter evening gown with matching gloves, acting like it had never happened. Tigerlily had perfectly curled my hair and pinned it to the side in my signature style. And when I wore that wig just right, I couldn't be stopped.

As I took my last steps onstage, I knew there was only one person I needed to impress: the Hermana Mayor, a woman with long black hair sitting on a balcony overlooking the stage. I stepped right to the edge of the stage and looked at her, as fierce and proud as a Kentucky Derby champion. I turned to the side, showing the Hermana Mayor my profile. I wanted to edge out the other finalist, not by a nose but by my lips and my hair. She didn't see Assunta de Rossi in that moment; she saw Horse Barbie.

I took my place alongside the other finalist, holding hands as we waited for the winner to be announced. As the host opened his mouth, the Hermana Mayor interrupted him, crying out, "I want Assunta to win! The one in red. She reminds me of myself when I was young! We have the same hair! I was sexy like her."

Huhummmm.

The other finalist, one of the Montecarlo girls, stood there in shock. Her ghostlike skin was even paler than usual. She had done everything right. Her Q&A was perfectly polished. The judges had picked her. But money and power were in the hands of the Hermana Mayor, and I had used my magic on her—a magic that came from spirits, skeletons, and self-confidence.

The legacy of my hair lasted far beyond my reign. The *palong* and Assunta curl were copied and repeated for years. And my wig? It was passed down to other queens, too precious to be put in a box. The Garcia girls wore it for nearly a decade after me, finally laying it to rest in a prized area in Tigerlily's dressing room. Wherever it is now, I'm sure it still has some magic left.

6

MISS GAY UNIVERSE

"MISS GAY UNIVERSE 2000 IS . . ." THE ANNOUNCEMENT CAME OVER the loudspeaker.

I swear I could feel the energy pulsating through my veins as I waited what seemed like an eternity for my name.

". . . Assunta de Rossi!"

The seven-hundred-seat theater of our famed Music Museum burst into applause. The panel of judges, packed with celebrities, had picked me! At seventeen, I had just won the most prestigious pageant in the country. As I walked to the front of the stage, my sky-blue single-shoulder gown shimmering under the bright spotlights, I beamed with pride. The sparkling crown was heavier than I expected it to be. It reminded me just how much this victory mattered.

The bus ride back to Manila from a pageant in San Fernando La Union was quiet, the dim purple cabin lights having soothed most of my pageant family to sleep, so I jumped when I suddenly heard the tinny metallic chirping of my Nokia cellphone in my pocket. It was January 2001, and zigzagging over the one-lane mountain roads in the gray predawn, I'd been lulled into a near-doze after an hour or so of watching the view alternate between cliffs and shoreline, cliffs and shoreline, as we careened through the switchbacks.

The call was from Mama—and I scrambled to pick up, knowing it had to be important news. Several months ago, in 2000, not only had I won Miss Gay Universe, the most prestigious pageant in the country, but two of my clan sisters had taken second and third place. The Garcias were legends now, and I was a myth in the making.

The Miss Gay Universe title opened doors for me. A month after taking home the crown, a pageant organizer who also worked as a casting producer called me.

"Assunta, may TV role ako para sayo."

He wanted me to play a young Melanie Marquez in a TV series for GMA 7. I had never considered acting before, but I liked performing—and to play not just a cis role but the woman who was the Philippines' first Supermodel of the World finalist? Of course I said yes! I filmed my scene in an ancestral home opposite the sexy siren actress Divina Valencia, a screen staple since the 1960s.

Two years before, I had been walking on imaginary high heels for Tigerlily in my friend's living room, and now here I was, acting among the greats.

But my success had a ceiling. To make money—*real* money—a young trans pageant queen in the Philippines typically went to Japan after her reign was over. There she could become a *japanera*, performing in cabaret theaters and karaoke clubs all over the country. The work was a natural extension of starring in pageants—and the pay was apparently fantastic.

I heard stories of trans Filipinas becoming the family breadwinners after they went to Japan. Everyone in the pageant world whispered in awe about *japaneras* who had sent enough money back home to build their mothers' dream houses, help launch a business, or send their nieces and nephews to college.

Maybe working as a *japanera* could give me the money I needed to become like Tula—to be in magazines.

What young beauty queen wouldn't want that? For the next few months, as I sensed my pageant career reaching its plateau, I imagined myself as a *japanera*. It seemed like the logical next step—the only way to hold on to that feeling from the night I was crowned Miss Gay Universe 2000.

When my phone rang on the bus that night, I was only a few days away from starting the performing artist training I needed to complete to get my documents for Japan. A dance company was providing the classes and sponsoring my visa. The whole process could take as many as six months, but before long, I was going to be a *japanera*.

Unless—

"*Anak,* your green card has been approved!" Mama's voice burst through the tiny speaker the second I accepted the call.

"Ahhh!" I yelled, waking up some of the other passengers.

Was I screaming from happiness or from shock? It was hard to tell. In theory, I knew Mama had been trying to get my green card approved ever since she moved to California, but life had gotten so busy, and it wasn't something I thought about as often as I had when I was twelve or thirteen, right after she left. It all felt so sudden now.

Mama began to tell me how thrilled she was that her baby could be with her again, but as I sat there listening, I felt sadness wash over me. Here I was surrounded by my closest friends—some of them still half-asleep, others visibly annoyed by my late-night screaming—and I couldn't bear the thought of being so far away from them. Going to Japan was one thing—but the United States felt a world away.

"*Ma, ano pong next steps?*" I asked, wanting to buy more time to figure out how I felt about this.

"Let me figure it out, *anak*. I'll call you again."

"*Opo ma.*"

When I hung up, I turned to Tigerlily. We didn't say a word as sadness filled our faces. We sat there in silence, longing for each other even though we were right next to each other. We both knew the life we had spent the last two and a half years building was coming to an end, and so much sooner than we had expected.

The next day I called Mama back. "Mama, can I go to America the following year *po* instead?"

"Why, *anak*? We've waited six years for this. Why?" She was understandably upset.

"Mama, I want to go to Japan *po* and be a *japanera*," I told her.

For a few seconds, only static came through my little Nokia. I knew it was an excuse. Yes, I wanted to go to Japan, but more than that, I wanted to continue my pageant life. I was on top of my game, and according to Mama, there were no trans pageants in America. I couldn't be Assunta de Rossi in the United States.

"I want you to think about it, *anak*," she said. "I'll call again."

She hung up. But I was firm in my decision.

A week later, Mama called again.

"*Anak*, I understand your reasons, but"—and here her tone shifted as she whipped out her trump card—"did you know if you move to America, you can be legally recognized as a woman in your documents?"

This time the silence came from my end. I couldn't believe what Mama had said. It was an impossible dream, and she had just offered it so casually. I could barely comprehend it. A legal gender change was just a plane ride away? Mama might as well have been a genie granting my deepest wish.

"Uh . . . uh, what, Mama?" I stuttered, lump in my throat, trying to swallow the disbelief. "You mean I could have a female name and female gender marker on my documents?!"

In a flash, my vision of being a *japanera* was replaced with the dream of being addressed by anyone and everyone in America with my female name and as my true gender. I could live a life being seen and treated as I am. The fork in the path ahead suddenly became a road paved with possibility.

Despite the ubiquity of government-organized trans pageants in the Philippines, trans people themselves are not politically recognized. We are culturally visible but legally erased. To this day, trans Filipinas have M gender markers on their documents and cannot change their names in court. We don't have robust antidiscrimination protections. No amount of pageant glory can make up for the fact that our government still doesn't see and treat trans people as full citizens able to participate in society as we truly are.

In a country of over 100 million people, only a few dozen certified endocrinologists offer gender-affirming care. Growing up, I relied on other trans people to find hormones, figuring out the right dosages through community hearsay, transitioning entirely without proper medical supervision. There was no other choice back then—and for many today, DIY is still the only option.

My community is littered with stories of injections gone horribly wrong. Even worse, when someone dies from an overdose or an unsupervised medical treatment, it's shrugged off as a sad fact of life. "That's what happens," the emergency techs will say, our lives stripped of value by the very institutions that ought to care for us. I will never forget when one of my Garcia clan sisters succumbed to death from a botched medical procedure, a victim of all the intersecting forces trans Filipinas have to navigate to get treatment.

That kind of discrimination was as casual as it was cruel. To escape it would be a literal dream come true. There was nothing more to consider—I told Mama yes. She was the first schoolteacher I ever met who wanted me to get an F!

A few months later, she flew back to the Philippines to help me process my documents. Together we traversed the bureaucratic night-mare of processing my passport and securing my medical clearances. Pageant life was replaced with endless lines outside office buildings on humid Manila streets as I collected the necessary paperwork.

My final interview was at the U.S. embassy overlooking the Manila Bay, adjacent to the park that honors our national hero José Rizal. It was the end of the day, and the sun was setting over the water, but I felt like my life was just beginning.

Inside, the flurry of *americano* accents around me offered a pre-view of what was to come. A tall man in a business suit—what we call an *americano* suit—sat behind a glass window as he asked me the set list of questions.

"Why do you want to move to America?"

I wanted to give him an answer as transparent as the glass be-tween us.

I want to move to America because I will be a woman in America! was what my heart wanted to shout. I would declare it like a revolu-tionary who had just won the battle. But Mama had told me in ad-vance not to complicate my answer.

Instead, I just gave him the boilerplate reply, "I want to be with my family in America."

Looking back, maybe my motive was obvious. I was wearing a fit-ted blue cotton top stretched over my hormone boobs. I'm sure I wasn't the first trans Filipina to interview at the embassy. But he just ran through the rest of his logistical questions for us, nodding along with all our answers. It was happening!

The gentle thud of his stamp hitting my documents seemed to cue the swelling of an unseen orchestra. I was ecstatic, my future of af-firmation as certain as the fresh ink on my papers. I was going to America!

· · ·

We went to church to say our blessings the same day Mama and I picked up our plane tickets. We got home that night exhausted. It was late May 2001, and the summer rain and muggy humidity made us all feel groggy and tired. By this time, Ate Rhomalyn, Papa, and I were living in Pacita Complex, a suburb outside Manila, and we showered multiple times a day to beat the heat.

Papa hadn't been feeling well and had spent the day in bed, resting. After dinner, Mama went to check on him while Ate Rhomalyn and I settled down in front of the TV. The next thing I heard was her voice screaming Papa's name at the top of her lungs.

"Mollie! Mollie! Oh my god!"

My sister and I rushed to the room and saw Mama in a panic, Papa on the bed behind her.

"I think your papa is having a stroke!"

I remember only flashes of what happened next. I know we ran out to scream for help from the neighbors. The men hurried into our house, carrying Papa's body out. It felt unreal, like a movie. Despite all the chaos, somehow everything was quiet, the sounds muffled. The one image that etched itself into my mind amid the blur was Papa's unresponsive body, his loose shorts dangling around his legs, his belly protruding out from under his white tank top.

When we got to the family care hospital, Mama came out to join us in the waiting area. The prognosis was dire. *"Manalig kayo mga, anak,"* she told us, comforting us to have faith.

But she also told us that this local hospital was not equipped to handle a stroke as severe as Papa had suffered. The doctor's immediate priority was to get him stabilized. We waited for a couple more hours, hoping for a miracle. I have never prayed as hard as I did that day, humming *Lord, Jesus, please heal my papa,* sometimes aloud, sometimes in my head, as the hours ticked by.

At around three A.M., the doctor came out to let us know that

Papa was stable but in a fragile condition. If he were to deteriorate any further, he told us frankly, he wasn't sure he could save him. He gave us the name of a larger hospital in central Makati that could treat him, but it would cost an obscene amount of money to use their ambulance to get him there.

Mama asked the doctor if we could use our SUV instead. He said that it was possible, but there was a risk Papa would go into cardiac arrest on the way. It was a risk we would have to take. We needed to get him to Ospital ng Makati.

A team of nurses and doctors helped to lay Papa down in the middle passenger row of our white Toyota SUV.

About halfway through the drive, as our car settled into a calm rhythm on the dark highway, I reflected on the gravity of our situation. Here I was, holding on to Papa as he passed in and out of consciousness, IV tubes jutting out of his body, yellow highway lamps passing by overhead. I felt like my heart could burst at any moment. There was nothing else I could do for Papa besides hold him. He could die in my arms at any moment.

"Lord Jesus, please heal Papa."

I was still humming, still praying.

When we got to the emergency room entrance, everyone sprang into action. The hospital staff quickly ushered Papa inside. Mama and I sat in the empty waiting room on green hard-backed plastic chairs that made our situation feel even more clinical. I laid my head down on Mama's lap, exhausted.

The sunlight pried my eyes open at seven A.M. I heard jeepneys honking in the rush-hour traffic outside.

"Mama, did the doctor update you *po*?" I asked.

"Not yet, *anak*," she quietly replied.

An hour later the doctor came to find us. He sat down next to us, his demeanor somber. We knew what he was going to say before he said it, but the foreknowledge didn't make it any less painful to hear.

"Your husband just had a massive cardiac arrest," he said to Mama. "We couldn't save him. I'm so sorry."

On June 1, 2001, Papa passed in Ospital ng Makati.

It was fitting in a way that his life ended where so much of it had begun. He was back in the same city where he had raised us. The city where he used to take me food shopping at our *palengke* in Guadalupe Public Market. The city where he first fell in love with Mama, catching her eye at a dance. The city where he had always made me feel loved in all my femme boy spirit, without judgment, offering affirmation in the humorous ways only he knew how.

Seven weeks later, on July 20, was my *despedida,* a farewell party at our house, where my family and my trans pageant family were combined into one beautiful crowd. Our living room was a carousel of motion as my loved ones refilled plates of *pancit* noodles for long life and ate barbecued chicken that made our crisp Red Horse beer even more refreshing. Tigerlily commanded the karaoke mic, singing along in her high-pitched femme falsetto to Original Pilipino Music songs like Regine Velasquez's "Tanging Mahal."

I watched her from the doorframe, where I had a view of both the indoor karaoke party and the outdoor food table, where my trans family was gathered, giggling, hugging, laughing, reminiscing about how we all met. I could hear them teasing and reminding me that no matter how queenly I was onstage, they would always remember the fifteen-year-old me—their one and only Horse Barbie. Every person around that table had taken me in like one of their own.

There were no words to describe my anticipation. In twenty-four hours, all this culture—the culture I was born into—would be replaced by the storied American way of life. I didn't even know what that meant. Would I be an *americana*? What would happen to my Filipino-ness? The last two years of my life had seemed impossibly vast compared to the tiny *eskinita* where I grew up, traveling and adventuring all over the Philippines, from street parties to remote pageant stages in the jungle. I had even been on TV. But I couldn't begin to comprehend what lay ahead of me.

My universe was about to explode.

PART II

SAN FRANCISCO

7
G-E-E-N-A

I SMELLED THE UNITED STATES BEFORE I EVER SET FOOT IN IT.

Our family in America regularly sent us *balikbayan* boxes—large, tightly wrapped care packages shipped by freight, bursting at the seams with clothes, electronics, and other goodies. I cared almost as much about getting a whiff of the box itself as I did about what was inside. My siblings and I would tear it open and sniff at the foreign air.

"It smells . . . *imported*," we'd say.

It smelled like America. It smelled like possibility. And then the pleasant aroma would dissipate, replaced by the dominant scent of the Philippines, which—well, let's just say it's a *different* smell.

When I stepped outside San Francisco International Airport for the first time that night in July 2001, I took a deep breath of fresh air and thought of those big *balikbayan* boxes. It was me who was imported now, starting over in a new country an ocean away—a place where I had been promised I could be free.

The flight to California with Mama had been long and anxious. I had never been on a plane before, so I had naïvely worn a light summery outfit and leather thong sandals. My feet were basically Popsicles by the time we landed in Taipei for our layover.

As we flew across the Pacific, Mama filled my head with our plans for the weekend. "Tomorrow," she said, "you're going to meet your cousins, you're going to see your grandma, and then we're all going to a nice buffet brunch."

I was excited but also anxious about what this new world would be like. I had seen San Francisco in pictures and videos that Mama and her family had sent—and in American movies like *Vertigo* and *Basic Instinct*. I wanted to ride down the Pacific Coast Highway in a red Pontiac Sunfire, but that was just a fantasy. I knew my life was going to look a lot different in California. There would be no pageant adventures.

Sensing my jitteriness, Mom took a break from reciting our agenda to comfort me. "*Anak, napaka* excited *ako* for you," she said. "*Huwag kang mag alala*—your *ate* Rhomalyn will follow after a few years."

Outside family, the only person I knew in San Francisco was Lucy—the trans queen who won the Miss Gay Evangelista crown in 1998, the year before I won second runner-up. I hadn't seen her in two years, ever since she moved away. She had left the Philippines before I ever got the chance to befriend her, but mutual friends had passed along her contact info when they heard I was headed stateside. She knew I was coming, and she promised to help get me set up once I was here.

Even though I knew I could change my name and gender marker in America, I had no idea what that process looked like. If it was anywhere near as labyrinthine as navigating an international airport, I was going to need some help.

Mama's boyfriend of two years, Tito José, picked us up from SFO in a silver Mitsubishi sports car and drove us out to the small room she was renting from Tita Maria, her best friend, and Maria's partner Cathy, in Vallejo, forty minutes outside the city. We knew Mama had started dating people in the States, but it was an unspoken understanding.

I thought meeting Tito José for the first time would be awkward, but during a drive-through stop at Burger King on the way home, I observed the tenderness with which he treated Mama. His romantic gestures and caring touches were a marked shift from the acrimony of my parents' final years of marriage. Plus, looking at his shiny bald head from the back seat of the car made me smile.

Stepping into Mama's apartment later that day felt like going back in time. I had spent high school sharing beds and floor space with my pageant sisters in Tigerlily's house, but now I was with Mama again, living together for the first time since I was twelve years old. She had come home to visit Papa and me in the Philippines regularly, but those trips were never the same as being with her for good, with no goodbyes on the horizon. There had always been a cutoff when I would have to go back to cuddling my hot dog pillow at night.

But in that little Vallejo sublet, I was her baby again. We shared a twin bed, and she cradled me in her arms, both of us making up for years of lost time.

"My little Bojojoy, *andito ka na, ang saya saya ko anak,*" she told me. I didn't need my huggy pillow anymore. I had Mama.

To change my name and gender marker, I needed money, and to get money, I needed a job. It's not like I could sell *kalamay* on the street or win cash prizes at Catholic fiestas anymore. San Francisco suburbia felt soulless and sanitized compared to home, where there was always a festival or a street party happening somewhere nearby.

Mama suggested I apply for a job at Target and try to get into a nearby nursing school. A seasoned American by then, she knew the most common trajectories for new arrivals like me, and they all began in grocery stores and customer service roles.

America promised me legal recognition, but it certainly wasn't going to give me glamour.

Still, I was hoping Lucy might have some more exciting options for an ex–beauty queen like me. I wasn't ready to leave my glory days behind before I even turned eighteen. One Friday soon after I arrived, I took the ferry from Vallejo to see my old friend, looking up in awe at the fog-shrouded Golden Gate Bridge as the boat pulled into the terminal.

"We're going out!" she told me as soon as I arrived at her downtown apartment, throwing her arms around me and pulling me into a fast embrace.

She solved my employment problem just as quickly.

"All the girls work in cosmetics, so you should work in cosmetics," she told me as we got ready to go dancing. That sounded a lot more exciting than looking up produce codes at a cash register. The makeup counter was at least pageant-*adjacent*.

There was only one problem: I never had to apply my own makeup when I was in the Philippines. My hair and makeup stylist had done it for me every night.

"Relax," Lucy said, like it was normal in America to get jobs doing things you didn't know how to do. "Everything's going to be fine."

She took me out to Divas, a famous trans bar in the Tenderloin, and within minutes I found myself surrounded by new Filipina friends, dancing like I was back home with my Garcia clan celebrating a major victory. *So this is where America is hiding all the fun,* I thought. Divas was no substitute for a fiesta, but it was at least a taste of home in a foreign place. Maybe I could have a trans community here after all, if I knew where to look for it. Lucy introduced me to everyone until our voices were hoarse, the crowd multiplying impossibly as the hours wore on. There were so many of us. It was exhilarating.

By the time dawn came, I knew two things: I had to move to San Francisco—and I needed more noodle soup. We wound up at a nearby 24/7 Thai restaurant, trying to prevent our hangovers with a hot meal, and Lucy was already plotting away, planning out my future.

"I know people at Macy's," she told me, perky as ever, totally unaffected by our all-night dancing marathon.

Macy's. Now, there was a name that meant something. It was an American legend—the stuff of Thanksgiving Day parades and Thirty-fourth Street miracles. I liked the sound of working there. I just needed help getting in the door. Back at Lucy's place, she started teaching me how to contour my face in a dark purple shade she called "blurple." This was the way they wanted you to do it at the department stores, she said: sharp, bold, dramatic.

"It's easy, see?" she would say after showing me a new trick, but I could barely keep my eyes open by then. I needed a nap. So I slept on her queen-size bed, and then we went out again, and I met more Filipina friends and got another crash course in cosmetics.

By the time I took the ferry back to Vallejo, it was already Tuesday.

"Where have you been?" Mama asked me.

"I'm applying for a job in San Francisco!" I told her.

It wasn't nursing school, but Mama was still impressed by how fast I had networked. More important, she was happy I had new friends already. She knew how hard it had been for me to leave the Garcia clan behind, and how raw my emotions still were from Papa's passing. She understood, too, how alluring the idea of getting new identity documents was for me, and she didn't want me to have to sacrifice everything I loved to get them.

I didn't have time to learn much more about makeup before I had to go in for my job interview. But as always, Lucy had the answer. Her grandma owned a beauty salon below her apartment where I got my makeup done and my hair blown out for free. We kept the look understated, as if I had done it myself. If anyone at Macy's had asked me to prove my skills on the spot, I would have failed. But they didn't—and I got the job.

My first day of work would be August 21, exactly one month after I'd landed at SFO.

I certainly couldn't have guessed that the path to being acknowledged as a woman would run through the aisles of Macy's.

As it turned out, a lot of the girls I met that night dancing with Lucy worked in the Macy's cosmetics department. There was a trans Filipina at nearly every counter. They felt like family right away. It was as though my community back home had teleported across the Pacific. We all worked together every day in an indoor *eskinita* that smelled like Chanel No. 5, laughing and joking whenever we weren't helping customers.

Lunch hour at the employee cafeteria felt like one big fiesta, with everyone bringing their own food to join in on the feast and *chismis*.

They all knew I was the shit—the top queen back home—but we were all equals here.

Not that that stopped Danmark from teasing me. Danmark was tall and beautiful, with blondish flat-ironed hair and buttery smooth skin. The sparkle of his blue contact lenses and the subtle shine of his lip gloss only added to his dazzle. He worked at Yves Saint Laurent, the next counter over from my post at Benefit, and he routinely read me for filth, mocking my fashion choices and calling me "fresh off the boat." I wanted him to be my best friend.

"Bitch, it's so cold in San Francisco!" he all but screamed one day when he saw my street clothes. "Why are you wearing that?"

I looked down at my pedal pushers, my thin V-neck shirt, and my leather *sinelas* and saw nothing wrong with my attire. But Danmark set me straight—well, as straight as a gay best friend can set someone.

He liked to take me to the thrift shops on Haight Street and help me pick out more fashionable clothing but stopped short of telling me exactly what to wear. "*You* have to pick your style, girl," he would tell me.

With big bags full of clothes, we'd go back to his apartment, smoke weed, and listen to American music. Making sense of English was still hard for me—once at Macy's I had to ask my manager to take over when a woman with a southern accent asked for help—but when I was high, the lyrics to J.Lo, Aaliyah, and Eminem songs made perfect sense. When the high wore off, we'd go out partying and head straight back to work in the morning.

I used my first two paychecks from Macy's to pay the $300 fee for a name change at the Solano County Courthouse. Mama took me to fill out the paperwork. She knew this was my dream—the reason I had left my pageant life behind—and she wanted to be there for the occasion.

I had written only the first two letters of my name on the application form when I felt her gently nudge me.

"Are you sure?" she asked, her eyebrows raised. "G-I-N-A sounds a little . . . basic."

First Danmark was throwing shade at me—and now Mama was, too!

But then she leaned over, looked closer at the form, and thought for a second. "Maybe put two E's," she said. "G-E-E-N-A."

She made it sound like a simple suggestion. But we both knew what was happening: She was renaming me and reclaiming me as her daughter. The look we exchanged in that moment said it all. Mama had already chosen what I was called once; it was only fair that she got a second chance.

I added three little horizontal lines to the side of my I and kept writing: "G-E-E-N-A."

It was more than just an extra letter; it was the affirmation I so badly wanted. My birth country had made it impossible for my own name to belong to me, extinguishing the boundless possibility of my ancestors' precolonial gender fluidity with a restrictive system that kept us confined in legal boxes. Seeing my new name in front of me for the first time felt overwhelming, a victory with no vanity in it. This mattered more to me than a million pageant trophies. After all this time, I was going to be seen as myself.

I filed the form away at the courthouse, but I took my new name with me out the door.

It was mine now. It was in me.

When my name change finally got processed and I received my new California state ID card in the mail, I screamed. Not only did my new ID say "Geena," but someone had made a clerical error, and I had an F gender marker, too, even though I wasn't supposed to be able to get one without surgery.

"I can't believe it!" I squealed. "Mama, I can't believe it!"

My excitement was way too big for that little sublet room in Vallejo. I ran outside, giddy, trying to cause a commotion the same way I would have back in the *eskinita*. I had big news. *Amazing* news. What else was I supposed to do but share it with everyone? The whole neighborhood needed to hear about this.

"Come look!" I yelled, holding the license in my hand, still incredulous.

Mama chased after me, but I was already running, jumping with joy. By the time she caught up with me, I was in the neighbor's front yard, looking for a way into their house so I could tell them what had happened.

"Stop!" Mama yelled, and I did, surprised by the note of fear in her voice.

"You can't do that, Geena!" she said, and elation swelled in me once again—yes, that was officially my name now. Geena! G-E-E-N-A. Shouldn't I tell everyone?

"Why can't I?" I asked her. "They're our neighbors!"

"I know you're happy, but you can't just walk into other people's homes," she explained, catching her breath. "If they have a gun, they could shoot you."

I was shocked. At home in the *eskinita*, everyone was in and out of one another's houses all the time. It was a community. Everyone had always told me how wonderful things would be in America, but Mama was showing me another side of our strange new home. Here in the suburbs, the houses might be lined up close to one another, but we were neighbors in name only. If you were of a different race or grew up somewhere else, you were an outsider. The white picket fences all around us were aptly named; white people were on one side of them, and on the other, there were people like me for whom this neighborhood was far from friendly.

I was a young trans Filipina immigrant, and Mama wanted me to understand what that meant for me here. No one was going to bring me a freshly baked pie to welcome me. Rather, they would cast piercing, doubtful eyes in my direction as I walked past. We could get money in America, I could be recognized in America, but those gains would come with perils we could not ignore.

It was the first time I really understood how dangerous life in America could be.

Soon my trans Filipina friends taught me that same lesson. We met every week at the Asia and Pacific Islander Wellness Center, a resource hub and hangout spot with regular events for the trans AAPI community that was only a few minutes from Macy's. Kasia, a trans Filipina with a Barbie doll body and bleached blond hair that came down to her waist, was the coordinator of the program and the moderator of the Metamorphosis Wednesday discussion group.

A lot of the girls used the time to talk about the men they were seeing. Back home in the Philippines, where we were more visible, we didn't have to worry as much about disclosing the fact that we were trans. People generally knew already.

Here in America, if you didn't tell a guy and he found out anyway, he would often get angry. And that anger could lead to violence. You had to be careful. Every girl had a different opinion about how to handle these situations.

"I disclose right away," some would say. "It's too dangerous not to."

Other girls, especially the super femme ones like Marta, waited before they told a guy, if they even disclosed at all. "He doesn't have to know," they'd say. "Why should I have to tell him? It's not some shameful confession I need to make up front."

I didn't know yet where I fell. As Danmark had said, I'd have to pick my own style.

The September after I arrived, I went on a weekend retreat to Lake Tahoe with the Metamorphosis group. Kasia had made all the arrangements, renting a van and a big cabin for all of us to share. When we got to Harrah's Casino that first night, some of the girls started flirting with guys on the floor, and others started working, exchanging knowing looks with potential clients.

Meanwhile I was staring at my surroundings, trying to figure out what a casino was, dazzled by all the lights and distracted by all the dinging noises.

Marta and her super femme friends came back to the main group after making some rounds around the floor, excited. "Some guys are flirting with us," she shared.

Kasia shot her a skeptical look. She knew Marta hadn't disclosed. But I thought nothing more of it until we got back to the cabin that night and Marta dropped a bombshell on the group: "I invited those guys to come over."

Kasia freaked out. She scolded Marta, telling her she had put us all in danger. Right on cue, there was a knock at the door. We peeked through the side window at the front porch. "Oh my God, there are six of them?" Kasia gasped.

They were dressed like lumberjacks, some of them carrying six-packs of cheap beer, their faces full of anticipation. They clearly thought they were getting laid tonight. Two trucks were parked in the driveway, headlights already off. Even Marta was a little scared now. She realized what she had done.

But Kasia took charge. "Tell them they can't come in," she told Marta and her friends, the most passable of all of us. "Everybody else, go hide. Now."

Kasia switched off the living room lights, and we all scurried like frightened mice into different corners of the cabin. I ran into a bedroom closet and pulled the door shut behind me. Over the sound of my own breathing, I could hear Marta's voice faintly in the entryway.

"No, no," she was saying. "We're really tired. Sorry, guys."

We waited. I held my breath. The front door clicked shut. And then we heard their trucks drive away. We emerged from our hiding places and breathed a communal sigh of relief.

But then they came back again. Kasia wasn't fazed—it was like she knew they would try again—and she told us to follow the same protocol. We all ran to the same spots as before, and Marta met them at the door.

"No, no, I'm really sorry," she told them. "You really can't come in."

By this point, I was terrified. We were a house full of trans women partying alone in the middle of the night. These guys knew our address and seemed determined to get in. Was this what life in the

United States would cost me? I could have the right name on my identification, but I would have to live in fear? Even as the adrenaline ran through my veins, the irony wasn't lost on me: I had left the Philippines, where everyone knew I was trans, only to find myself in a literal closet in America.

I was legally recognized here but culturally misunderstood. Worse, I was invisible, one of thousands of trans people working behind counters and cash registers, who kept the gears of society turning, but who would be thrown away the second we asked to be seen. I was a dirty little secret, desired but ultimately disposable.

It made me wonder how much my new name was worth to me. If America was going to mock my very being, deny my womanhood, and shame me for expressing myself, what good was it to officially be Geena on my paperwork? I thought I could dream here, but my dreams were hemmed in. The guys outside the door weren't just threatening; they were a symbol of what might happen to me if I dared to step out of my place.

Welcome to America, I guess.

I missed my home. I missed Tigerlily and the Garcia clan. I missed Papa and wished he were here to protect me from these men. He would have made sure nothing bad happened to me.

Finally, the front door closed. Marta had convinced them to go. The truck engines started, their low rumbling fading into the distance. "Are they really gone?" someone asked.

We all came out again, shaken, the word *retreat* we'd used to describe this weekend getaway now taking on new significance.

One month later, on October 4, 2002, a trans teenager the same age as me was murdered in Newark, California—less than an hour south of Vallejo. Her name was Gwen Araujo. She had bravely come out on the eve of the new millennium, naming herself after Gwen Stefani, her favorite singer, only to face constant mistreatment at school.

A classmate said that Gwen's transition had made total sense—that it seemed like the most natural change in the world. "She was a girl just trying to be herself," the classmate later told a reporter, "and people didn't understand that."

Four men killed Gwen one night using methods too brutal for me to repeat here. They buried her in a forest almost three hours by car from the crime scene. When they were finished putting dirt back on her shallow grave, they went to McDonald's.

In court, some of the killers would claim a "panic" defense, arguing for a lesser sentence because of the supposed shock of finding out that Gwen was transgender. It would take over a decade—until 2014—for that defense to be fully banned from California courts.

In the meantime, Gwen Araujo's murder sent shockwaves through the Bay Area trans community—and it made me wonder whether there was anywhere on earth I could be respected and free at the same time. I had crossed an ocean for recognition. But what good was that recognition without safety?

8

WA BUKING

I WASN'T IN AMERICA LONG BEFORE I FOUND OUT I HAD LOOKS that could literally stop traffic.

During my breaks at Macy's, I liked to walk along O'Farrell Street to an outpost of the famous Boudin Bakery for a little treat. One day when I was so close to the café I could smell the sourdough, I heard a motorcycle revving on the street behind me. *Vroom, vroom.* Clearly I had caught somebody's attention.

I turned around and saw him there—leather jacket, Harley, the classic combination. We exchanged an intense look but said nothing. I could tell this man was enthralled with me—and I knew why: I was *really* feeling myself on my walk. My all-black work outfit was hugging my body in the right places. I had red lipstick on, as was my custom when I worked the cosmetics counter. My hair was curled into gentle waves, tousled by a gentle breeze from the hills above. *Vroom, vroom* was right. I wasn't just having a good hair day; I was having a good *everything* day.

I kept walking the last half block to Boudin, listening to the sound of his engine trailing behind me the entire time. I could almost hear his thoughts, too: *Who is this beautiful woman?* But he must have been thinking it a little too loudly because, as I turned to open the door to the bakery, I heard a loud bang. Turning, I saw his motorcycle jammed up against the rear bumper of a red sedan, the handsome rider fuming beside it. He had taken his eyes off the road for too long. He had been too busy watching me.

For a second, I froze, mortified, feeling somehow responsible for what had happened. *Should I say something? Should I go help him?* But my break was almost over, so I sheepishly ducked into Boudin instead. And as the cashier rang me up, I realized I must have been *wa buking*—unclockable. The man on the motorcycle had no idea I was trans.

At eighteen, that idea was more thrilling to me than anything else: In America, being *wa buking* was a superpower. Yes, I could use it to snag men if I wanted to—and I *did* want to—but more important, being unclockable felt like a way out of the impossible double bind America had put me in. If my choice was either to be invisible in public or to be seen as a cis woman, I was going to pick the latter every time.

Being *wa buking* could help me access not just relationships but experiences and privileges that would otherwise be denied to me.

Back in the Philippines, I had grown accustomed to shouts of *Bakla!* anytime I walked down the street. Transness was hypervisible there in a way that it wasn't in the United States of 2003. And so for our entire community of trans Filipinas in San Francisco, *wa buking* was a common goal: To be unclockable was to ascend to the highest levels of affirmation that American society had to offer. It was a measurement of how far we all had come from a place where everyone knew our T.

We'd even tease one another when someone did their hair or their makeup especially nice. *"Oh, wa buking, ka dyan sis,"* we'd say, in the same tone as *Don't you look nice?*

Of course, everyone who worked at Macy's knew. All the other employees had heard that trans Filipinas ran the cosmetics counters. When I went up to the fourth floor to see what kind of clothes I could afford with my employee discount, I'd hear murmuring from the women who worked up there.

"That's the girl, that's the girl!" one would say to another, glancing sneakily at me from behind a rack of jeans, as if I were one of P. T. Barnum's exhibits.

We were the *chismis* of Macy's for sure. But I couldn't have cared less. We had so much fun hanging out together.

During off hours at work, the main aisle through the cosmetics department became a makeshift pageant stage. All the trans girls, gay boys, and queer people would come out from behind the counter, moving in formation, strutting our stuff to music like Miss Universe queens vying for the crown. In our imaginations, our work attire became sparkling sequined evening gowns and plunging swimsuits.

The few non-Filipino people who worked in cosmetics loved the free entertainment, so they'd take turns keeping a lookout for our manager, a white woman with fiery red hair and a high-pitched voice. Still, we showed up on the security camera, and we'd sometimes get reported anyway. The manager would chastise us—but we'd just do it all over again, undeterred. Cosmetics was our queendom.

But we drew a different kind of attention from the customers, who almost never clocked us. One day while I was working the counter, a tall guy—like, almost *seven feet* tall—walked straight toward me, surrounded by his entourage. He was a famous NBA player I recognized because his team was popular in the Philippines. As he took a seat at my counter, he motioned for his entourage to leave. He wanted to talk to me alone.

"Where are you from?" he asked me.

"The Philippines," I told him.

He kept talking, but I was too nervous to follow what he was saying. I hadn't been in the United States long enough to be fully conversational in American English, let alone to chat up a basketball superstar. Back home, the way we spoke English was very proper. We didn't use slang or take any verbal shortcuts. Instead, we spoke like schoolteachers trying to help children pronounce new words. Still, I could tell from his intense eye contact and his wide smile that he was flirting with me. It was mind-boggling to me, and honestly thrilling, that he could be looking at me so closely without realizing I was trans.

"Do you want to join us?" he was asking me, when I tuned back in to what he was saying. By this time, the entire department had fallen quiet as they tried to eavesdrop on our conversation, waiting on tenterhooks for me to respond.

"I'm sorry, I'm really busy," I told him. "I can't do anything tonight."

He looked almost as shocked as he did disappointed, as if he couldn't believe the girl at the cosmetics counter was saying no to him. But he got up and left anyway, his entourage rejoining him on his way out of the store. I had enjoyed using my superpower on an NBA superstar, but going with him would have been a bad idea. Eventually, if you got close enough to someone, you were no longer *wa buking,* you were a freak.

"What did he say?" everyone asked me. "Geena, what did he say?"

Even my cousin, who worked upstairs in juniors, rushed down the escalator because he had heard through the grapevine who exactly I had been talking to.

"Cousin, what the fuck did you do?!" he shrieked. "Don't you know who that was? Why did you say no? You could have taken me with you!"

But of course, accepting his invitation had to stay a fantasy: As a trans woman, there was no such thing as a carefree night spent among American men. I could stop traffic on the street, but the bedroom was a much more dangerous place.

. . .

What confused me the most was that American men did desire trans women, just not openly.

Most nights my first stop after work was Divas, the iconic trans bar in the Tenderloin where Lucy had taken me during my first night in San Francisco. Divas was a four-story legend, with mirrored walls that made its already large crowd of trans-amorous men seem even bigger. I was only seventeen when I started going there with Danmark and Lucy, but my fake ID and some flirtation did the trick.

Once inside, men would buy me drinks with lightning quickness, and here the drinks didn't come with strings attached: Every guy there already knew I was trans, and they thought that was sexy. In Divas, I didn't need my *wa buking* superpower; I could already command the kind of attention I craved.

One night before I could even say hi to the bodacious trans bartender, a glass was already waiting for me. "Hey babe, this bubbly is for you," the bartender said. "From handsome in the corner."

She nodded over at a gentleman in his midthirties, wearing a suit, who looked uncannily like Ryan Phillippe. I gave him a nod, nothing more, as I raised my champagne flute and took my first sip. Then as I walked past him on my way to the dance floor, I stopped for a moment to run my finger slowly down the nape of his neck to the end of his tie. Catching the end, I tugged it, and mouthed a silent *thank you*.

It was hot. I could be such a flirt when I felt safe. Lucy and I danced, the mirrored ball casting sparkles all over my face, as I lost myself completely in the moment, singing along to Aaliyah's "Try Again."

Every so often I'd turn to face my admirer, lip-synching along to the lyrics: *"I'm into you, you into me, but I can't let it go so easily."*

Outside Divas, though, American society sent me the opposite message: Trans women were disgusting. Television was basically transphobic propaganda. The Philippines had no equivalent of Jerry Springer or Maury Povich, parading us around onstage as a spectacle for a riled-up studio audience; no, we were in pageants and even had legitimate TV roles. So it was a shock to watch daytime TV on my days off and find out that women like me were something of a weird, almost taboo fixation, despite our relative invisibility in public life.

Jerry Springer typically liked to bring a trans woman out onstage alongside a man she had slept with, buttering her up at first with compliments about her looks. Even before I could clock her visually, I knew from the way Springer was talking—and from that devilish twinkle in his eye—what was happening. He was building up to the reveal.

"Have you figured it out yet?" he'd nudge the audience, and then voilà, he'd announce that she was "secretly a man" or that she had "gotten a sex change." In an explosion of moblike rage, the studio audience, her boyfriend, *everyone*, would turn on her, booing and jeering and hurling insults. It was gutting to watch it happen to these gorgeous women. They were on national TV, just as I had been in the Philippines, but I certainly never wanted to be on TV like *this*. This was a fucking circus.

Maury Povich was almost worse because he'd make the audience play literal guessing games in segments like "Glamour Girls or Sexy Studs?"

"We've invited twelve beauties to our stage today, and some of them were born female, some were born male, and it's up to me and you to decide who's who!" he cheekily announced in one episode, then solicited guesses from the audience, even giving out cash to people who got it right. They pointed at the women, most of whom used stage names like Mango and Raven, looking for Adam's apples and shouting, "That's a man! That's a man!"

I remember how shame sank into my heart, like a stone to the bottom of a lake, when I saw that segment. It seemed like no one could be proud of being trans here, not publicly. And if this was how trans women were treated in American entertainment, I didn't want any part of it. Better to stick to the cosmetics department of Macy's, participating in our impromptu runway walks and in the small handful of trans Filipina pageants held in California. Jerry Springer and Maury Povich, these two older white men, were a barometer for American attitudes around gender and for the reactionary beliefs people held toward trans women. We were perceived as gross, unattractive fakers.

It was hard to square that attitude with the fact that Divas was always packed full of men hoping to take someone home that night. Anywhere outside that bar, being a newly immigrated trans woman from the Philippines was hardly an advantage. But inside, I was a goddess. Before I ever came to America, I watched a lot of *Baywatch*, admiring the way Pamela Anderson and Carmen Electra dropped jaws on the beach in their high-cut red swimsuits. I had expected desire in the United States to look like *that*—me running in slow motion, doing sexy hair flips for all to see. Instead, it looked like me commanding the attention of everyone in a cramped nightclub. But there was still a lot to like.

The men at Divas worshipped us, tending to our every need. One prominent tech CEO was a regular—and he *loved* trans Filipinas. He became something of a sugar daddy for me, as he had been for countless trans Filipinas before me. There was no jealousy between me and my friends because he had plenty of money to go around, and it was only fair that I get my due as the latest to arrive. I quickly became his favorite. It was fun to flirt with him, but the extra income was nice, too. Back in the Philippines, in the trans pageant scene, we had a custom of paying for all our boyfriends, but here I was getting spoiled—and it felt nice.

You'd think my Catholic guilt might have kicked in at Divas, but it felt so much like the transactional exchanges of my pageant world that I never really felt bad about having a sugar daddy. Danmark, Lucy, and I would stay there long enough to collect our free drinks, then head out to the nightclubs and dance until they closed. Finally, at two A.M., drunk off our asses, we would go to an infamous sex club called Power Exchange—and only then would I be tempted to make the sign of the cross and whisper a prayer.

We went there to watch. The vulgarity of public sex shocked and thrilled me all at once. Simultaneously, I thought, *Oh my god, this is so hot,* and *Oh my god, I'm seeing too much!* Around one corner, I'd watch a trans woman surrounded by sexy men just going at her, and obviously that fantasy did something for me. I wanted to drive men that wild.

But around another corner, I would see a man whipping a hand-cuffed woman, and the Catholic guilt came surging up. *He's hurting her!* I thought, wincing with each strike. I instinctually covered my eyes at some points, but then peeled my hands back off my face because I didn't want to look like the prudish dork in the sex club.

And once I watched, I realized this scene was hot, too. It all was. But it was hidden. Desire in America was a thorny thing: It seemed like people were really honest about what they wanted only under cover of darkness.

I told Mama next to nothing about my late-night adventures. I mean, the kind of stuff I saw at Power Exchange was not exactly dinner table talk. By this point, we had moved into a two-bedroom apartment on Fifth Street, eight blocks from my work. Mama had left her job at the factory due to a knee injury, so I was paying the bulk of the rent.

"I'm going out with Danmark!" I would tell her on my way out the door, and leave the rest to her imagination.

She might not have known specifics, but she could sense that

Danmark was a bad influence—at least in her eyes. I loved hanging out with my new gay best friend. He knew how this place worked and how to navigate it.

On Mondays, after meeting Danmark at his place on Haight Street, we'd join Lucy at the Café, the biggest nightclub in the Castro District, on the corner of Market and Castro. They played hip-hop and poured strong drinks on Mondays—strong enough that we'd be shit-faced within an hour, throwing up in the bathroom, drinking some more, dancing, and smoking weed. We'd light up—literally— whenever they played Christina Aguilera. Standing on the outdoor side patio, looking in through the glass at the crowd on the dance floor, we'd watch the commotion through big puffs of smoke and sing, "Ring the alarm, and I'm throwin' elbows!" as we felt the high go to our heads.

I'm not sure how we ever managed to stumble back to Danmark's apartment from the Castro, but we did, and we'd all pass out at his place. It's a miracle any of us made it to work the next day.

Danmark had moved to the United States when he was only eleven years old. But before he did, he lived in Pacita Complex, a suburb of Laguna, just outside Manila, so we shared common roots. In fact, he and my very first boyfriend in the Philippines had been in the same elementary school class. Because he had gotten here so early, Danmark wanted to teach me everything I needed to know about America. He was like a gay Filipino version of Professor Henry Higgins from *My Fair Lady*, but the opposite, teaching me how to *stop* speaking formally and start using slang. We smoked weed and listened to Destiny's Child until I no longer sounded so studious and aloof.

When I first met Danmark and he asked what we should do after work, I would always say, "Let's play it by the ear."

But as we belted out the lyrics to our favorite songs in a weed haze, bumping to "Bug a Boo" and "Emotion," I would realize which idioms I had been saying wrong. "Play it by ear" was how the phrase went, Danmark would correct me, and we'd laugh not just at my mistakes but at the fact that I seemed able to absorb American slang only when we were smoking weed.

Some days he'd take me to hang out with his high school friends in Alameda, a suburb outside San Francisco. He'd bring me just so I could see what it was like outside our Filipino bubble, and I'd work my way through conversations with his mostly white friends. They knew I had just come to America, so they were always spoon-feeding me the words I was reaching for, finishing my sentences for me, and filling in any missing vocabulary. They talked about college life. It was still novel to me that teenagers would leave home for college and live together in dormitories. That piqued my curiosity. I talked mostly about Justin Timberlake and Christina Aguilera. Pop culture was my wheelhouse, and if we ventured too far outside it, I couldn't keep up.

As a bright-eyed eighteen-year-old who had been raised on American movies, I was eager to adapt to my new surroundings. When Christina Aguilera dropped *Stripped* in 2002 and changed her look with that chunky, dirty bleached blond hair, I got my hair done the exact same way. I explored and absorbed everything I liked about this country. Call it assimilation, call it survival, call it curiosity, but I wanted to fit in. And to do it, though I didn't recognize it as shame at first, I felt like I had to leave my Filipina immigrant identity behind.

I'd come home from work some days to find Mama watching soap operas on the Filipino Channel, a station based in nearby Daly City that broadcasts programming all over the world. Here we were in California, the entertainment capital of the planet, with an enormous new TV in our living room, and Mama was watching shows from home?

At Danmark's, we liked to watch *Felicity* and *Will & Grace*, both shows about young people looking for love in New York City. We'd watch new episodes and reruns, dreaming about chic studio apartments and taxicabs and better nightclubs than San Francisco's. My dalliances at Divas were fun, but this was what I thought I wanted: To be a sexy young American woman enjoying a glamorous urban existence. To be free of the contradictory knots that trans women like me were expected to accept as our fate.

If being *wa buking* was the way to achieve it, so be it.

"This is going to be our life one day," Danmark and I would tell each other. "This is going to be our life."

Still, it's not like I could put my own desires on pause until I could afford surgery. I was a young woman coming into my own sexuality. In my naïveté, it wasn't always easy for me to tell the difference between my own desire for men and my desire to be desired by them, but I felt the undeniable pull either way.

At Macy's, the manager of a local four-star hotel came by my counter all the time, always sipping on an enormous candy-colored Jamba Juice from the location downstairs. He wasn't interested in buying makeup, he was interested in me, dialing up his flirtations a little more with each midafternoon visit.

I knew from all the girls' stories at Metamorphosis that I was playing a dangerous game. He didn't know about me yet, of course. I was *wa buking*. But if I went on a date with him, there would be a limit to what we could do together without him finding out. It felt unfair, though, that I had to deny myself what I wanted. This man was bold, and he was sexy. He had a good job and a nice car. Was I really going to say no to everyone until I got the money I needed to become even more unclockable?

One day when he asked me out, I said yes. He drove me across the Golden Gate Bridge to the Tiburon Peninsula, and we had a beautiful date, watching the marine layer come in across the San Francisco skyline at sunset. My heart was pounding the entire time, half from the excitement of being with him, but half from the fear of being found out. I was getting what I wanted, and now I would have to deal with the consequences. Apparently, you don't believe some lessons until you learn them for yourself.

Back at his place, we started making out on his bed, and I knew I had to tell him before we got too far. I was already risking my life; I knew from my friends at Metamorphosis that some men would react violently even to the realization that they had *kissed* a trans woman. If he tried to put his hands up my dress, or if he started thinking too hard about any suspicions that might have arisen during the evening, this man's face could be the last thing I ever saw.

"Wait," I said. "I have to tell you something. I'm transgender."

In that moment, my worst fears were confirmed. His face turned tomato red after the words came out of my mouth, and he flew into a rage, shouting, calling me ugly names, and berating me for not having told him sooner. It wasn't enough that we had stopped; he hated me for having even let things get this far. I stepped backward away from him, eyeing my exits. There was a chance I would need to run. Adrenaline pumped through me. When he saw how scared he was making me, he collected himself, but the disdain in his eyes remained.

"I think you need to get out of my bedroom," he said.

I hurried out the door, and he appeared a few minutes later, fully clothed, telling me gruffly that he was going to drive me home. He lived in Sunset in Ocean Beach, only a twenty-minute ride from my downtown apartment, but time seemed to stretch out infinitely as we made the trip. Even the air coming out of the A/C felt heavy, like thick smog weighing down the flirtatious energy we had shared earlier. He didn't say a word to me, and I didn't dare speak, either. But that only made his sidelong glances more hurtful. He was scanning me the entire drive, trying to figure out which part of my body he hadn't clocked. What hadn't he noticed? His silent judgment was eating me alive.

At the same time, it seemed almost arbitrary to me that one little word should change how he felt about me. He had spent weeks flirting with me. He had clearly liked what he saw. But once he found out, we couldn't even have a discussion. One second I was the most desirable woman in the world to him; the next, he could barely stomach sitting in the same car as me. The whiplash had me reeling.

Finally, we pulled up to the apartment, and I got out of the car. As I turned to say goodbye, his face was full of scorn.

"That's why your knees are so big," he said as I swung the door shut.

After that, I never went into a guy's bedroom unless he knew I was trans. But I also realized I didn't have to share something so intimate with men who were incapable of reciprocating that level of honesty. I disclosed to keep myself safe, not because I felt they had a right to know. In this new country, I deserved to use all the power I could get.

9

BABAYLAN KISS

WALKING INTO A TANNING SALON FOR THE FIRST TIME FELT LIKE A forbidden act.

The entry to Tropical Kiss was on Geary Street in Japantown, an anonymous, purple-lit door between all the boba shops and Asian gift stores. Two girls sitting behind the front desk greeted me when I entered.

"Um, hi," I stammered. "How does this work? I've never gotten tanned before."

"Well, it's simple," one said. "You choose how dark you want your skin to be. Since it's your first time, maybe try ten minutes, then you can do more on the next go-round."

I stood there, dumbfounded, stunned by how casually she had told me that I could choose "how dark" I wanted to look. For a new arrival from the Philippines, that was a radical notion—and one that needed quite a bit of unpacking. I had grown up getting teased mercilessly for having dark skin—and I had developed my Horse Barbie persona as a reaction to that colorism—but here, getting darker was the point.

As I imagined walking out of Tropical Kiss with a tan, I could practically hear my parents yelling in my ear and feel them thwacking me on the ass as I came home sweaty from playing street games while the sun was out. *"Ang itim itim mo na!"* they would chastise me. Look how dark you are!

"We also have packages," the girl at the front desk was telling me, but I was still back in my childhood living room, a chubby-cheeked sunburned kid watching TV shows where only light-skinned actors got to be the stars.

In the Philippines, light-skinned actors were the object of desire in every romance, the only ones who could slap people on soap operas without being portrayed as villains. The rare dark-skinned actors I saw were relegated to service roles or sidelined as pitiable, dirt-poor tertiary characters.

From a young age, I got the message loud and clear: Having dark skin meant you were ugly, undesirable, and dirty. And now I was about to intentionally make my skin darker. It had been one thing to give up on the bleaching powder and adopt my role as the dark horse of the pageant scene. It was another to choose it.

Going to a tanning salon might not seem like the most monumental life event, but for me it was the first step toward deconstructing and dismantling some of the harmful beliefs I had unknowingly inherited from our colonizers.

You choose how dark you want your skin to be was a sentence that flew in the face of everything I had been raised to believe.

Back when I used Etta's prepackaged bleaching powder, I would apply it to my whole body. The noxious stuff came in a red box with a white hourglass figure of a woman emblazoned on the side—a figure who seemed to promise that I could be beautiful, too, once I was as light as her.

Every day for a week, Tigerlily and I would mix the powder and liquid chemical solution until it had a thick, pastelike texture. She helped me apply it evenly as I stood, limbs extended, in her living room.

Thirty minutes in, the paste would start solidifying. Then, as the chemical seeped deeper into my skin, an acrid smell would fill the room. My body would itch, first in patches, then everywhere, but I couldn't scratch it off. No, I had to let it sink in. It felt like the whitening powder was burning away the top layer of my skin.

At the hour mark, the pastelike texture became more like a hardened mold. By then the itching became full-on burning, and I would run to the shower, leaving little trails of bleaching powder behind me on the floor.

In a way, you could trace those tracks back centuries to the Spanish colonizers who first taught us to hate our own dark skin. They had forced the people of the Philippines to adopt Catholicism, then brainwashed us into adoring and worshipping white saints. They stole our land and then mocked our dark-skinned indigenous ancestors. We were a Spanish colony for 333 years, only to be bought by the United States for $20 million after the Spanish-American War in 1898. Our new colonizers saw us as savages and tried to erase the rich diversity of our languages, imposing American English on our education system, a tongue that felt bereft of variation and devoid of beauty. The Spanish, the Americans—they all wanted us to value whiteness.

The more we internalized their racism, the more power we gave to the paradox that became part of Filipino culture: We were people of color who came to subconsciously esteem and support white supremacist ideals. We shamed one another for living under the sun. All those centuries of indoctrination are not easily undone.

In the Philippines, every afternoon at three, a national TV channel would broadcast an image of a gleaming white Jesus who spoke in a Johnny Carson–like voice, preaching the "Daily Prayer Habit." Radiant beams of light would dance around the picture of Christ as the voice encouraged us to repent of our sins and pray for world peace. Looking at and listening to that image every day encouraged us to associate heavenly glory with whiteness, furthering our subjugation.

So imagine how much whiplash I felt when I moved to San Francisco and learned that white Americans liked to go tanning, the darker the better. At the time, being white and tanned signaled that you led a leisurely life full of sun-drenched vacations. Of course, they could undo their tans anytime by simply staying out of the sun.

More promising was the fact that American pop culture seemed to be starting to acknowledge the desirability of people of color. Ashanti was churning out sexy videos, always all bronzed up. I adored Brandy and Kelly Rowland for embracing their dark-skinned beauty. It was the beginning of something that felt bigger—the seeds of a movement that could assert that Black and brown skin are beautiful—and it thrilled me. When I saw these stars proudly showing skin, I felt my heart swell.

Still, whenever I went to Filipino supermarkets and grocery stores, I saw all the imported bleaching soaps, lotions, and beauty products displayed right by the entrance. It was like they had been placed there on purpose to remind me that while I might be in America, I was still Filipino in my mind and culture.

Nowhere was that more apparent than our gatherings to watch the major world pageants. For Miss Universe 2003—which was basically the Super Bowl of pageants—more than twenty of us got together at Kasia's tiny apartment in the Tenderloin, arriving with trays of *pancit*, barbecued chicken, white rice, and various desserts. It was our own mini fiesta in San Francisco.

We all listened with rapt attention as we heard the opening voiceover: "It has been called one of the wonders of the modern world, connecting the Atlantic to the Pacific Ocean, the Panama

Canal! Tonight, this wonder is home to seventy-one of the most beautiful and breathtaking women in the world, all here to compete for the title Miss Universe 2003!"

Then, as the seventy-one ladies in white floral-print swimsuits paraded down the cobblestone streets of Panama City's colonial old town, we let comments fly as freely as bets in a Vegas gambling hall. Whenever it was a white European contestant, we'd talk about how beautiful she was or speculate that she'd probably make the semifinals.

But when a Black contestant came on screen, proudly announcing her name and home country, the casual insults rolled off our tongues.

"*Ang ganda nya kahit maitim,*" some would say. She's beautiful even though she's Black.

"Dirty *ah ah,*" others might say if her skin tone was even the slightest bit uneven.

When Miss Philippines appeared, the whole room erupted, even more satisfied when we discovered she was light-skinned. If she had been dark, we would have taken the same jabs at her as we did at the Black contestants. We had truly internalized colorism to the point that we would insult our own entrant in the pageant. I myself made these comments, not yet able to think more deeply about what we were doing.

We were judging beauty based on what we had been taught all our lives.

Which only made it more confusing to realize I *wanted* to go to tanning and showcase my natural skin tone. That day in Tropical Kiss, I was hesitant but eager, a game of tug-of-war playing inside me. It was a mind-fuck of the highest order to unlearn the belief that my brown skin was inherently ugly.

As I laid my body down in the tanning booth, I felt confused but ultimately indignant at the cruel legacy that had made this decision so complicated. Tears swelled in my eyes. I could still hear my family scolding me. "Stop playing outside or you'll get dark like those Aeta!" they'd shout, referring to our dark-skinned aboriginal ancestors. I could still hear my aunties and our neighbors during a community vacation to Batangas Beach, screaming at us and the other kids, "*Hoy pumasok kayo dito, sige mangingitim kayo!*" They were mad not because we'd done something wrong but because they wanted us to get inside the house before we got too dark. Our innocent playtime in the sun was always laced with a disgusting threat.

"I'm letting my body be darkened," I whispered to myself, still in disbelief that this was happening. What if someone heard me? "I'm letting my body be darkened." This time I said it firmly, with an assured tone, as if I were preparing myself for the shame police to pop my tanning bed open. I was shedding generations of toxic beliefs. It was an ultraviolet rebirth.

I started to question more of our colonial beliefs as time went on. Catholicism, with all its detailed systematic doctrine, had been the predominant cultural force in my life for eighteen years.

But once I realized, through books like Dr. J. Neil Garcia's *Philippine Gay Culture,* that Catholicism was a religion forced upon our indigenous islands—and that before colonization, there had been a thriving cultured society in the Philippines that honored gender fluidity—I had an awakening.

I learned more about *babaylans,* gender-fluid healers and shamans who played a crucial role in our societies before the Spaniards came. The Catholics who colonized our land saw *babaylans* as a threat because they were considered spiritual leaders, so they supplanted them and enforced a rigid gender binary on our people.

Considering the full scope of our history, I could choose to honor my beautiful indigenous culture, just as I had chosen to free myself from hatred of our dark skin. Embracing precolonial Filipino culture complicated my process of adapting to the United States; I felt that I was not so much assimilating as learning to see the insidious impact of history for the first time. Only then could I decide what felt true to me and what didn't.

In the Philippines, going to church was our utmost social responsibility, each mass a thread in the fabric that held our communities together. But in San Francisco, mass was more of a duty—a thing we were expected to do every Sunday that, to me, didn't really feel like a pure form of divine worship.

Inside St. Patrick Church on Mission Street, a sea of strangers singing "Ave, Ave, Ave Maria" felt odd to me. I grew up knowing the people I went to church with. They looked like me, they sounded like me. Exchanging "peace be with you" with strangers felt disingenuous. I didn't see them in school or on the streets or at fiestas; they were just there to sit, stand, kneel, and go home.

But knowing the history of colonization made mass feel not just strange but also alienating. At the same time, I was surrounding myself with a more diverse group of people, outside the confines of Catholicism, who exposed me to new beliefs and new ways of looking at the world that helped me contextualize everything I had experienced back in the Philippines. For better or worse, I had had to leave my motherland for me to truly know it.

I returned to Tropical Kiss until I was exactly as dark as I chose to be. And little by little, I stopped attending mass. Mama still periodically attended, but not me. It must have been painful for her to watch me reject centuries of spiritual teaching that had been passed down to her, but she disguised it well, continuing to love me even as I strayed from her faith. I knew that if I wanted to keep growing, I had no more time for dogmas that taught me to hate my skin and myself.

10

BUTTERFLY

MOST CATHOLIC MOTHERS PROBABLY WOULDN'T FLY TO THAI-land so their daughter could get irreversible gender-affirming bottom surgery. But mine did.

At ten P.M. on July 6, 2003, we arrived in Chonburi, a seaside suburb an hour south of Bangkok, where English wasn't widely spoken. We were here so I could see Dr. Suporn, who was famous the world over for his handiwork. We girls liked to say that if you went to Suporn, you had "the Maserati of vaginas." His results were that good.

Nong, a petite Thai woman in her thirties with short hair, had driven us all the way here from the Bangkok airport. The hospital had hired her to be our guide through the whole experience. On the drive, Mama watched out the window as the lights of the capital city receded, sleepy towns emerging out of the darkness every few miles, then fading away into the black. At first, the occasional flickers of light felt familiar, as if we were passing through rural towns in California, but Chonburi was on the other side of the world. I was about to get a life-changing procedure I had wanted for as long as I could remember.

After checking in to our suite at Chon Inter Hotel, Mama flopped down onto the bed while I went out to the balcony, feeling equal parts jet-lagged and buzzed, anxious and excited. The neighborhood was quiet, a welcome escape from the hustle and bustle back in Bangkok. But my thoughts raced to fill the silence.

"I can't fucking believe I'm actually doing it," I said to no one, taking a long draught of the ice-cold Singha beer I had brought outside with me. "It's really happening."

In truth, I was nervous as hell.

I had been fifteen years old when I met the first trans woman who I knew had received gender confirmation surgery. I was backstage at a neighborhood pageant in Pasig Line, Manila, hanging out with the multigenerational crowd of *baklas* gathered in the hot and humid dressing room, when suddenly a woman with pale, ghostlike skin sauntered backstage, her shiny black bob bouncing with each step. She looked like a 1990s Versace supermodel in her skintight jeans and red-and-white-check halter top. I was mesmerized.

But after she greeted everyone, she turned around and the whispers began.

"Oh, that's Gina Pu-keh," someone said.

Gina was, of course, her name. But *puke,* as it's spelled in Tagalog, means "vagina." People were calling her that because she was one of the only trans girls in the scene who had gotten bottom surgery. In that moment, listening to those whispers, Gina seemed even more like a mythical goddess to me, a mysterious being who represented the fulfillment of my wildest dreams.

But then I heard another whisper: "You know . . . her vagina made her crazy."

I didn't know what it meant. Those words shook me. I absorbed that rumor at an impressionable age. But as I stood on that balcony in Thailand years later, I knew I was making one of the sanest decisions of my life. I wasn't crazy—maybe a little jittery, but not out of my mind. I truly wanted this. But as every trans woman who's gone through this knows, wanting it your entire life doesn't make it any less scary the night before.

After another chug of Singha, I joined Mama in the big hotel bed.

Later the next day, we walked into the sleek Chonburi Hospital for my presurgery checkup.

"*Sawadee ka*," Nong greeted us, escorting us directly to the section of the floor reserved exclusively for Dr. Suporn's clients.

Between the warm welcome and the smooth logistics, we felt like VIPs. So far this experience was living up to the Maserati name. It was downright luxurious. That was because I had worked hard for treatment this good.

Back in San Francisco, when I finally decided to speak into existence my dream of having the surgery, I started going to Divas more often after clocking out at Macy's. Plenty of the trans-amorous men who hung out there were willing to spend cash in exchange for my valuable erotic time.

Every night at Divas, bathed in the purple light that bounced off the mirrored dance floor, I exuded undeniable sensuality. Guys noticed me. Men in finance, men in suits, men in leather jackets, men in tech—they all contributed to my growing "surg fund."

But it was Eddie Jackson, the founder of a prominent software company, who paid me the bulk of the money I needed. Eddie had an affinity for trans Filipinas—and I was enticing enough for him that he regularly drove from Silicon Valley to spend the night with me at the W Hotel. I didn't mind Eddie. He was respectful and funny, and we had a good time together.

During the weeks we spent together, I followed Eddie's journey from being a fan of fencing to taking up the sport himself. I would lie naked on the silk bedsheets in our room at the W and watch him show off his counterattack stance and his sharp lunges. Once I had the money I needed for my "Maserati," I stopped seeing him, but I'll always remember his ridiculous showmanship as he jabbed an imaginary épée at the minibar.

It took two months of long sleepless nights to afford my trip to Thailand with Mama and my surgery with Dr. Suporn. My private hospital room in Chonburi wasn't quite as nice as the W Hotel, but it was still swank, and Nong showed up at my door with the gift of barbecue chicken.

The night before my surgery, anxiety and anticipation filled the air. Mama was all nerves. When Nong arrived, Mama was restlessly pacing back and forth while in the background the TV on the wall played the news.

"Mama, sit down and eat *po*," I said, pointing to the empty bed beside mine.

Our guide had brought the meal more for Mama's benefit than for mine; we both wanted her to relax. At this point, I was more nervous for her than I was for myself!

Once Mama was still, Nong gave us the rundown of the next few days, explaining everything from how long I'd be recovering in the hospital to when I'd have to come back for my follow-up visit. Still sensing my mother's nervousness, Nong said in her most assuring tone, "Mama, you no worry too much. Geena lucky to have you here. Very, very soon, she'll be a butterfly."

"*Kap khun ka*," Mama said, thanking her for the kind words, then bowed slightly with her palms pressed together, all but praying to Nong as she left the room.

Alone again, Mama lay down on my bed and held me.

"Mama, thank you *po* for being here with me and for loving me," I said, tears welling in my eyes.

"I love you, *anak*. I'm here for you."

Love and presence. That was all Mama could give me, and it was more than enough. I fell asleep lying there with her, waking about an hour later to the sound of a BBC anchor's voice. But inside me, there was a humming only I could hear.

I got up from the bed and went out onto the balcony to take in my moment. The revving of *tuk-tuks* echoed from the street below as the salty ocean breeze blew through my hair.

"Night before, Geena," I murmured to myself, trying to keep my nervousness at bay.

The procedure was irreversible. Once it was done, that would be it. No turning back. It was one of those rare moments in life when you can feel a chapter closing as it happens, not just in hindsight. At only nineteen, I couldn't help but be proud of myself for making the boldest decision of an already adventurous life.

I was doing the damn thing.

On that balcony, I prayed for my safety but also for Mama, because I knew how momentous it felt to her, too.

Looking up into the midnight sky, I thought about Papa and prayed for his guidance.

"My Bojojoy is getting a *vajayjay*!" I could hear him teasing me, tickling my ribs, always with jokes at the ready.

I thought about all the kids who'd bullied me and told me I wasn't a girl. This surgery would be impossible if I had stayed in the Philippines. My pageant winnings had been enough to get by, but they weren't surgery money. It would've taken me years and years of saving—and even if I had gotten it, it still wouldn't have been enough for my birth country to recognize me as a true woman.

Most important, I allowed myself to wallow in my sadness, acknowledging and living with the slight possibility that I might not experience pleasure in the same way again.

Many trans Filipinas back home ignorantly believed that if they got bottom surgery, they'd lose the ability to orgasm, and that they'd go crazy—like Gina Pu-keh—if they couldn't. Growing up, I had internalized that idea. That fear seeped into my body as I stood there on the balcony, along with older fears, too. *Who am I to change what God gave me?* I thought, the old Catholic guilt wrapping its familiar tendrils around my heart. I thought I had let go of my indoctrination, but here it was, pulling me back again.

I knew I was taking a risk. Although the vast majority of trans women do still orgasm after bottom surgery, it's not always an easy journey. But when you're trapped in a cage, anything outside it feels like utopia. Regardless of whether I'd have success on the other side, I knew there would be freedom in trying. So even though I wasn't a practicing Catholic anymore, I prayed for my orgasms.

At seven the next morning, as I lay in my hospital bed, prepped for surgery, Dr. Suporn greeted me. "Ready to be a butterfly?" he asked, grinning wide.

As they slowly rolled me into the operating room, Mama held my hand and pressed something into my palm. Her rosary. "Pray, *anak*."

When I woke up, it felt like someone had pulled my hips all the way through my ribs up to my shoulder blades. The sensation was otherworldly. Once the morphine wore off, I wasn't in as much pain as I thought I'd be. To be honest, the boob job I'd gotten a year before, in San Francisco, hurt way more than my groin did. Still, that first night at the hospital after my surgery was the most uncomfortable sleep of my life. I'm a full-on side sleeper so the nightly hip pain was a recurring battle.

The next few days were a blur of pain pills. But in rare lucid moments, I could look over and see Mama, nestled in her own bed next to mine, looking back at me.

After about a week, Dr. Suporn came in to take off the gauze.

Mama was just as excited as me, if not more. *"Eto na sya Geena!"* she said, making a drumroll sound.

She'd always been curious as to how they could possibly make this happen. My surgery might as well have been a magic trick to her. For a Catholic mom, she was incredibly open-minded about it all. I knew her religious friends always said something disapproving whenever she talked with them about trans topics, but here she was, eagerly awaiting the unveiling of her trans daughter's vagina as if she were about to find out what was behind door number one on a game show.

The second my gauze was removed, it looked like Mama's eyeballs were going to burst out of her head. She held her hand to her mouth in awe, then suddenly exclaimed in joy, *"Nanghihina yung tuhod ko!"*

She had to sit down on a chair in the corner because her knees had started shaking when she blurted out, "I can't believe it! It looks exactly like a vagina!"

The nurse gave me a handheld mirror, and when I saw it, my grin must have gone all the way up to my ears.

"She's so beautiful!"

After a few days in the hospital, Mama and I moved back to our suite at the Chon Inter Hotel for the rest of my recovery. I was getting stronger each day, taking little walks up and down the hallway.

Every day Nong came to check in on us, our conversations growing friendlier with each visit. She'd bring us crispy fried snapper dipped in vinegar and tell us about all the other "butterflies" staying in the hotel. We learned she was the sole provider for her family, and that she had been working for Dr. Suporn for a few years. A lot of her Thai friends dreamed of getting the surgery, she said, but unfortunately they usually had to go to a more affordable doctor.

"Dr. Suporn the best," she would say, both thumbs up.

I smiled and nodded. He was the best.

During one of my hallway walks, I met Kate, a Danish computer engineer in her fifties. She had gotten her surgery a week ahead of me and was happy to assure me, "You only get stronger from here."

For her, surgery felt like a life-or-death choice. "I can't continue without truly living," she told me.

She was by herself, in an anonymous hotel in a foreign land. Because her family didn't accept her trans identity, no one had come to help her recover.

"I just wish my family were here," she said. On her walks up and down the hall of our floor, she had heard Mama and me.

I reached out and took her hand. "Come meet my mama," I said.

Kate had a family here, too, just not the one she was expecting.

Three days before our flight back to San Francisco, after tearful farewells with Nong, Mama and I explored Bangkok. We walked all over the city as I carried around an inflatable, doughnut-shaped cushion to sit on. I didn't realize its purpose would be so immediately recognizable.

When we went to Calypso Cabaret, an establishment famous for its stunning trans performers, my doughnut cushion drew attention right away. The trans cabaret girls spotted it after the show and swarmed me.

"Which doctor? Which doctor?" one asked.

"Suporn," I proudly replied.

Her face melted. "Oh! Dr. Suporn! My dream! My dream!"

To commemorate our trip, Mama took me to the biggest gold jewelry store in Bangkok, Gems International. Inside, rows and rows of glimmering gold pieces greeted us. She picked out two eighteen-karat gold pendants, each about an inch in diameter. One was a textured butterfly that seemed to flutter as it dangled on its chain. The other, of course, showed Jesus Christ on the holy cross.

Those pendants were us, the trans butterfly and the Catholic, a pair as perfect as it was unexpected.

11
CRAIGSLIST GIRL

WHEN I GOT BACK TO SAN FRANCISCO AFTER SURGERY, I FELT LIKE my world and my ambitions were bigger than ever. All the things I'd ever wanted, that I thought I would never have, now seemed within reach. A female gender marker, sex and pleasure—my dreams were coming true. And the first thing I wanted to do was take my new Maserati on a test drive.

But I had to heal first, both inside and outside. Growing up in a conservative Catholic culture, the only sex education I got was abstinence, abstinence, and more abstinence. An orgasm is one of life's most fundamental pleasures—a pure moment of uninhibited pleasure—but when it comes to sex, Catholicism mostly preaches shame. And even after all the time I spent at Divas and Power Exchange, I still hadn't fully silenced the inner voice telling me my own wants and desires were wrong.

"It's against the Bible!" people would have said in the culture where I grew up, where scripture was treated as the only truth. To them, getting bottom surgery was the ultimate affront to God.

. . .

Ever since moving to America, I had been on a long journey of discovery, embracing the skin I lived in, questioning the religion I was born into, and reclaiming my precolonial past. Coming home from surgery wasn't the completion of that process, but it was a key dividing line between who I had been before and who I would be moving forward. I wasn't going to let the beliefs of the past hold me back any longer.

I was ready to seek my own truth.

The only problem was that I had so much more to learn, beginning with my own body. Now that I had come home from surgery, I wanted to access the parts of myself that tickled, the parts that I knew could unlock pure bliss, releasing all the joy I was meant to experience. *How does it all work? Should the guy go slow? What if it hurts? What if I bleed? Do I keep going?*

One day when I got out of the shower, my skin felt extra soft from the steam, and I made the decision to look for that tickling sensation. I was told that my clit would feel extra sensitive, so I started looking for *her* with my fingers. Once I found it, electrifying shockwaves spread through my body. She was small, but she was mighty. As I touched myself, I felt like I was riding in a wooden roller coaster, the wheels ratcheting up as it climbed the first hill, slowly, but surely. The vibrating crescendo made my legs shake of their own volition. At the top, there was clarity. Then I was suspended over the edge with a glimpse of eternity. Just a little more.

And then the downward motion, the sudden, freeing bliss of letting go. The pure happiness was unbelievable. I knew then that I could access that pleasure alone. But what would it mean to find it with another person?

For a sex-shamed trans girl with a brand-new vagina in the year

2003, answering that question meant logging on to Craigslist.com. I browsed to "casual encounters" in San Francisco one night and entered the "T4M" section—transgender women seeking men.

The loud clacking of my Dell desktop keyboard sounded like a drumroll as I typed, *"Cute post-op Asian trans girl looking to try her new vag."*

I looked at it for a moment, stopping my drumming, and then added, *"Must have pic."*

Within minutes, my email inbox was flooded with messages and pictures from men of all ages and ethnic backgrounds, some of them creepy and aggressive, others hopelessly romantic. My post had been up for only about an hour when I saw Jake's picture. He didn't write anything elaborate; he just attached his picture, a form-fitting military shirt showcasing his slender muscular build. He looked like Jake Gyllenhaal, scruff and all. His message was simple: *"Hey, wanna chat? This is me."*

He sent me more pictures, all filled with lumberjack hotness. Finally, I sent him a picture of me in Hawaii wearing a skirt and a bikini top. That sealed the deal.

The following night, around seven o'clock, I walked to a two-story Victorian townhouse on Haight Street. I was relieved to find my Gyllenhaal doppelgänger waiting for me by the front door, his looks even more stunning than advertised.

"Hey, what's up?" he greeted me in a deep voice, tugging at his collar.

"Hey there," I flirted back in my sweetest girly tone.

His roommates were away so we had the entire place to ourselves. Inside with him, alone, I noticed how strong he was, his muscles bulging through his plaid shirt. It was the kind of strength that could hurt me. I wanted him to be gentle, to remember that I had never done this before. Everything I knew about having sex with men was useless now; I was a blank slate, and that felt as freeing as it was nerve-racking. My whole body was vibrating, humming at the thought of doing this with him. It felt so right. I had waited years for this. But my mind was trying to picture how the night would unfold.

As we stood there in the living room, exchanging glances, I wanted to say so many things. I wanted him to know how badly I wanted this, and what it meant to me to finally feel so deep an alignment between my soul and my body. I wanted to beg him to make this first experience as pleasurable as possible.

Instead, too nervous to say much at all, I just squeaked out a reminder—"Please remember, this is my first time"—and followed him to the bedroom.

"Don't worry," he said, looking me in the eye. "It will feel good."

It was like he was trying to tell me he had done this before, and given that I had met him through the Craigslist T4M section, he probably had. Still, I was trusting a stranger with something sacred. We took off our clothes, and I lingered for a moment, psyching myself up one last time.

As he drew close, I whispered in his ear, reminding him again, "Please be extra gentle."

I knew how this felt when I did it by myself, but it felt almost impossible to let go with another person.

"If it hurts or anything, we can stop," he told me. "It won't be awkward. You just say it."

That calmed me down a bit, and I started breathing deep, matching the rising and falling of his bare chest. We stayed in sync as we began, communicating through that shared breath, reassuring each other that we were both present. After a minute, he checked in with me to find out how I was doing.

"This feels *sooo* good," I told him as our bodies locked into the right rhythm.

I gazed into his eyes, trying to communicate the pleasure I was feeling, parting my lips just enough to inhale and exhale in unison with him. My orgasm was different than I expected it to be—deeper, more grounded, and explosive all at once. It was exactly the tenderness I needed.

A few months after that night, my petition for a gender marker change was approved by a San Francisco court. Back in 2004, you had to wait until after bottom surgery to officially change all your documents. When I received a California driver's license and a green card, both bearing an F, I felt a very different sense of completion from the one I felt with Jake. This was the fulfillment of everything I had come here for.

This was the promise Mama had made me—that if I moved to America, I could be recognized as the woman I truly am. It had seemed unimaginable to me when she said it, but now it was real. I was Geena with an F now. No one could take those letters away.

This was my new license to live.

Maybe it was because I had taken the bold step of getting surgery, but as I settled back into my life in San Francisco, I started to feel restless.

When I first got the job at the Macy's cosmetics counter, I thought that was it for me. I was content with my newfound friends, enjoying being young, and feeling no real pressure to do more. Danmark and I took some community college courses, and I idly imagined being a psychologist one day. Mama, meanwhile, was always telling me that I should be a nurse—the expected career route for every Filipino immigrant—but that wasn't of interest to me.

For the most part, I didn't really have any great aspirations—but mostly because I had forgotten all my old ones. My dreams of being on a pageant stage again, or of becoming an international super-model like Tula, gathered dust in the corners of my mind.

Sure, I joined a few trans pageants in San Francisco here or there, but they were once-a-year kind of events, put on for the community, by the community. I would never have been able to make a career out of competing in those casual and infrequent events.

Working at Macy's, living with Mama, hanging out with Danmark—what more could I want? But after Thailand, and after my gender marker change, working the makeup counter by day and partying at night was starting to lose its luster. I didn't know when or how my life would change, but I could feel it coming. Maybe I willed it to happen.

One day at work we had one of our Makeover Day events, when we encourage customers to sit down and get their makeup done while we make a little pitch: Buy five products or more, and they'll walk away with a mini gift bag full of products. It was a fun and frantic event, but I needed three cups of coffee just to survive because I had to be on my feet nonstop.

That day, in a rare moment of calm amid the customers, I spotted a tall, skinny brunette idly walking up and down my aisle, holding a perfume in one hand and a stack of tester sheets in the other. She worked for the perfume brand and came to Macy's only when there were special cosmetics and fragrance events. Midway through one of her laps, she stopped in front of me and asked, "So what are you selling here?"

I launched into my usual sales pitch. "Let me introduce you to Dr. Feelgood," I said, referring to Benefit's bestselling smoothing primer.

She sat down in my chair, and I started applying all the products I normally used, like the liquid blush that could double as a lip tint, and the pinkish-silver cream highlighter that worked with a wide range of skin tones. I got lost in the rhythm of all the brushing and daubing and blending.

Then suddenly she grabbed me by the hand and looked me straight in the eye. "Listen, you should be sitting where I'm sitting," she said. "You look like a model."

I stared at her, surprised, shaken out of my routine.

"Seriously," she went on. "My name is Salina, and I'm a model. Have you ever thought about modeling?"

I thought she had just wanted to sit down in my chair because she got tired of walking through the department. But apparently she had a mission in mind.

"Well?" she said.

I didn't know how to respond because her question had reawakened something in me: My vision of being like Tula. My instinct to aim high. But it simply wasn't reasonable for me to think someone like me could be a mainstream model in America. It made more sense to leave that fantasy buried deep in my brain. In some alternate universe, there's a version of me that stayed in San Francisco, kept working at the Macy's counter, and maybe even went to nursing school—and I like to think she would be happy, but she wouldn't be me. I hadn't lost the self-belief I had as a pageant queen. I just needed someone to remind me of the scale of my dreams.

"I'd like to be a model," I said, "but I don't know how."

"I'll be right back," she said, power walking back to fragrances.

When she returned, she handed me one of her modeling composite cards showing her full name—Salina Monti—and her measurements, next to an array of pictures showcasing her different looks.

"My number's on the card," she told me. "Let's get coffee sometime, and I'll tell you more."

On my next day off, we met up for a coffee that changed everything. Salina told me that she had just moved back to San Francisco after spending many years modeling in New York. She flipped through her portfolio, showing prints of herself on the cover of *Elle* Spain and *Vogue* Brazil. On one side of the spread, she looked fresh in an ad for Pond's face cream, and on the other, she looked sultry in a swimsuit.

"You could do this," she said, as she turned the pages.

In my mind, I was asking myself if she even knew I was trans. She must have. Everyone at Macy's knew that trans Filipinas ran cosmetics. We were unmissable, always huddling and laughing together, not to mention our impromptu pageants. But I didn't bring it up. And I knew deep down that she was right: I could do this.

She asked if I had any modeling pictures she could send to her agent in New York, and I told her I didn't, but it wasn't a problem. The best way to start would be to get some experience right away. She slid her portfolio aside and opened her calendar.

"There's a store modeling job at Armani Exchange tomorrow. How would you like to model with me? I could ask if they need someone else."

I said yes right away. And the next day I did my first modeling gig at that store on Grant Avenue with Salina. We modeled their newest summer collection of distressed jean jackets, studded boyfriend jeans, and fitted tank tops—a very rocker chic vibe. I felt right at home in the fast-paced quick-change scenario. It was like being in pageants again. And just as quickly as I had left them behind, my dreams were back.

When I told Mama that I was moving, she cried.

Then she said, "Why New York?! People there are mean!"

But when she saw that I was firm in my decision, she assured me that I should try to reach my goal, however unlikely it must have seemed to her that I would achieve it. "After all," she said, "you could always come back home."

The hardest part was telling Danmark. I took him to dinner one night at the California Pizza Kitchen in Emeryville. We were seated near the kitchen, but I couldn't blame my sweat on the open pizza oven; I was just nervous to tell my best friend I was going away.

Danmark could immediately sense something was off. He knew me that well. "So what's up, babe?"

The sly, insistent tone in his voice was basically his signature. One I was going to miss. For a moment, I was back in the bus zigzagging through the mountains with the Garcia clan, missing Tigerlily before I'd even left—except that I had a feeling Danmark wouldn't be as understanding.

"Um, you're gonna hella hate me," I started, hoping I could buy some mercy in advance.

"Why?" he prodded.

It was time to rip off the Band-Aid. "I've decided to move to New York."

Danmark's face turned as red as the flames in that pizza oven.

"I'm sorry, Dan."

"I thought we were gonna move there together?" he said.

In his wounded eyes, I saw all the hours we spent watching *Will & Grace* together, dreaming of the glamorous city life. I thought I saw tears start to form, but he held them back. He was too pissed. Neither of us said much after that. We just nibbled on our pepperoni pizza, letting thick silence hang in the air between us, then got the check, having barely touched our food.

Back in my room that night, I turned the lights off and looked up at the glow-in-the-dark stars that were stuck to my ceiling. I put on a CD that Danmark had burned for me, full of songs for us to listen to while driving around San Francisco, and Tamia's "Officially Missing You" started to play: " 'Cause this pain I feel, it won't go away."

I hummed along, crying myself to sleep. It felt like I had just found another chosen family only to leave it behind again. But I had to follow my heart, even if it felt like it was pulling me away from comfort and community. When I left the Philippines for America, I was choosing to cut off my career at its apex for what I thought would be a better life. But life in the States wasn't necessarily better or worse; it was different, with its own challenges. Getting that F on my identification was a nice baseline of respect, but it hadn't satisfied my ambitions. When I looked back on my life, I wanted to be able to say that I had done something big.

The next day Danmark and I met up at Union Square and stared at the glass facade of Macy's—the place where our friendship had begun.

He turned to me, conciliatory. "Clearly, I didn't handle it well," he said. "I just couldn't bear the thought of not seeing you every day."

We wrapped each other up in our arms as if it were the last hug we would ever share. The sound of our sobbing blended into the din of cars and people passing by. It felt like the end of everything. I couldn't bear the thought of leaving him, either.

But Salina had told me that if I really wanted to give modeling a shot, I had to be in New York. With her encouragement, and my new F gender marker on all my ID, my horizon had suddenly expanded. I was imagining things that couldn't be explained with logic. My vision for my future had been darkened for a long time. The light was waiting for me somewhere on the other side of the country.

PART III

NEW YORK CITY

12

GENNA

OUT OF ALL THE STORIES ABOUT A GIRL MOVING TO THE BIG APPLE to pursue her Big Dream, I promise you've never heard one like mine. For starters, I was already a celebrity halfway across the world; I just had to do it all over again. But this time I'd have to hide, going "stealth" as we call it, coming out only to a trusted few.

Trying to make it as a model in New York would be like competing in one long, thrilling, exhausting pageant. It would be my greatest performance ever.

But that journey began humbly on a dark runway at JFK surrounded by a thick blanket of snow. As we taxied to the gate, I stared out the window at my first view of New York, at the white ground blinking red from all the lights lining the tarmac. It was March 2005, I was twenty-one years old, and I was ready to start fresh. I had a new vagina and an F on my California driver's license—all essential tools for my undercover mission.

Very few people in New York knew my history. Nowhere else in the country could I be so anonymous while still having so much opportunity to make a name for myself. I could get lost in the crowd at first—and then start climbing once I established my cover.

That first night in New York, I ended up on my friend Vanessa's couch in Astoria. Vanessa was a trans Filipina I'd met in San Francisco who had moved here before me. She made me a meal of chicken adobo, perfectly tender and salty—a proper welcome. Before long her trans Filipina friend, Ericka, came over to see the doe-eyed newcomer.

Ericka was super femme and petite, in her early thirties, with long black hair and eyebrows as thin as sewing threads. I joined her outside to smoke, and I was fascinated by her Capri cigarettes, as slim as her eyebrows. When she held them between her long red fingernails, with her pinky held up, thick puffs of smoke swirling around her in the wintry cold, she looked as legendary as Joan Collins in *Dynasty*.

"Why did you move here?" she asked me, taking a drag.

"I want to be a model."

She looked me up and down, clearly sizing me up. At the time, I didn't have the "look" that one would expect from a high-fashion model. Maybe if I were a size 0 or 2 instead of 6, but even still, I was light-years away from embodying the white European couture ideal that was even more dominant in 2005 than it is today.

I might as well have told her I wanted to be an astronaut. "Are you serious?" she asked.

This shady bitch, I thought at first, stung by her incredulity.

But there was also something refreshing about her brazenness; this was how trans Filipinas talked to one another. And I could tell that her sassy remark came from a place of truth and concern that only another trans woman could understand. She was asking me: Didn't I know what happened to girls like us in the modeling industry?

Ericka wasn't wrong to be dubious. All the trans role models I looked up to had been professionally ruined when they were publicly outed. There was Tula, of course, who had appeared in a Bond movie before being outed by a tabloid. The trans model April Ashley got into

British *Vogue* before a friend sold her out to the tabloids, cratering her career. Tracey "Africa" Norman was outed through a whisper while she was at a photo shoot, the loose lips of her hairdresser's assistant costing her countless jobs. Did I really want to risk the same kind of thing happening to me? At the time, full of bravado, yes, I did.

"I'm serious," I said.

It wasn't just that I had seen Tula's face in the newspaper at an impressionable young age. I wanted to feel what I felt on those pageant stages again: to inspire awe and, yes, adoration. I told myself that all my mentors and predecessors, from Tula to Tigerlily, had sacrificed so that young trans girls like me could dream, so didn't I owe it to them to at least try to push the envelope a little further? Maybe, just maybe, I could do it.

Despite her skepticism, Ericka offered me a backup plan while I chased my dreams. She worked as a hostess at Libation, a newish multilevel nightclub on Rivington Street on the Lower East Side. In a bit of good timing, she was about to take a month's leave to go get her own gender confirmation surgery, and she needed someone to cover for her. I would be perfect for the job.

My pageant training translated: I knew instinctively how to welcome guests with the same grandeur and grace I had once used to introduce myself onstage. And the dimly lit hostess table would give me the perfect cover. If an acquaintance from San Francisco walked in, I could tilt my profile, hide behind my wavy hair, and let the darkness disguise me. It was kismet.

Without even trying, I had two friends and a job lined up—and I hadn't even unpacked. At the rate I was going, I felt like I was going to be on the cover of *Vogue* tomorrow. Surely Anna Wintour would come knocking any minute now.

I might not have wound up on the cover of any magazines within my first week in New York, but somehow, magically, I did get my lucky break. About a week into my new hostess job, I welcomed two guys at the door. A few minutes later one of them approached me to ask if I was a model.

"I'm a fashion photographer," he said. "My studio's just around the corner, actually."

I held back from rolling my eyes. By this point, I'd been approached by random guys on the street claiming they were "fashion photographers," only to check their websites later and . . . well, let's just say their work was not the kind of modeling I wanted to do.

But this guy—"Barnaby," he said, handing me his card—was different. When I looked him up, I saw that he'd photographed celebrities for *Harper's Bazaar* and, yes, even *Vogue*. I called him the next day to set up a shoot. In my naïveté, I thought I would be expected to wear multiple fabulous looks, as I had seen Naomi and Gisele do in magazines, so I showed up to his studio with big bags full of outfits and shoes, ready to play dress-up. He shot my bags a quizzical look, ignored them, then produced a single gray button-down shirt for me.

"I'd like to just shoot something portrait and natural," he said. "Agents only want to see your bare face."

I'll admit I was disappointed. I had brought some great clothes. But I said yes, let's do it.

Even as I agreed, I knew that my go-to makeup tricks for feminizing my face weren't going to be enough for a shoot this simple. I was instantly self-conscious; in the pageant world, I had the protection of my mystical wig and the dazzle of my evening gowns to distract from my imperfections. Here I would have nothing to hide behind. No amount of contour could make my cheekbones look like Naomi's, and the slight smudge of eye shadow I had worn wasn't anywhere near as smoky soft as Gisele's.

But let's not forget I was a pageant performer of the highest caliber. I was the Horse Barbie who could whip up a full face of makeup on a bumpy bus ride. I quickly ducked into the bathroom and managed to smudge some dark brown eyeliner with a shaky finger to give me a cat-eye look. I applied some just below my cheekbones, too, contouring as best I could under the circumstances. The result wasn't perfect, but I instantly looked more feminine. It would take a more discerning eye than Barnaby's lens to clock me. *Pwede na yan.* I made it work. I felt dysphoric and iconic all at once.

If Barnaby noticed my impromptu makeover when I returned, he didn't say a word.

He posed and directed me, the shutter of his Polaroid punctuating the silences between instructions. Together, those clicks were like a ticking clock measuring this surreal moment. This was happening. My dream was coming to life.

He used a black-and-white film, pulling the photos out as they were ejected and setting them aside to develop. The first few shots he showed me were astonishing—raw and intimate. The interplay of shadow and light on my skin, the way my eyes were focused on the lens, holding its gaze like a lover's—the composition was totally captivating.

In the photos, I looked as if I were about to say something but decided against it, midbreath. Somehow, by suspending me in a single moment, Barnaby captured a kaleidoscopic perspective: who I used to be, who I wanted to be, and what I feared. There was a deeper trepidation in my eyes—the look of a spy on her first undercover mission. But there was also a determination, and a hunger, to make these images matter. I felt vulnerable and yet powerful, or maybe the power came from my vulnerability. I had never seen myself this way before.

Still, these were the only fashion portraits a professional photographer had ever taken of me, and I had hoped they would show who I was—that they'd convey some semblance of my presence. Not just my hopes and fears but my soul. I had come to New York to prove myself—to prove that I could rise to the top all over again. Even in my silence, I still wanted to declare my existence. But instead, the photos almost looked as if they were from a treasured but forgotten album found in the attic of a dilapidated house. I looked femme and mysterious, alluring but inaccessible. Not *me*. I liked the ethereal quality of the images, but I didn't want to be a ghost of myself. I wanted to feel alive the way I had on my very first pageant stage.

The next day Barnaby called. "I sent your pictures to some modeling agents I know," he said. "They want to see you."

That was how my dream began. Or at least what I thought would be a dream.

I should have known from the beginning that it was a devil's bargain: Modeling meant hiding who I was. Few choices in life are so binary, but this was one of them. If I had come out—or been outed—in 2005, there would not be a book in your hands right now. The stakes of staying stealth in the industry were that high.

Thank goodness there were no YouTube videos of me competing in hundreds of trans pageants in the Philippines, and no modern-day social media to dredge up my past. In Asia I had been celebrated for being trans, but in New York I would have to stay airlocked in the closet as if there were no oxygen outside it. The same country that had given me the freedom of an F marker could also stamp me with a scarlet T.

But my modeling dream was a singular, all-consuming vision.

Back when Tigerlily first showed me pictures of Tula, I had had no idea what America was like—how big it was, or even that New York and California were on opposite coasts. I knew even less about how the modeling world worked. But because of Tula, I knew what would be possible for me if I went abroad—and who I could become.

My ascendancy through the trans pageant scene had been improbable, too, but I had done it. Throughout my rise, I had felt as if Tula were guiding me, with her big, fluffy hair and that soft sensual smile. Even though I had never met her, even though I had seen her only in the newspaper, she felt as real to me as a close friend. She was going to show me the way again, I was certain.

Before I knew it, Major Model Management, one of the top agencies at the time, had signed me. They sent me around first to shoots with various photographers, then to editorial castings for magazines like *Glamour* and *Lucky*. Next came Target and Hanes Lingerie for advertising work. Then a huge billboard in Times Square for an electronic ad that wrapped around the entire MTV building on an enormous LED screen. That led to catalogs and bridal clients, which weren't quite as glamorous as *Vogue,* but once a catalog client books you, they ask you back repeatedly. Catalogs weren't the runway at Paris Fashion Week, but they were steady work.

At first, modeling did feel as breezy as winning pageants back in the Philippines. I excelled at the ads and catalogs. But as I booked more gigs, I could tell that I was throwing myself headlong into a high-pressure existence. Even as I started down the same path Tula had walked, I could feel paranoia setting in. I lived in fear of that tabloid headline. I realized that for Tula, being outed had been not a one-time event but a daily risk. Every job came with a new set of dangers to navigate.

Modeling was going to be like playing Jenga with my life on the line instead of a bunch of meaningless blocks: The higher I climbed, the more disastrous my fall would be.

But that won't happen to me, I told myself. *Not for a while.*

Once I was making enough money to move off Vanessa's couch, I found a new place to live through Craigslist—a room for rent in a three-bedroom apartment on 101st Street on the Upper West Side. On the day I toured it, I wore a midi floral dress to really amp up my femininity. I didn't want to get clocked.

Evan, a white dude in his midthirties who worked as a chef, greeted me at the door and gave me the tour. That's when I realized how generous New Yorkers are with their definition of the word *bedroom*.

The available room was a tiny five-by-eight-foot space with no AC. It was crammed right up next to the entryway, almost as if it were meant to be used as a mudroom. But I was already living in a figurative closet, so why not live in a literal one? Besides, the room had a big window and some sparse furniture—a twin bed, a small lamp, and a corner table, all of which were included in the rent. And a space this nondescript was only fitting for a spy like me.

By that time, my mission to become a clandestine supermodel dominated my personal and professional life—and I was doing it all alone with no Angels by my side and no Charlie to save me. I was hiding, lying, and performing, all in plain sight. It was stressful, but at times it could also be fun. When I forgot what was on the line— and I often had to for my own sanity—I could enjoy the spycraft. This anonymous room, tucked away on the Upper West Side, would be a perfect base of operations.

Modulating my voice to sound as delicate and femme as possible, I asked Evan, "Could I move in next week?"

Luckily, he was as desperate for help with the rent as I was for a place of my own.

That room became a private space where I could envision bigger things—an incubator for my ambitions. The perpetually bespectacled Robert was my only other roommate—a white guy in his early thirties who worked as an assistant professor at NYU. I saw him only during breakfast as we crunched our cereal in a kitchenette that could only fit two of us at a time.

Chewing was about as much sound as I was willing to make at that time of the morning, when I could swear my voice sounded more manly, the lower bass tones that much harder to pitch upward when my vocal cords were still shaking off sleep. It was a toxic combination of science and internalized transphobia that I dealt with daily.

When I saw Robert in the morning, I'd grab my coffee, all but whisper a hushed "Hey, morning," and then eat my Kellogg's.

Robert was kind enough to clear out his closet next to the kitchen—which was about half the size of my so-called room—so I had space for all the clothes I unpacked from my two huge suitcases. The only way to latch the closet door shut all the way was with a firm hip check. But it was mine, as the room was mine. Having a space that belonged to me and me alone was still a novel thing.

From my window, I could see men playing cards on the street below and women gossiping away on vivid beach chairs beside them. It reminded me of my little *eskinita* back in the Philippines. Occasionally a guy in a white tank top and loose-fitting denim would walk down the street with a stereo swinging in one hand, filling the street with salsa music or reggaeton. Any given afternoon could become an impromptu dance party. This liveliness was familiar, but it could only do so much to cheer me up. I was still in a city I didn't know. A city that I didn't want to *truly* know me just yet.

I longed for the unapologetic trans flamboyance I had known back in the Philippines. What had happened to the pride that I had literally worn like a crown? In New York, I had to silence so many parts of myself to remain inconspicuous. I felt as if I were looking after seedlings I watered under the cover of darkness, hoping people would see only the flower when it bloomed. But this was also part of the immigrant experience in America: We find life in society's cracks, and we keep going no matter how hard it feels, no matter how impossible it may seem.

Ultimately, the apartment won me over with its ready access to Central Park—the North Meadow was basically my front yard—and with my Dominican neighbors, who made the streets feel like a family and who were always deep-frying something delicious-smelling. New York wasn't home, but maybe one day it could be.

. . .

One of my first big modeling breaks was a sexy shoot for a *Complex* cover story. For its August–September 2005 fashion issue, the magazine had tapped famed photographer and creative director Steven Baillie to capture "The 10 Most Beautiful Women in the World," as the cover promised, "One Page at a Time."

I wish I could say I felt beautiful heading into that opportunity, but all I felt was butterflies. Here I was being introduced to the world not just as a woman, without any qualifiers, but as one of the *most* attractive women on planet Earth. I should have been elated. But all I could think about was what the tabloids would say if they ever found out.

When I arrived on set that day, I was the last to sit down in my hair and makeup chair. All ten of us were arranged in a long room with a mirror hung against the opposing wall, as teams of stylists powdered our faces and blended our eye shadow to perfection. Clouds of hairspray, sprayed in orchestral unison, filled the air with an aerosol fog. Never had I been to a shoot this intense.

"Pout your lips," one of the makeup artists asked me, holding up a tube of gloss, and after she applied it, the effect was incredible, almost otherworldly. I looked good. Maybe I wasn't ready to call myself beautiful yet, but the makeup boosted my self-esteem.

On the other side of the door, I heard the popping of studio flash-bulbs and a buzz of activity in the wardrobe area. The energy was busy, loud, and chaotic, like a fiesta in the Philippines.

"Gorgeous, yes, give me more!" I could hear Steven calling out to a model. "Give me more of *that.*"

And then, to an assistant, "Wind! We need the wind! *More wind!*"

If anything could make me feel gorgeous, it was this atmosphere. This *electricity*. The wind machine would probably give my ego a boost, too. What girl doesn't want to be seen with her hair artfully

flowing all Beyoncé around her face? Still, I was a total novice compared to these other models. I didn't know if I could give the photographer what he wanted. What did it mean to give him more? Give
him more *what*?

I looked sideways at the nine other girls sitting in their chairs—a
cadre of models from Victoria's Secret. I had seen their faces before
on TV and billboards. Each was from a different country, and our
skin tones covered a wide spectrum, like an artist's palette for all of
humanity. None of them looked as scared as I felt.

The model next to me was a petite woman with deep brown skin,
accented by a glow that seemed to emanate from her body. There was
an effortlessness about her—an ease I coveted. I looked into her eyes,
hoping to find some reassurance, but her expression was icy. Maybe
she thought I was a diva because I was the last to arrive? I wasn't
late—I had shown up when my itinerary said to be there—but they
had all stared at me when I walked in and took the last empty seat.

"Who's your agency?" my neighbor asked me, her tone suspicious.
She might as well have said, *I haven't seen you before. What are
you doing here?*

I could have told her, *Major Model.* But the way she asked the
question told me she'd only hit me with a dozen follow-ups: *Is this
your first magazine shoot? Where are you from? Oh? Did you do any
modeling in the Philippines?* The floodgates would open, and she'd try
to find out everything there was to know about me, not because she
wanted to be my friend but because I was a possible enemy. Only in
the modeling world can such a benign question be so barbed.

I lowered my chin, quieted my voice, and pretended like I barely
spoke English. It was the only way I knew how to stop the conversation in its tracks.

When my agent first told me that *Complex* wanted to feature me
as "one of the 10 most beautiful models from around the world," I felt
as if I had been selected as a finalist in a pageant. They had picked *me*!

I was teleported back to countless stages, where the mood had been fun and generally supportive. But the make-do spirit of *pwede na yan* had no place in this hair and makeup room. No, this felt more like being chum in a shark-infested sea. The model next to me had sniffed blood in the water and was circling.

Just as she was about to try to talk to me again, I was called in to shoot. "Geena, we're ready for you!"

Once in the studio, the hairstylist finished my look by teasing the top of my hair, giving me a full ponytail bouffant à la Gwen Stefani in her *No Doubt* days. Another stylist laced up red Rollerblades around my ankles while her assistant stood by with a boom box—not a hollow prop, but an actual, working *heavy-ass* boom box.

They handed it to me, and I had to lift my arm to hold it, straining under the weight. The gesture stretched out my tight-fitting deep V-neck shirt so wide that it almost exposed my boobs. Faster than a Secret Service agent could dive in front of the president, the stylist's assistant swooped in to help me hoist the thing onto my shoulder. My boobs were safe. Crisis averted.

If you've never held a twenty-five-pound boom box while wearing roller skates, I don't recommend it. It was nearly impossible to find my balance, let alone pose gracefully. But I needed to look hot. I was supposed to be one of the most beautiful women out of billions, after all.

I focused on keeping the line of my body vertical and calming the shaky wobbling of my ankles. Somewhere in there, I must have followed Steven's instructions because I did end up in the magazine. But all I remember was trying not to fall on my ass.

When I look back at that issue of *Complex* now, what I notice first is my impeccable smoky eye. The makeup artist really did make me look gorgeous. But if you keep looking, there's something else in the image, too. You can see my sheer performance as I deliver exactly the aura the photographer wanted. It's almost *too* much—at least by

American standards. I had come from the pageant world, so I brought a certain theatrical flair to my work, trying out new ways of being, inhabiting different characters with each shoot. But American fashion culture looks down on such earnestness. I had to tamp myself down to the point that it almost crushed my soul.

There was a light inside me, full of hope and wonder, that I was supposed to dim when I modeled—but it still found a way to peek through.

I had been on hundreds of pageant stages, honoring what felt like an artistic calling. The pageants made me money, but more important, they allowed me to tap into my desire to express myself—to connect with the world through performance.

Modeling in New York felt like performing only for myself, wrapped up in my own inner dialogue as I tried to make each shot better than the last, really *becoming* a bride or a sexy boom-box-carrying Rollerblader.

The photographers didn't care about any of that; they just wanted strong angles and the right mood. My image was only going to end up getting flattened anyway, consumed on a page instead of a stage. The viewer would be so many more steps removed from what I was doing; their gaze would be distant enough to keep my secret safe but too far to really see me.

But they will see me one day, I told myself. *They will.*

I thought I could be the one to change things. I had an almost messianic belief in myself that I had been chosen for this. The speed with which I had reached the top of the pageant world was unheard of. Even Tigerlily, who had mentored so many girls before me, was in shock. She couldn't think of any other way to explain it besides some sort of innate capability—or, hell, even destiny. When I was wearing my Manang Sally wig and striking my Horse Barbie pose, I had felt it, too: the power, the clarity, the purpose.

With the enormous odds stacked against me in the New York

modeling world, I had no choice but to believe in that force again—an ethereal power that emanated from within, flowing outward but still lingering like an ember in my very core. It was my guide, especially in moments when I couldn't find my true north.

I thought if I became successful enough, the fashion world and the media would accept me when they found out, because by then, they would adore me too much to trash me in the press.

That's why I told Ericka I was serious when she asked me if I wanted to model on that snowy night—and why I kept going even when I had so much to lose. I felt like the exception to the rule, mistaking my own confidence for invincibility. I had to stay silent until it was time to be loud, I thought. And it wasn't time yet.

A few months later I read that issue of *Complex* for the first time, noticing that my name was spelled wrong in blaringly large print: GENNA. For a second, I was disappointed, but it quickly dawned on me that it might be better this way. The misspelling could help me hide a little longer. If someone were to look up a "Geena" from the Philippines, I couldn't be her! I was "Genna" now!

The way I had answered the two questions they asked me for the article also made me laugh.

"What she likes about home: It's a really tropical, laid-back country. There's no pressure about getting a career right away and money isn't everything. It's more of an easy life at home.

"What she's got to say: One thing I like about modeling is the role-playing. It's sort of an act. It's not just the glamour, runway, and prints; it's trying to fit into character. I love that."

I was definitely role-playing during that shoot. And I was also imagining how Tula must have felt every time she was photographed for a magazine. Had she ever been able to relax? Or was she too afraid of being seen?

13

JAMES BOND

MAYBE I HAD BEEN A BALLERINA IN ANOTHER LIFE, BECAUSE MY movements that day flowed in perfect harmony with the camera. *Click.* My arms moved to my hips. *Click.* I turned my profile ever so slightly, letting the lens catch me in a new light. I felt as if I were in an Edgar Degas painting, each angle of my body a masterpiece in motion.

It was spring 2006, and I was shooting the monthly catalog for Demetrios Bridal.

Most important, I was feeling myself.

I mean, there was no greater validation than being chosen to model for the multibillion-dollar bridal industry. Out of all its options, Demetrios had picked *me* to adorn the pages of its glossy oversize catalog. *My* face. Women browsing the catalog would look at me and dream about their own weddings. At every turn of the page, I would be a different facet of their fantasy personified, a fun-loving bride with a sweet ponytail on one side of the spread and an untouchable goddess on the other.

It was my job to be that moldable. Over the course of the eight-hour workday, my hair had to be restyled countless times, from an updo to a French twist, from curly to wavy, from headbands to hair ties. I had to be whoever they wanted me to be.

When I first started modeling, I had booked jobs with "looking for Eurasian" written on the casting sheet. I never anticipated bagging that market. But my agent was also sending me to castings that said, "Looking for Latina." There had been no space for my Filipinoness back then; if you weren't East Asian, you weren't top choice. Brown Asian models were not the kind of Asian the industry wanted. But I had the kind of look that could blend in—a blank canvas of a face that makeup artists loved, especially because of my small, almond-shaped eyes. I couldn't help but feel that I was erasing myself all over again with each new job, so the client could paint who they wanted to see instead.

At the same time, that flexibility was what made me so good at the tedious bridal shoot. I could look like thirty different women in the same day. And the affirmation I got in return was incredible. I felt as if I had infiltrated the inner sanctum of the gender binary, like James Bond slinking through a secret underground facility, not in a tuxedo but in a thousand dollars' worth of puffy chiffon. My mission was working.

Back on the streets of New York, though, that high faded, and my self-doubt surfaced. Because as much as I felt destined to change things, I couldn't escape the mental toll of all my covert maneuvering.

I was living two lives at once. Every moment held split realities, even in the most mundane conversations. Around fellow models or my agent, I was constantly on guard. Could they see the pain behind my smiles? Did they notice the fear flashing across my eyes between casual sips of coffee? Sitting across from them, I often felt as if they could peer into me, as if they could feel my longing to be seen as I was. But I was too good at hiding for them to notice.

The only industry figure I ever thought about telling was Dmitry, a sexy Ukrainian model whom I had come to think of as a friend. We had built up a rapport after running into each other at several "sexy" castings, chatting away during the dread-filled minutes we spent waiting to be called. He looked—if I'm being honest—like a mobster, his arms covered with mysterious scars, but he was a softie at heart: crunchy on the outside, gooey on the inside, like a Ferrero Rocher.

Still, I didn't trust him enough to come out to him.

No, it was only in my own head, and around Ericka, that I could still be myself. Even then, I was starting to lose my grasp on what my own reality looked like. The lies I was telling other people were beginning to obscure everything else.

That's why, when I was walking down the street that day after my Demetrios shoot, I did something that might sound a bit off-kilter: I felt my boob job. Maybe I looked bizarre—the woman cupping her left breast in public. I drew some stares for sure. But it gave me comfort, like placing my hand over my heart. I wasn't wearing a bra, so I immediately felt the weight of my breast and breathed a sigh of relief. My boob was tangible. Real. Something I could hold in my hands for a few seconds to remind me that I had chosen my own happiness, at least once.

At the same time, it made me think of the gravity of staying stealth. The surgeries I had gotten to reduce my dysphoria—to feel like the real me—were now granting me access to experiences that heightened it. As a model, those surgeries allowed me to blend in, to fit the industry's restrictive molds. But as a trans woman living in a world that denies my agency and personhood, that trip to Thailand also saved my life. I felt freer, and more authentic, but I was using that bodily freedom to lock myself in the closet all over again. Even my body was two things at once, a joy and a burden.

I wondered, as I walked down the sidewalk that day, what it would be like to be honest with everyone. To tell the people at Demetrios that they had a trans bride in their catalog and then watch the shocked look on their faces.

The entire time I modeled, I always had that voice in my head. Even as I lied to save my career, I was trying to tell the truth to myself, whispering it to no one. I constantly drafted two answers to every question, simultaneously processing how I felt and projecting how I *should* feel, all while trying to stay in the moment. Whenever someone asked me about life in the Philippines or about my family, the pragmatic part of me would kick in, pushing my emotions to the side so I could survive.

And when your every waking thought is bifurcated, cleaved in two by constant pressure, it's easy to lose track of who you are. Which Geena was I: the fantasy bride in the catalog, or the woman anxiously clutching her boob on the sidewalk?

Was I the one who told the truth—or the one who hid?

My friendship with Ericka was like a release valve for the tension of juggling my twin lives. I could relax around her. But our friendship also had its own fascinating duality.

We had met at the crossroads of our lives. I was new to New York; she had been living here since she was fifteen. But because she was so Americanized, she barely understood queer Tagalog, which I knew well. I was the first to teach her Swardspeak, a coded queer slang that blends several languages—Tagalog, Spanish, English, and Taglish— with brands and celebrity names, blending them all like a *halo-halo*. American colonization had left an indelible mark on our lingo, so in return we conquered English by infusing our witty, twangy Tagalog with an array of pop culture references.

If Ericka's date for the night was late because it was raining out, we'd say, "Julanis Morrissette," mixing the popular singer's name with the Tagalog word for "rain." "Oh my God, Barbra Streisand" was our snide comment to a person who just cockblocked us. In Tagalog, *bará* means "to block," and only a diva's name could capture the drama of missing our last chance to go home with somebody. Whenever a guy didn't deliver on his promise to buy us drinks at the club, I'd point him out to Ericka and say, "Beware, he's Oprah Winfrey," because her first name sounds like the Tagalog word *pramis*.

It made me feel even more like a spy to share a secret language. Ericka could ask me how much I had paid for my chic slinky club dress, and when I told her, "Oh, it's Mariah Carey," only she knew I meant it was *mura*, aka cheap as hell. These exchanges were our everyday banter, reminding my friend of her vibrant *bakla* roots.

I taught her something else, too. I had gotten my surgery two years before Ericka handed off her hostess job to me. By then my vagina had been a few places. I liked to joke that it had a "transpacific point of view."

So even as Ericka showed me around the city, I was able to tell her about some of the more figurative places I had been. Places where the depths of pleasure run even deeper than she knew they could.

I already had experience playing the role of vaginal mentor. Once, Julie, a fellow young trans Filipina I knew, was freaking out on the phone with me a few months before her surgery.

"Will I ever have an orgasm for real?" she asked me.

Even though I had answered her countless times before, she still wasn't fully convinced. I couldn't blame her. Even within our own community, people carelessly spread the myth that you'd never experience orgasm again after surgery. That damaging lie has been passed down from one generation to the next, from the Philippines all the way to Manhattan, making many trans women feel that they're not just unworthy of pleasure but incapable of it.

So instead of reassuring Julie yet again, I went over to her apartment. I walked through the doorway, looked her in the eye with calming assurance, and said, "As your trans sister, let me share this with you," explaining what I wanted to try.

She considered it for a moment, then agreed. And so we sat back to back on her bed as I started to pleasure myself. Together, we were going to shatter this generations-old myth. If the evidence of her own eyes couldn't convince her, nothing could.

After about ten minutes, I asked her to turn around. In my hand was a silky truth serum. She looked at it, mesmerized, as if I had produced diamonds out of thin air, her eyes sparkling. She started to cry, overjoyed from the certainty of her new knowledge. I started crying, too. There was a purity in that exchange—love received as freely as it was given. I had taught her a spell to break the chains of self-hatred.

Once Ericka came back from her own surgery, we were insepa-rable. I tried to give her the same assurances. I wanted her to have the craziest of all orgasms—that's one way to know your friendship has become a best friendship. We were two trans Filipinas, bonded to-gether by the queer humor of our shared mother tongue and by a desire to experience more.

Every Tuesday, Wednesday, and Thursday night, I would take Ericka out to dinners with male club promoters at whichever trendy restau-rant needed a "model boost." A big group of us—about twenty mod-els and promoters in all—rotated between Hiro Sushi, Gansevoort, and Buddakan, making sure we were seen as we entered.

Afterward there would be limousines waiting out front to take us to West Twenty-seventh Street in Chelsea between Tenth and Elev-enth avenues—a notorious stretch of nightclubs called Club Row. The people in line waiting to be let into B.E.D., Marquee, or Cain would watch in envy as we stepped out of our limos and walked right inside. We knew the bouncers. The velvet rope moved for us as auto-matically as a sliding door at a supermarket.

The only club that was hard for us to get into was the exclusive celebrity hotspot Bungalow 8. That only made it more tantalizing. In *Sex and the City,* Carrie Bradshaw famously describes it as "com-pletely pretentious" and says "you need a key to get into" it. Fortu-nately, I had a key: One of the club promoters I knew had a standing invitation to Bungalow 8, but he could take only a few models with him.

I was lucky enough to get picked quite a bit, but not without caus-ing some drama. This was the hierarchy within the hierarchy: There were models, and then there were *models.* You'd think that people who got paid for their good looks would be more secure, but really, we were just grade school cliques, roving through Chelsea, looking for validation.

As prestigious as it was to walk into Bungalow 8, Cain was my favorite club. It was safari-themed, which might sound tacky, but the interior was all class. It looked like the tribal council set on *Survivor South Africa,* with warm yellow lighting that flattered everyone. Nightlife guru Steve Lewis called it "the best club in New York for a time," and for a beautiful, heady year, it was my nightly sanctuary.

A bunch of us had a regular table in the corner. The male models would rub one another's bodies, laugh, and then get lost in the sea of beautifully lanky creatures on the floor. The finance guys—friends of the club promoter, usually—would come by to say hi, but mostly to ogle us. They were usually douchey, but some of them at least tried to put on a front of worldliness and sophistication. Ericka and I saw right through their facade, but we didn't care.

There were perks to hanging out with the Wall Street bros: For one, they let Ericka, with her skinny Capri cigarettes, light up and smoke inside because they knew the owners.

Here I was in New York City, dancing at the VIP table of a club with bottle service that would bankrupt me if I had to pay for it myself, flirting with *über*-confident Wall Street types. I had become a cliché. But there's a reason clichés become clichés: For a time, it felt *good* to be that girl. It was pleasurable to float through that world, drinks getting handed to you, compliments pouring down on you like warm tropical rain. As I made laps around the club, I felt as if I were walking the red carpet, to the staccato rhythm of flashbulbs as the paparazzi vied for my attention.

"Geena! Geena! Over here, Geena!"

Inside Cain, I felt powerful but also safe. Pretty but invisible. I was protected from the prying eyes of the fashion folks I worked with during the day. No one asked me their little "innocent" questions. Nobody gave a shit where I grew up. They just cared that I was there. In the club. With them. Add to that the pleasure of intoxication, and an atmosphere of extravagant consumption, and you have Cain.

Yes, it was pretentious, and yes, it was all riding on a wave of money that would evaporate in the financial crash a few years later. But for me, for now, it was a place of peace. I was accepted there, and I liked that feeling.

One night I looked at Ericka, both of us drunk by this time and barely keeping our balance. She had a blissful look on her face, as if she'd just sprouted two big fluffy wings and flown off to paradise. Then we heard the drums. A guy in cotton-wrapped pants with an African *djembe* tied around his waist was walking around the floor, stopping at each table, then hitting his drum harder and harder until the bass seemed to fill our whole bodies with its concentrated power. When he finished his rounds and took his place on the central dance floor, the place erupted.

It was like the room had an orgasm: He was beating his drum, loud and hard. Drunk clubgoers careened onto the floor, drawn in by his gravity, surrounding him in a surging kinetic throng. I was in there, too, a lanky lady who had downed one too many vodka cranberries. Ericka and I were screaming at the top of our lungs, wild and free, letting out all the happiness inside. We were in heaven, lost in the moment, but most important, no one in this room—and I mean *no one*—could clock our fucking T!

Ericka and I liked to walk around the club, all but prancing as we made our rounds. We held hands like two sexy lost cubs amid the safari. We would lock eyes with a guy, sip our drink through those tiny cocktail straws, and then time would slow. That playful exchange—our luscious, dreamy gaze meeting his cartoonish gawking—was one long, tension-building tease.

Usually, he would follow us right away, trying to strike up conversation. Too often he'd go straight for the tacky off-the-cuff line, "Can I buy you ladies a drink?"

Even more reason to ignore him.

We let him think he was chasing us down, but really we were in control, always staying a literal step ahead. We loved it—the validating feeling that we not only passed but could command a big testosterone-laden man to move hundreds of pounds of muscle mass to pursue us. At the end of the day, we humans were animals, too, predators and prey. We were the hunter and the hunted—and it was nice to feel more like the former for once.

Growing up in Manila, I expected—well, actually, I *still* expect—to be clocked on the streets.

Which was why it was so exhilarating to walk through Cain. It was like someone had cast an invincibility spell on me when I was on that dance floor. I had gone from living in a poor neighborhood alley to being a fashion model in New York City. How else could you explain that besides magic? And to be an *unclockable* fashion model in New York City—that must be the result of some powerful, legacy-building magic. I felt even surer that I was going to be mythical. One day the next generation of trans babies would whisper my name in hushed reverence.

But that grand vision for my future could be punctured at any moment.

In the middle of our second—okay, maybe it was our third—vodka cran, I was flirting with a male model who couldn't stop complaining about the exhausting day he had running around to castings. A cigarette dangled in my free hand.

I felt an insistent tap on my arm. It was a club promoter I knew. "Hey, Geena. Meet my buddy, Tommy. He's also Filipino."

The word rang loud in my ears: *Filipino!* All my senses went into overdrive at once. The hair on my arms stood on end. This was danger—the sort of fight-or-flight situation I should get away from. *Now.* But freaking out would only draw attention.

Every word out of my mouth from that point on was trans Filipina stealth survival 101. I was instantly sharp as a knife, transdrenaline rushing through my veins.

Bring it on, Tommy.

"Oh, hey!" I said, turning to greet him. "Nice to meet you. *Kamusta?*"

The last word was a test. If he was a Filipino who spoke the mother tongue, that could spell disaster for me. I looked at him expectantly, hoping to see a look of confusion on his face. Instead—

"*Musta,* nice to meet you," he said.

Fuck, fuck, fuck. He spoke Tagalog.

I had to go even deeper into survival mode. Time to play naïve.

"I love this place," I said, as nonchalantly as I could muster. "The music is so good."

Meanwhile I was screaming inside. Why, why, *why* did he have to interrupt this perfect night? And of course, now that he knew I was Filipina, the questions would come hard and fast, like blows in a boxing match.

"When did you move to New York?" Tommy asked me.

"A couple of months ago," I said, keeping my voice in a whisper-like tone. I used a voice that made me sound like a twelve-year-old girl, ultra–high pitched, femmey, suffused with innocence.

"Cool, that's cool," he replied.

Was there a knowing coyness in his voice, or was I just being paranoid?

I had to stop him from talking before he could ask more questions. The music picked up, and I tilted my head toward the dance floor, then pulled him away from the table, like a cheetah dragging her prey through the grass. Ironically enough, to keep him at a distance, I had to get closer.

Within seconds, we were in the dance pit, surrounded by swirling bodies, performing the kind of lustful gestures that make babies. My new Filipino friend thought I was into him, but I was manipulating the situation, flirting to keep my New York dream alive. Every time he tried to talk to me, Ciara's "1, 2 Step" remix would drown out his words. I made mock attempts at getting to know him, still using a girlish voice, pulling his head closer so I could speak into his ear.

"What do you do?" I squeaked. I was asking not because I genuinely wanted to know but because I was praying he wouldn't say, "Fashion." If he did, maybe I'd have to kill him. Just kidding. But I'd have to watch out for him. I'd have to calculate how to avoid him.

"Real estate finance!" he shouted, his voice piercing through the loud music.

"Hi, guys," Ericka said in her sultriest voice, joining us after the song ended.

We looked at each other in silent agreement, knowing we both had to put on our game faces to avoid being clocked. These were the kind of moments we had trained for. When Tommy asked Ericka how old she was when she moved to America, she said, "When I was very young."

Being seen as an "Americanized Filipino" can be a helpful tactic for steering someone away from associating you with childhood customs like trans pageants and flamboyant *bakla* culture. Ericka couldn't possibly be trans if she had come over that early.

Her lack of a thick Filipino accent already gave her a leg up. I, on the other hand . . . well, after a few drinks, forget about it. My *p*'s become *f*'s, my *v*'s start to sound like *b*'s, and my accent is fresh off the boat. That's why I had to rely so heavily on my innocent little girl voice. That high, squeaky pitch was textbook unclockable. But I could do it only inside a club, with music as my partner in crime. The next song started up, and I nestled up next to Tommy again. No more talking for a while.

After hours of dancing for my life that night at Cain, Ericka and I finally left. The longer we stayed, the greater the chance I would end up as the prey in that safari of illusions.

14

FIREFLY

"MODEL GO-SEE" IS A BIT OF JARGON THAT MEANS EXACTLY WHAT it sounds like: You go and get seen by a photographer. Go-sees are the grunt work of modeling—the auditions *before* the auditions.

As my career picked up, my agents were sending me all the time to these quick advance meetings. They've got a brusque show-me-your-portfolio, let-me-see-your-vibe kind of feel. You walk in wearing neutral clothing, whip out your lookbook, and chat for a few minutes. The hope is that if you gel with the photographer, they'll use you in their next booking or at least agree to do a test shoot with you.

The really enterprising models—and I was one of them—wouldn't just do the go-sees our agents scheduled for us; we'd also email photographers ourselves. You've probably noticed by now that I'm not the type to sit around and wait to be told what to do. Maybe that's the immigrant habit of making the most out of each situation. Or maybe I just didn't want to run out of money. If I didn't keep hustling, my ass would be back in San Francisco before I knew it.

But finding out how to get in touch with photographers was a full-time job. I spent all my spare time online. I scoured industry

websites, searching for contact information, listed or otherwise. Not
to mention the hours I pored through the websites of photographers'
agencies. It felt like the only way I could get an edge.

I felt frustrated every day I wasn't shooting. And when I *was*
shooting, I was thinking about all the other kinds of shots I needed.
I needed more high-fashion pictures. No, I needed more commercial
pictures. No, I needed more beauty pictures. No, more sexy pictures.
I had to cover as much of the market as possible. In hindsight, it
might not have been the smartest move to spread my image so thin,
but I worried that if I didn't try to do everything, I'd end up doing
nothing. As a Filipina model especially, I couldn't let any opportunity
pass me by.

By this time, my bookings were leaning toward the "sexy" market.
But when I did lingerie or swimsuit shoots for an ad, the work felt
mechanical. The lingerie had to be shot from a hundred different
angles for the packaging. We'd start, take a few shots, and then the
photographer would move the light for the next set.

"This shot is for the three-in-one panty package."

He'd move the light again.

"This one's for the in-store signage."

We'd repeat the process ad nauseam. I felt less like a model than a
mannequin. I was there to be bent, flexed, and posed. Hey, at least I
could pay my rent. But I was always searching for more—a way to
capture the essence I hadn't yet expressed.

Then one day Randy Paris responded to one of my cold emails
asking for a go-see. Randy was the fashion photographer and creative
director for a luxury outerwear brand I had long admired. His photography was unmissable. You'd see it in magazines and on Manhattan billboards—striking black-and-white images that were all sex and
leather jackets.

He and I met, hung out a couple of times, and became friendly enough that I felt comfortable airing some of my frustrations with the modeling world. I told him I felt I wasn't getting the kind of pictures that I wanted in my paying work. It was solid and steady but not nearly expressive enough. I wanted pictures that felt like *me:* regal, powerful, feminine. I wanted to see that unquestionable drive in my eye. I longed for the Horse Barbie spirit to show up in my pictures—to move with the kind of mighty gait that meant no one could tell me shit. I wanted mysterious side profile shots of me whipping my hair like a tail, in full command of my powers.

I felt ready to do the kind of intimate shoot in which the possibility of being fully naked would come up. I trusted Randy to do it, and he wanted to help me explore that part of myself—the part that was sick of panty packages and wanted something deeper.

We set a time for me to come to his studio. He asked me to bring black clothing, shoes, and lingerie. When I got to his artist loft in the middle of SoHo, I could see why he had requested that wardrobe.

The place was a huge, echoey relic of Manhattan real estate, with thirty-five-foot ceilings and spare partitions scattered everywhere. It looked like Marcy's loft in Martin Scorsese's *After Hours*—the kind of place that I didn't think existed in SoHo anymore.

Randy had already set up a light stand beaming soft yellowish light that bounced off the caramel finish on the hardwood floor. The leather couch was the same caramel color, oversize and plush. Behind it hung a vintage black-and-white Aqueduct poster of a jockey racing down a straightaway, his steed midgallop. The frame was almost as wide as the couch.

The stage was set. The backdrop felt like a sign: The horse was behind me, midgallop, as I extended my long Barbie legs, stepping back into my power. I was the Horse Barbie again, ready not just to pose but to create art.

"How are you feeling?" Randy asked me as I got settled, a note of genuine care in his voice. As if we both knew that we were about to create something special. No swimsuit photographer ever asked me how I was doing.

For the first few shots, Randy asked me to stand just off-center from the light to create a high-contrast shadow running lengthwise down my face.

"I want you to look directly into the camera," he told me. "In between each click, I want you to think of three very different emotions."

He was trying to teach me something about the power of a photograph. He wanted to show me the soul of an image. If we could take three radically different photographs in the same position with the exact same lighting, then what would make the portraits unique was *me*. *My* gaze. *My* energy.

On the first click, I imagined being a queen, respected and feared in equal measure. On the second, I thought of pure sex, focusing my eyes intently on the lens and saying in my head, *I want you, and I know you want me*. Finally, for the last shot, I made my eyes soft and thought about having a secret that I was too coy to share.

I realized then that I played just as much of a role in creating a photograph as the person behind the shutter did. I wasn't just providing a limited, rigid projection to fulfill someone else's demand; no, this shoot felt more like an open-ended artistic collaboration. I might not be the one pressing the button, but I had an active part to play, too—a role that went beyond delivering the right angles and lines. For the first time, someone had given me the chance to truly bring *myself* to what I did, and I was thrilled. This felt like modeling as an art form.

We looked through the shots we had taken so far, in perfect agreement that we were on the right track. Next, he wanted me to pose with the couch. The leather looked worn, as if it had survived a decade's worth of SoHo ragers.

How am I going to move around on this? I thought. *Will I be exposed?*

By that point, I was wearing black stilettos and a skimpy cotton shirtdress tank top. Would my heels punch through the delicate leather? Climbing around on a sofa with shoes on wasn't exactly something you got much practice doing in everyday life. If I thought about it too hard, I'd never be able to let loose, so I decided to pretend I was dancing between each click of the shutter.

My mocha skin glimmered lusciously as I gently traipsed from one side of the sofa to the other. When I climbed onto and around it, I was almost camouflaged against the coffee-colored leather. Every time I stopped moving, I peeked at the camera, as if I had just realized someone was watching me. As if there were a voyeur hiding behind the curtains. My movements were perfectly synchronized with the camera's, the staccato clicks of the shutter creating a timed, rhythmic flow.

One, two, three. *Click.*

One, two, three. *Click.*

I got lost in the moment. Lost in motion. I stopped looking at the camera so often, wandering through my own golden-lit, sensual paradise. At times, when I heard the shutter, I'd turn and give the camera a menacing stare—the kind of look that could burn straight through the lens and scorch the viewer on the other side. A light sweat glistened on my skin, making me feel as slippery as the leather. Whenever my legs rubbed against each other, I felt a pleasurable tingle. This was worlds apart from panty packages. This was something *else.*

I felt somehow at home in this anonymous loft. A meditative basslike thrum filled the space between shutter clicks; I knew it was in my head, but I swear I could *feel* the sound permeating the images, imbuing them with an ineffable, indescribable magic. In over a year of modeling, I had never been so completely in the moment, so lost in my craft. I felt like a movie star who was working on a buzzy indie film after a decade of phoning it in on popcorn blockbusters—as if I were finally responding to my calling and satisfying the artist within. The shoot was rougher and scrappier than what I had been doing lately, but it was collaboration in its purest form. Even my veins were vibrating with energy. It just felt *right*.

For the next group of shots, I wanted to wear my sheer black-cotton boyfriend panty and nothing more. I was feeling confident enough at that point to go topless, and I said as much.

"Are you sure?" Randy asked.

He was a tall guy, strong and built, but with a quiet voice and a gentle soul. He understood I needed to say something that night that only my body could express.

"Do you have liquor?" I asked him by way of reply.

I wanted a slight nudge to elevate me. He poured us tequila on the rocks. We locked eyes as we lifted the glasses, clinked them together, and drank, the alcohol burning our throats. *Let's shoot,* I thought.

But before moving on, Randy wanted to check in with me again. He had noticed me finding my rhythm as we got the last shots.

"You seemed to be really having fun playing and moving on the couch," he observed.

I was. But it was so much deeper than fun. After growing up in a cage of guilt-ridden Catholic dogma, for the first time I felt free—*fully* free—to express my sensuality without any guilt. No part of me was wondering what my parents would say about me taking such sexy pictures. The "trans talk" in my head was nonexistent. The shutter was the only thing I heard anymore. We kept shooting, time collapsing into an eternal present.

I'm kneeling on the couch. *Click.* My hair's wet from splashing water on myself from the bathroom faucet. *Click.* I'm on my back on the couch. *Click.* My body glistens from all the sweat and water, leaving condensation on the sofa as I stand up. *Click.* My right cheek presses against the framed horse poster. *Click.* The glass frame is textured with oil, my moisturizer leaving a mark. *Click.* I am playing. I can keep shooting forever.

In that huge loft, our bright spotlight could penetrate only the area we were using for the shoot. The rest of the room was dark, lit only by blinking red and yellow headlights passing by on the street below. If you were a nosy neighbor peering at us from the building across the street, I would have looked like a cabaret performer under the light, dancing for an unseen audience.

"Principles of Lust" by Enigma started playing through the sound system, and I asked Randy to blast it.

The mystical swell of synthesizers reverberated around the loft, my body following the song deeper into an experimental trance. The punctuated choral voices sounded like they were singing to me, the high-ceilinged loft transformed into a cathedral. "Do what you feel, feel until the end," the hypnotic lyrics instructed, and I obeyed. I was floating, an ethereal spirit freed from the confines of shame and guilt.

Holding my tequila on the rocks, my hips started swaying like Salma Hayek's during her dance routine in *From Dusk Till Dawn,* but instead of gracefully maneuvering a snake around me, I was keeping the cocktail glass perfectly upright, the ice glimmering like diamonds under the spotlight.

Suddenly, it didn't feel like a glass of tequila in my hand anymore, but a candle in a clear glass jar. I had become the physical embodiment of fireflies glowing in the night from our Filipino folk dance Pandango sa Ilaw.

Arms up and open wide, I was ready to receive the blessing.

That experience in SoHo gave me the confidence I needed to take more control over my modeling career. Between castings, whenever

I wasn't working, I kept reaching out to photographers. I could finally see the trajectory laid out in front of me—the path toward expressing myself more fully as a model and artist.

The photographer Mark Deni responded to me one day, confirming he would be willing to do a private shoot. His work was more fashion than lingerie, but why not combine the two? I thought. I was ready for an experience just as transcendent as my SoHo shoot.

After climbing three floors of steep stairs to his Tribeca studio, I entered a sun-filled loft with hardwood floors that creaked out a halfhearted welcome. It was my first time meeting Mark in person, and I thought I detected a certain coldness as we shook hands. He projected calm and little else.

Maybe he's just being professional, I told myself. *He just wants to get this done.*

My suspicions were confirmed when I saw only three outfits hanging on the rack. This would be quick. First, I slipped on a black-and-red-velvet long-sleeved gown with a thigh-high slit. It made me look like a grungy goth Victorian queen. The effect was heightened by his heavy-contrast lighting, the kind you'd see in the pages of Italian *Vogue*. I didn't really care for the second outfit—a neon-pink-check biker-chic dress. And after that, we shot a couple of nudes that were more mechanical than sensual. Mark moved haltingly, and I felt stilted, too, mirroring his curt energy.

The last outfit was red mesh La Perla lingerie. There's no other way to describe how I looked wearing it besides *expensive,* as if I had just come out of a dom session in *Fifty Shades of Grey.* The high-contrast blue-gray tones of the shot made the whole scene look cinematic. Maybe something good would come out of this after all.

Afterward Mark told me he'd email me the shots as soon as he had time to retouch them, and with that, we were finished. I was left to wait for the photos to appear in my inbox.

Two weeks later Mark sent me a message that haunts me to this day. I was on Ericka's couch when I got it, and as I started to read, the midafternoon traffic outside her window fell conspicuously silent.

Mark had noticed something while editing the photos. "Just curious, and it may not be any of my business, but in re-touching your images, I got really familiar with your body," he wrote, "and I was just curious about what your scars were from near your privates? They look like pretty big scars."

I started sweating. I clicked "reply," not knowing what I'd even write, my fingers shaking as they hovered over the keyboard. Maybe if he had asked me in person, my fight-or-flight would have kicked in. Maybe I could have whipped off some witty in-the-moment reply like "Bad bicycle accident. You don't want to know."

But faced with those words staring at me from a screen, I felt frozen. The air was still, too, the humidity of the apartment sending sweat oozing out of my pores. All I could hear now was the gurgling of Ericka's goldfish aquarium. It was usually such a soothing ambience, but there was something suspenseful now about the popping of each bubble as it surfaced—a slow-burning horror building to a crescendo in my mind.

What can I even say?

By that time, I thought I had a handle on how to hide my surgical scars while moving and posing. I had mastered that skill specifically so that I *could* let go. But when I read Mark's email, I lost all my newfound comfort with expressing myself more sensually. It evaporated into the air just like those damn bubbles in the fish tank. This was what I had always worried might happen if I let my guard down.

It stung even more because I loved my scars—and still do. I wear them like a badge of honor because they made me who I am. They remind me what I have done for myself—that I have gone through the hard work of aligning my body and soul.

But that day the same scars that had given me so much pleasure became a source of pain and gut-wrenching shame. Maybe I was losing my grasp on the meaning of it all, pursuing success at the expense of happiness. My mission to become a model was going according to plan, but it was putting a strain on everything else: my grip on myself, my emotional health, even my friendship with Ericka. She and I were supposed to be hanging out, and now here I was, sweating over my laptop.

But I couldn't stop now, I told myself. I just had to stay stealth a little longer. Another year, maybe two, and then I could change things. The trans model messiah. I just had to be more careful.

I calmed my quaking fingers and typed out a reply: "The scars are from waxing irritations. Ouchy."

Never have I told a more important lie.

15

BEBI

FOR ME, MEN WERE EVERYTHING MODELING COULDN'T BE: CA-
sual. Carefree. Cathartic. They were fun to be around, to be under,
and to be on top of. In a lot of ways, I was just like any other girl in
her twenties living alone in New York City, navigating the waters of a
large—but not always deep—dating pool.

For me, dating was the only part of my life in which I felt something like control. All day long I waited for other people to make
decisions about me. My agent would call, relaying news from casting
directors and fashion brands. My schedule was determined by the
whims of others. When it came to men, though, I got to choose.

Maybe that's why I slapped Jacques when he asked me to hit him.

Jacques was a hot French guy—and the VP of a luxury real estate
company. We met at the Soho House rooftop on one of those summer nights when the warm breeze makes everything feel effortlessly
cinematic. When I spotted him, I executed my go-to move to perfection, letting the wind blow my hair into my mouth and nibbling on it
playfully. I gave him a smoldering look, commanding him to approach, and his feet obeyed.

He left behind what looked like a group of his work friends—and it was even hotter that he abandoned them for me. When he got up close, he slowly brushed back his thick dark brown hair, and I wondered who would speak first as we held each other's gaze. Both of us were drinking Manhattans, and the aroma of smoked whiskey grew even more intense the closer we leaned into each other.

I had hooked him. By the time we got to his townhouse in the West Village, he was calling me "Bebi" and asking me to call him the same. A yellow streetlight poured in through the open floor-to-ceiling French shutters, bathing his dark wood furniture in a warm glow and casting soft shadows across the floor. Which was where his clothes started piling up before long. By the time he got down to his boxers, Jacques looked like Richard Gere in *American Gigolo*. He summoned me to the edge of his bed, and it was my turn to listen—but really, I was getting exactly what I wanted.

Our makeout session lived up to all those movie clichés, our breath synchronizing in a harmonic back-and-forth. He tasted like a Manhattan with a hint of Listerine.

But then when I was *really* on top of him, both of us naked, my body cast in silhouette from the streetlamp, he switched on the light on his bedside table.

"Bebi, can I ask you something?"

My mind raced with a million worst-case scenarios. No doubt he had clocked my T. I nodded yes, even as I prepared to flee—*fast*.

But then he finished his request: "Will you slap my face?"

If relief and confusion could be combined into one hybrid emotion, that was what flooded my heart in that moment. I was safe.

But I had never done anything like that before. Slap him? I did it once—*pak!*—thinking it was just a one-time thing. But then he begged for more. I slapped him twice between thrusts before I stopped again.

"I can't do this," I said, with feigned hesitation.

"Come on, Bebi, I love it."

Eskinita where Geena grew up. To the left under the flowers is the door to their sublevel home.

Baby Geena with Mama.

Bojojoy with Papa.

First communion at Our Lady of Guadalupe Parish Church.

Fifteen-year-old Geena. Taken after she won her first pageant title at SM North EDSA. Part of the 20,000 pesos was used to buy her magical wig.

Geena's pageant family. From left to right: Ruel, Tigerlily, and Jojo.

Geena in the middle winning the most prestigious pageant Miss Gay Universe 2000.

Geena in her iconic red halter gown wearing her magical wig.

Geena's unbeatable striped bikini, always a shoo-in for Best in Swimsuit.

Geena and her best friend, Danmark, who she met in San Francisco in 2001.

The Polaroid taken in New York City that got her modeling career started.

PHOTO BY BARNABY DRAPER

First magazine editorial in New York. Her name was misspelled.

PHOTO BY STEVEN BAILLIE

The first time Geena gave Norman a haircut. She's been cutting his hair since.

Norman playing guitar while Geena is dancing in nature.

Geena and Norman's first weekend together.

Geena speaking at
the TED Conference
main stage in Vancouver,
Canada.

PHOTO BY RYAN LASH/TED

Geena speaking at
the White House for
the first time.

Geena telling a joke to
President Obama.
She spoke at the DNC
LGBT Gala.

PHOTO BY ALLISON O'BRIEN/
AOB PHOTO

Geena as the first trans Asian Pacific Islander Playboy Playmate.

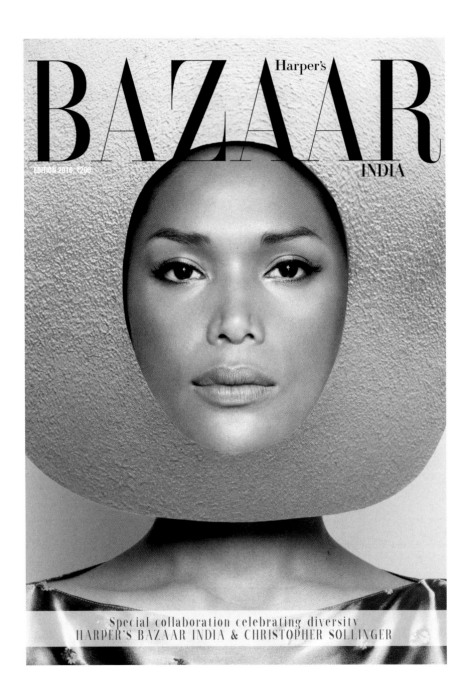

Harper's BAZAAR INDIA

EDITION 2016, ₹200

Special collaboration celebrating diversity
HARPER'S BAZAAR INDIA & CHRISTOPHER SOLLINGER

Geena on the cover of *Harper's Bazaar* India.

PHOTO BY STOCKTON JOHNSON

"I can't," I said, making my voice sound girlish.

I knew exactly what I was doing.

"Bebi, please, please," he begged, still elegant and handsome even as he was asking to be dominated. He was a man in power who wanted pain in the bedroom—and more of it. I could tell this was pure pleasure for him. But the trust in his eyes was thrilling, and it revealed who was really in charge here.

I slapped him harder. He especially liked it when my smack landed perfectly in between his left cheekbone and jawline, his plump cheeks producing that perfect high-pitched slap. *Pak!* His face got redder; his moans grew more intense. After my sixth slap, I started to feel uncomfortable—hello, Catholic guilt!—but by the tenth, I eased back into it, letting go of more inhibitions with each thrust. My self-imposed judgment vanished into the night.

Wrapped up in that consent between him and me, we had a sense of freedom. Our needs were being stated—and satisfied: His were literally written on his cheeks. He received all my slaps pleasurably, their rhythm a grounding soundtrack to a perfect, if unexpected, evening.

I was in control.

I was trusted.

There was a thrill to entering a bar and coming out with a guy. Especially when that guy looked like Ricardo. "He's a Calvin Klein model," his friend had whispered to me over the din of the Mets game at a joint on the Upper West Side—but I didn't need to be sold on him. He looked like a beautiful blend of every race on earth, like the male version of "The New Face of America" on that famous cover of *Time* magazine. A bit Asian, part Brazilian, maybe some French, too. I wanted him—and I got him.

As we stepped out onto the street, the roar of the bar faded into the background, replaced by the sound of our footsteps finding each other's rhythm on the sidewalk. He pressed his hand against the small of my back, a quiet but insistent reminder of his intentions, and I felt wanted, oh so wanted. It was a perfect moment.

But some nights that moment could only be fleeting, because as we walked the few blocks between the bar and his apartment, the reality of the situation hit me. Not even our impromptu makeout session could distract me from the nagging unease in my stomach. The truth was that men were fun—but they could also be dangerous. I hadn't forgotten having to hide in that closet at Lake Tahoe, or seeing the look on that guy's face in San Francisco as he drove me home in complete silence.

My steps slowed down. The horns of the cabs blaring past us sounded more like fire alarms now. *Geena, what are you doing?*

And then I looked over at his face—that beautiful face that looked like it was from everywhere and nowhere all at once—and kept walking. There was no way of knowing whether he'd be worth the risk, but tonight I wanted to take it anyway.

He lit some candles when we got into his apartment.

This guy got game, I thought, admiring the way the light flickered against the exposed brick wall of his loft. It was so New York—the kind of apartment you'd see on TV.

Then we were undressing, drinking in the sight of each other's silhouettes. I tried to shush the "trans talk" inside my head—the inner voice that yelled at me, warning me not to keep putting myself in situations like this. Because if I listened to it, I would never experience anything—never *feel* anything. That's the tragic paradox at the heart of transness: To live, we risk dying. To feel pleasure, we accept the possibility of pain.

Ricardo was gentle with me. His thrusting flowed like dance. When he was on top, his face moved in and out of my vision, the brick wall behind him coming in and out of focus. For a second, my mind went still. As we climaxed, it was just the two of us in that room—not us and the nagging voice in my head.

Afterward Ricardo asked me to stay overnight, and I agreed. He wrapped me up in his enormous wingspan, and I snuggled up into him, inhaling his musky, peppery scent. To me, this was a continuation of the sex, an exchange of heat and intimacy just as vital as the act itself. If you had eavesdropped on us, you would have heard us humming to each other, gently, back and forth, call and response. I felt as if I had defeated the "trans talk" for good and could finally just . . . relax.

But then a jolt of fear hit my heart.

Ricardo is a model, I realized, remembering his friend's bragging in a panic.

I needed to get out of there. It didn't matter that our bodies were intertwined, or that seconds ago I had been floating off to sleep on an ocean of postcoital bliss. He was in the industry, and if he caught on to me, I could be outed. Word of my transness would travel from his lips to infinite ears. Suddenly wide awake, I peeled his arms off me as he started to drift off.

"I have a super early call time," I lied.

He looked confused. Hadn't we just shared something special? Couldn't I just set an alarm?

"Sorry, I have to go," I said, searching for my clothes on the floor.

This wasn't as jarring for me as it was for him. My life was full of these extreme swings between comfort and fear, between pleasure and danger. I could let myself stop performing for a few hours, maximum, and then I had to shift back into stealth mode.

Ricardo tried to get in touch afterward. He was nice, and he couldn't help it that he was a model—anyone that hot was basically legally *obligated* to be photographed for a living—but I had to hold it against him. I couldn't take the risk. Did I ever envision us walking around the Reservoir together, holding hands and sipping coffee?

Yes. Was he a guy who got away? Not quite, but I always wondered how he would have reacted if I had told him.

But I didn't tell him. I couldn't.

Then I wondered if I should tell Jacques, whom I met again for dinner one night not long after seeing Ricardo. In between bites of pasta, I opened my mouth a half-dozen times to say it. But the words never came out. I felt comfortable around him. He wasn't a model. And we had a sensual connection—the sexy slapping was proof—but I still didn't know very much about him.

This was our first official date, and people hide things on first dates: addictions, gambling problems, even histories of violence. Not that my being trans was anything like those things, but still, we were both holding our cards close to the chest, and I didn't want to play mine too early. I would soon learn the dangers of getting vulnerable too fast.

Sometime amid my liaisons with Ricardo and Jacques, my best friend Danmark flew out from San Francisco for a visit. I wanted him to taste all the best perks modeling had to offer. I took him—where else?—to Cain. We were determined to relive our glory days in San Francisco, dancing all night. The drinks came in a steady stream, the sweat we built up evaporating into the air, alchemizing into pure fun. The music thumped so loud, it filled our chests.

Then from a distance, a familiar face came toward me, clearing the crowd—Dmitry, the sexy Ukrainian model and one of the only people in the industry I considered a friend.

I introduced Dmitry and Danmark to each other, and the three of us danced together in the crowd, chugging vodka crans. When we sat down for a break, we still got jostled around because the place was so packed. In a rare moment of calm, humming from the alcohol running through our veins, I felt a wave of pure joy at the sight of Danmark and Dmitry sitting next to me, an old friend next to a new one. The whole world was at peace—but maybe that was just the vodka talking.

Danmark went back to the dance floor, leaving me alone with Dmitry.

As we sat together and talked, reminiscing about the families we had left behind, Dmitry boasted to me about one of his scars. He had gotten it during a fight, he said. Each scar was a story, he said, usually a scary one, and together they made him who he was. He might have been rough-and-tumble, but I found him disarming. He was being vulnerable with me, disclosing pieces of his past unprompted.

Maybe it was all the talk about scars, but then in a moment of stupidity, I felt like I should return the gesture.

"I love that you met Danmark!" I shouted to him over the music, leaning over to put my mouth close to his ear. "He's my best friend, and you've been a good friend to me, too!"

And then the words just spilled out of me before I even knew it. Nonchalantly, naïvely, suddenly: "By the way, I'm transgender, but no one knows, so keep it a secret, okay?"

He pulled his head away to look at me and make sure I wasn't kidding, but my steely expression proved it wasn't a joke. His eyes widened slightly for a split second, and then he looked calm again.

"Don't worry," he said. "You're good, you're good."

And I believed him. I thought maybe for once someone could just see me as normal, that my transness wouldn't be an asterisk permanently attached to Dmitry's perception of me. He had shared with me; I had shared with him. We *were* cool, right?

I saw Danmark off in the distance, laughing, having a blast as if he were in a Mariah Carey music video, blissfully unaware of the bomb I had just dropped on my own life. Already, only seconds later, I regretted what I had said.

When I saw Dmitry after that, something felt off. We went through the same rituals, our same comings and goings, even grabbing a slice of pizza for lunch after one casting we both attended. While he didn't acknowledge the secret I'd shared with him, he did act overly reassuring, as if he wanted me to know everything was still cool between us. But the air of goodness he put on felt a little *too* good. Could this be real? Could I really tell people and be accepted? Was he masking his true feelings with a performance of coolness?

Sharing my secret with Dmitry had come from a place of wanting to feel more connected to him, but the prospect of being fully seen felt too intense, like staring directly into the sun. I had been performing for so long, I wasn't sure I knew how to be the real me.

Maybe it was the overwhelming internalized shame I still carried. Maybe I couldn't let someone else accept me because I hadn't accepted myself yet. But after that night at the club, my relationship with Dmitry changed. We saw each other less and less. We'd say hi inside Cain sometimes, but I wouldn't go running toward him as I had before, all eager to catch up and hear the story of his latest scar.

Usually, I'd spy him from a distance, whispering to someone after he'd spotted me. I began to get paranoid. Dealing with him from that point on felt less like friendship and more like a high-stakes negotiation. I had to make sure I stayed on his good side now. He had my secret. He could destroy me with a single word.

But who was manipulating whom? I couldn't tell anymore.

This is why spies never drop their cover story, not even for a second. Dmitry had been a friend; now he was a liability.

One night after another dinner date with Jacques, right before we walked into his townhouse, he stopped and looked at me.

"Bebi, I'm being relocated for work," he said. "Not sure when."

It's like he knew I had been thinking about telling him—about getting too close too fast. I appreciated his honesty. At least we both knew now that whatever happened inside his place was purely for fun. Just a fling. It would be exactly what I had thought I wanted when I first met him: pleasure with no strings attached.

In his bedroom, our bodies hungrily latched onto each other, the intensity stronger in every way than in our first encounter. Maybe that was because I knew it could be our last time and that it was pointless to hope for more.

When I was on top of him, he left his bedside lamp on. He wanted to look at my face as I gave him exactly what I knew he wanted. I didn't hesitate this time. I slapped him. *Pak!* Each thrust felt like it was all we had—all we'd ever have. *Pak!* For some reason, knowing that we might never see each other again only made the pleasure more powerful. After all, you can't have a climax without an ending.

Still, a certain wistfulness lingered with me after that night. Jacques went radio silent for a week afterward. When I finally checked in, he said that he had been traveling, and when I pressed a little more, he said he wanted to put some distance between us. He didn't want the relationship to get any more serious because he was being relocated sooner than he anticipated. There was no point letting our feelings for each other get any stronger. I said I respected that.

But some part of me hoped for something more than a casual encounter. I let myself fantasize about what it would be like to keep meeting up with him, flying off to some faraway country to give Bebi the best slap of his life. Falling in love with a man felt somehow even scarier than having sex with one. I was too afraid of what love would require of me emotionally to even speak that desire aloud. I couldn't let myself do much more than imagine a life with someone who embraced all of me. But deep down, buried somewhere beneath all my modeling ambitions, I wanted it.

16
JERSEY GIRL

A MODEL'S LIFE IS MEASURED IN MILESTONES—AND MINE WERE racking up. After I shot the John Legend music video in late 2005, more work had come my way: I was on the cover of *Modern Luxury* and in the pages of *Glamour* and *Cosmo*. I modeled lingerie for Hanes. My face was on a Times Square billboard. Jobs led to more jobs. When it rains, it pours, they say, and I felt like I was standing under that gushing gutter in my *eskinita* letting the bookings wash over me.

Just as I had done in the Philippines, I had risen fast. *Too* fast. There's a reason spies don't star in music videos. I thought that the higher I climbed, the closer I'd get to breaking through—to becoming the out trans model who won everybody over. Instead, as I got closer to the mainstream exposure I thought I wanted, I felt even more pressure to stay hidden. I was certain my cover was about to be blown. At times, that feeling of inevitability was unbearable, and my only catharsis was Cain.

I came home from dancing one night and collapsed onto my twin bed, arms dangling limply over the sides of the mattress. As I lay there, caught in that delicious liminal space between wakefulness and sleep, every sensation was heightened: The stillness of the dark room. The slight breeze coming in through the window, carrying with it the scent of lamb, onion, and curry rice from the famed late-night halal on the corner. The aroma was like a cloud of hypnotic bedtime incense guiding me to sleep.

Suddenly I felt a strange warm liquid splashing over my face. In a stupor, not knowing whether I was dreaming or not, I pried my eyes open and saw a blurry swatch of yellow light coming from the doorframe. *Why was it open?*

The second thing I saw was my roommate Evan. He was peeing on me. *What the fuck?* I leaped out of bed, pushed him out of the way, burst through my open door, and screamed at the top of my lungs, "Robert! Robert!"

I rushed through the hallway, dripping wet, and knocked on my other roommate's door. I was still screaming, but even amid my utter confusion and panic, I made sure to pitch my voice upward. I didn't want to get found out in these circumstances.

"What happened?" Robert mumbled, half-asleep.

"Fucking Evan!" I yelled. "I woke up to him peeing on me!"

Jolted awake by my words, eyes wide, Robert bolted toward my room to confront Evan, who was still urinating on my bed, drunkenly oblivious to the fact that I was no longer in it. Grabbing Evan by the shoulders, Robert guided him out of my room. I was still shaking, covered in now-cold piss, and one thing was clear: I couldn't sleep in my room.

After a shower, I lay down on the living room couch and called Ericka.

Like a true friend does in the middle of the night, she picked up right away. "Hey, what's up?" Her voice was sultry even when she was half-awake.

"Flaka, I woke up and my roommate was peeing on me."

"Oh my god, are you safe? What do you need?"

I just started crying. I felt so far away from anything familiar and safe. It was as if every emotion I had been holding on to up until that point just flowed out of me, a river bursting through a crumbling dam. The constant hiding, all the maneuvering to keep my identity secret, even my decision to leave home—it all felt so utterly pointless. For months now, I had been telling myself, *You're doing fine, keep going,* whispering it like a mantra when the stress grew too much to bear. But now, after being drenched in my roommate's piss, it was hard to believe my own words. I had held on to my dream for so long, but it was such a lonely dream, cutting me off from everyone except Ericka. My dream required me to worry about getting clocked even when I was in shock. This nasty, cramped, concrete jungle—this city where I had once seen so much opportunity—now seemed to be twisting around me, choking me with its vines.

I missed Mama. I wished I could have heard her voice right then.

But there was no way I could call her to let her know what had happened. The second she heard, my ass would be back in San Francisco, and even as I felt myself hitting rock bottom, I wasn't ready to give up. When I was in pageants, I had survived plenty of harrowing situations in the remotest parts of the Philippines and kept going. What was one more obstacle in my path?

On the other end of the line, Ericka waited for my sobs to die down, then asked, "Wanna move here so you can be closer to me?"

She lived in a high-rise condo building in Jersey City and had been trying to get me to move across the river for months. This time I was tempted.

The next morning when I told Evan what he'd done, he had no memory of it and was mortified. He sputtered horrified apologies and scrambled, desperately, for a dozen different ways to make it up to me. He would buy me a new mattress, he said. He would give me a discount on next month's rent, as though a coupon could compensate someone you had pissed on. Words spilled out of his lips, but it was as if he were set on mute. I was watching his mouth make all its hollow little gestures, but my mind was elsewhere—and it was made up.

Compared to getting peed on in New York, Jersey City sounded like paradise. I thought it would be my golden ticket away from all the stress of my New York life. And I was right—at least for a while.

Some people dismiss New Jersey as "the Armpit of America"—but after I moved there, that armpit became my oasis.

Every evening when I went home after modeling in the city, my breathing and heart rate would slow down in time as the PATH train decelerated in the tunnel beneath the Hudson River. My fingers would uncurl from my portfolio, and I'd let it rest on my lap for the rest of the ride. For a night, I could relax and just *be*.

It was so much easier to lead two lives when there was a river between them. In New Jersey, where I lived in an apartment building one over from Ericka's, I felt free.

As I got off at the Newport train station in Jersey City after a day in Manhattan, I felt absolute serenity. The high-rises along the waterfront seemed like a shield from the stress of the big city across the water. I had died and gone to Jersey heaven.

But in New York, the stress of staying stealth only intensified—an ever-escalating fear of getting found out.

One day at the MAC Cosmetics corporate office in SoHo, I found myself in an elevator full of models, all of them wide-eyed and full of big dreams. Many had come from countries thousands of miles away. It was a cattle call. You'd know it, as soon as the doors slid open, from the hums of a dozen different accents.

In a room packed with close to a hundred other models, all waiting to be summoned, I took a seat in the crowded waiting area by the receptionist. Everyone's faces were as anxious as they were beautiful, awash in the glow of enormous LED screens playing a life-size air-brushed MAC ad. We all wanted to be one of those women on TV. But out of all those vying for a spot, the cosmetics giant wanted only a lucky seven.

For its upcoming campaign, MAC was looking for four white models with blond, red, and brunette hair. They also wanted one—*only one*—Black girl, one Latina, and one Asian. At the time, it was one of the most diverse campaigns I'd ever heard of.

In the mid-2000s, there was almost no talk of improving representation and diversity in the modeling industry. Typically, for every job, a brand would be looking for several white models, from blond to brunette to red, and they were in abundant supply. White-passing girls could compete in that category, too. Apart from that, there was typically space for only one model of color, and companies typically wanted that model to have light skin. That put me at a disadvantage as a self-professed Jungle Asian; if they wanted an Asian girl, they usually chose a light-skinned East Asian model. Complaining about the lack of diversity was out of the question. All of us on the outside of whiteness had to follow an unwritten rule: *If you want the job, don't speak up*. It was the opposite of all those "If you see something, say something" messages plastered all over the subway; in the modeling world, the unspoken motto was *See nothing, say nothing*.

As a dark-skinned model, when you booked a job, you zipped your lips, smiled for the flashing lights, and ignored all the rejection and pain you'd experienced along the way. What else could you do if you wanted to work?

We had no social media platform where we could voice complaints or advocate for greater inclusivity. We had no way to put a brand on blast. And as a stealth trans model, I was always conscious of the fact that I couldn't even whisper about a company the way some of my peers did. I literally couldn't afford to be a critic.

As I waited to be called, I surveyed the room, scanning for familiar faces—and I did a double-take when I saw who was sitting across from me. Lucia Santiago, *the* supermodel of the Philippines, was mere feet away. All the Filipino gays used to call her "the one," and every designer in the country cited her as a muse. When she walked the runway in fashion shows, it was as if she did it twice, her performance echoing in the excited murmurs of the audience. Everyone was in awe of her bone structure and her command of the light—and for good reason. She was stunning in person.

My model-obsessed gay best friends back home would have freaked out if I told them I was at a casting with Lucia Santiago. Inside, I was fangirling hard. I wanted to approach her, adore her, giggle with her. But she would've clocked me right away.

Here in New York, I could only worship her from afar, tortured by the fact that I couldn't even say hello to one of my idols. In any other world, this would have been a cause for celebration: two Filipinas modeling together in New York. Sisters in the struggle. We were literally the only ones I knew of. We could have bonded over being brown-skinned models who knew that castings like this were biased toward light-skinned Asians. But I couldn't share any of that with her.

If we had been anywhere else, doing *anything* else, I would have greeted her with the same jubilation every Filipino does when we recognize each other in foreign lands: *"Huy, kamusta ka?"* followed by the grounding *"Taga san ka satin?"* to find out which town within the islands, which *barangay* district in the city, which dialect of our language—all the rich geography that makes up a person. I couldn't do that with Lucia. Even a Filipina Power fist bump could happen only in my imagination.

I hid my face from her and pretended not to exist.

Please call me now, I thought.

Mercifully, before I knew it, I was in the room.

Turn to the right profile, *click.*

Turn to the left profile, *click.*

"Please pull your hair up," the casting director asked.

I could feel the lens zooming in, as though the camera were judging my every pore, tracing every one of the laugh lines between my cheeks.

Thank God my Shiseido moisturizer is working its magic, I thought.

But even as I stared the camera down, I felt like I was taking a lie detector test.

Can the camera tell?

I tried to feminize my stare—as if that's even a thing you can do.

"It was good to see you," the casting director finally said, dismissing me.

And then, just as fast, I was out of the room. I had passed another test.

But as I pushed open the transparent glass double door in the hallway, I saw a second unexpected face: It was Larry Hashbarger, the fashion creative director at Macy's in San Francisco. I knew him from working at the cosmetics counter. He knew my T.

"Hey, Geena, how have you been?" he greeted me warmly.

I felt the color drain from my face. "Hey, Larry, how're you doing? What are you doing here?" I barely managed to force the words out of my mouth.

"Oh, I'm just here to meet the brand executives" was his casual reply.

The screaming chaos in my head felt so loud, I was surprised he couldn't hear it. I wanted to run straight back through those double doors like a Looney Tune, leaving a human-shaped hole in the glass. But acting scared in front of everyone would have been career suicide. So as Larry pushed through the hallway with his colleagues, I simply said, "It's good to see you."

And in my tone was a plea: *Don't tell anyone. Please, Larry, don't tell anyone.*

His response might as well have been uttered in slow motion. "It's good to see you, too," he said, holding my gaze for a moment, his eyes twinkling.

A high-stakes negotiation was hidden in that casual exchange. As a gay man, Larry knew what it was like to be persecuted, and I hoped he'd picked up on the subtext layered into our brief greeting. He owned a trans cabaret in San Francisco, so I felt confident he was an ally, but you never knew. Maybe he'd be proud of me, seeing me at a coveted MAC Cosmetics casting, when the last time I saw him in the Bay Area, I'd still been selling makeup over the counter. But then he might also say something off-the-cuff to the MAC execs that would give me away, like, "She's come so far!"

"What do you mean?" they'd ask him.

And then he'd tell them.

Back at street level, the golden-hour sun illuminated the reflection of my face in the glass SoHo storefronts, and I tried to calm down. As my silhouette strutted from window to window, a hazy profile in motion, I sneaked little side glimpses. It was more than a moment of vanity; it was an affirmation—and an honest assessment of my situation. I was both women at once: the flesh-and-blood model walking down the street and the phantom skittering between the windows. I wanted to be seen and to be a blur at the same time. I wanted to be in a MAC campaign but have no one know my name. My life wasn't split in two; *I* was split in two. Moving to New Jersey could only buy me a little time; a river couldn't keep my worlds from colliding.

I turned to face a shop window, then took a few steps toward it, my reflection disappearing right before I could ask the face looking back, *What did I get myself into?*

Ericka's studio apartment was a five-minute walk from mine, but we might as well have been roommates. We slept in the same bed, cooked together, and partied together. We would make fried rice with marinated tapa beef, filling her space with the mouthwatering aroma of garlic and vinegar. She was my family. And her family became mine, too.

On weekend mornings, when we were still in bed, her mom would swing the door open carrying bags bursting with Filipino treats from the nearby Balikbayan store: soft tamarind candy, our favorite instant Lucky Me noodles, and colorful sweet delicacies like purple *ube* cake. Forget breakfast in bed—this was Sunday Filipino brunch in bed.

There were different kinds of treats near us, too. Hoboken was full of Jersey boys—and I liked Jersey boys. Ericka and I would go out together at night to sample the local men. Away from the prying eyes of the modeling world, I could just be me, single and flirty. We made the rounds, hopping from one bar to the next, one-night stand after one-night stand. Fun, and nothing more.

One day I got a call from my agent. "Want to see your family?"

I was surprised by the question. "What do you mean?"

"You've just booked multiple Macy's catalogs!" he said. "You're going to San Francisco!"

Oh, boy.

A big part of me was grateful for the booking. It was a huge opportunity, both financially and in terms of visibility. And I could spend time with Mama. My clothes would smell like garlic fried rice again—a maternal aroma I badly missed. I wanted to be a baby bear again, nestled up against her mama. Getting spooned by Jersey boys was fun but not as comforting as home.

But did I really have enough fortitude to deal with the meta, full-circle, "are you fucking kidding me" feeling of being back at that San Francisco Macy's—a place where *everyone* knew my T?

Despite my higher-profile jobs, I was still mainly a catalog girl, so I couldn't pass up the opportunity. I was good at it, too. I had pretty much perfected the laughing midair profile hop that you see on billboards in Herald Square. You've seen the pose—it says, *I'm just a fun flirty girl jumping in the middle of the street!* I could already see myself doing hundreds of those midair profile hops for JCPenney, Nordstrom, and Kohl's. I had to tell my agent yes, even though I knew it was risky.

Before long I was opening the door to a hotel room in downtown San Francisco. From the window overlooking busy Market Street, I watched the trolleys pass by, indulging in a fleeting moment of nostalgia. But before the anxiety could kick in, I picked up my luggage and took a short cab ride to Mama's apartment on Fifth Street and Harrison. Checking into the hotel had been a paranoid bit of overperformance: I wanted the client to *think* I was staying there so that they'd be less likely to connect me to anyone in the area. That way there wouldn't be any questions about who I was staying with or who I knew.

When I walked into Mama's apartment, her warm hug seemed to squeeze the tears out of me. *"Anak, kamusta flight mo? Miss na miss na kita, kain na, kain na,"* she said, expressing her longing, only to follow it up with every Filipino mom's greeting: guiding me to eat.

We hadn't seen each other in so long, and all I wanted was her approval of my decision to move to New York. I hoped she would be proud that I had left San Francisco as a cosmetics counter employee and was returning a bona-fide fashion model. She had been scared for me to move so far away, especially because my career path seemed like such a gamble. Whenever we talked on the phone, she always asked me nervous questions: "How was your audition?" "Are you eating well?"

Every time she asked, I felt a twinge in my heart because I wanted to say more, to tell her how I was struggling to balance everything, but I didn't want to worry her too much. Now, together again at last, I could just hold her. I slept well that night, feeling safe for the first time in God knew how long.

Fortunately, the photo studio for our shoot wasn't at the Macy's in Union Square. Instead it was miles away, deep in the industrial Bayview district. Somehow I had got it in my head that I would be shooting the catalog on the top floor of the store, which would have meant dodging everyone I used to know so that I didn't trigger a cascading game of telephone that would cost me the job—and my career.

But even in a studio across town, I was worried about being discovered. With each click of the camera, each robotic turn to capture every angle of the blue and brown two-piece swimsuit, I quickly followed my "stomach in" gesture with a dread-filled glance at the studio entrance.

Was someone coming?

I managed to put on my million-dollar catalog girl smile even as I remained convinced that someone from the Union Square Macy's would walk through that door any second. Would it be Larry Hashbarger? Had *he* gotten me this job? I felt like I was being photographed naked, totally exposed to the people nonchalantly coming and going at the door.

The next outfit was a brown floral halter dress. The fabric was soft and flowy. I twirled as the camera clicked, turning the room into a buzzy blur. For a few seconds, I escaped to a different, more elevated plane. I could breathe as long as I was spinning. The door disappeared in my dizziness. But by the fiftieth dress, I was losing myself in the personas I was inventing for each look, trying as hard as I could to get out of my own head.

And I would have to do it all over again the next day.

After two days of shooting, I sought comfort in the depths of a swirling pot of spaghetti sauce. It was Mama's sweet Filipino-style recipe. The pasta was perfectly al dente, and the tomato sauce was silky with banana ketchup, all topped with ground beef and sliced hot dogs seasoned with the exact right balance of salt and sugar. My work trip was turning out to be a wild seesaw ride between the fear I felt in the studio and the comforts I enjoyed at home. I spent all day with a pit in my stomach, then at night tried to fill that pit with Mama's food.

"What do I tell people when the catalog comes out?" Mama asked me that night after a big bite of pasta.

"Ma, I really don't know *po*."

I took a frustrated tone with her, as if I had hit a dead end in a maze and just given up. I didn't know what to say anymore. Even the guaranteed joy of a Filipina mom's home cooking wasn't enough to keep my woes at bay.

I tried to remind myself that Mama was carrying my burden, too. Inasmuch as I had to be in the closet, she was in one, too. She had never told anyone I was a model because I couldn't risk the word getting out. Our cover stories and our alibis always had to align. We had to work in perfect sync, like the sugar and salt in her spaghetti sauce—our own sweet and salty secret.

But this time the secret felt bitter. This gig wasn't just hitting close to home, it was a bull's-eye, dead center. On some level, I knew it would be even harder to stay stealth in the industry if I came here. Everyone in the Macy's cosmetics department would see my smiling face in those pages. They would spot me and probably be excited to see how far I had made it in the modeling industry, but in the middle of their innocent celebration, one of them would whisper, *Do they know?*, meaning capital-M Macy's.

Do they know she's trans?

Back in New York, I received the kind of text message I had always dreaded.

"You're in Page Six!" a friend messaged.

The words hit me like a semitruck. Had something come out

about me already? I knew going to San Francisco had been a mistake. I flipped open my laptop in a frenzy and found the article online. The *New York Post* headline read PUBLIC SQUABBLE.

> Comedian Dave Chappelle had nothing to laugh about after he fought with his wife, Elaine . . . at Coffee Shop in Union Square the other day. The lunchtime crowd was shocked to see Elaine in tears after the duo battled because Dave had left her side to chat up gorgeous model Geena Rocero. "Geena's very attractive," said our spy.

The article was exaggerated and full of lies. A couple of days beforehand, I had been at Coffee Shop with a girlfriend having lunch. Yes, Dave Chappelle and his wife had been sitting at the adjacent booth. But we didn't interact.

This was not the kind of press attention I needed. Now that I was linked to a celebrity, a media vulture might decide to dig deeper into my life at any minute. They could research my name, ask around, figure out my history—and feel like they got the juicy scoop about the trans model who had "fooled" everyone in town.

It would be Tula and April Ashley all over again. The salacious media would take my story and rewrite it without an ounce of respect. Why was this happening now? I needed another year or two to get more established, to become less dispensable, I told myself. But by now, I was finding it harder to believe my own excuses. How long had I been trying to convince myself of that?

After the *Post* piece, I only grew more paranoid, knowing I was working on borrowed time. At every event, I kept an eagle eye out for reporters and tabloid photographers. Would they tell more lies? Would their cameras catch me at the wrong angle?

At every casting I attended, the other models' stares felt more intrusive than usual, as if they were drilling into my skull and eavesdropping on the never-ending loop of *what ifs* playing in my head.

All the while I pretended I was okay, as if nothing had changed. I had to take it one day at a time.

The iconic Linda Evangelista once said, "I don't get out of bed for less than ten thousand dollars a day." That's a dream for every model, and I was lucky enough to have some of those days. At some points the money was good enough that I *had* to get out of bed. Some checks were too large to leave on the table.

And then I reached another modeling milestone, one of the most coveted of all: booking a cosmetics campaign. Rimmel was launching a lip gloss with a mirror and a tiny flashlight hidden in the tube itself. It was brilliant, designed so you could fix your gloss in a dark nightclub without interrupting the flow of your evening. I was the exact target customer for the product, so I was thrilled to get the offer. Rimmel was a major brand.

The day I shot the commercial, my taxi pulled up to the address I had given the driver, and to my surprise, I realized we were filming inside Cain. This was the last place I would ever associate with my job given how many unscrupulous NSFW moments I'd had there. But I had to laugh at my personal and professional lives bleeding into each other yet again. Fortunately, we had the place to ourselves—and unless any of the background dancers were also Cain regulars, I wouldn't be recognized.

The plot of the commercial was simple: A hot girl—that's me!—is taking sips of her tequila and having one too many flirty chitchats with men, when she realizes she needs that crucial touch-up. Cue the lip gloss with its all-powerful flashlight. The beam hits my face, and the camera captures a perfect *Hey, look at me* moment in the middle of the dark, crowded dance floor.

After the hundredth take, I felt bad for the background dancers. All I had to do was stand in place and apply the gloss again and again until my pouting lips looked silky and luscious; meanwhile they had to dance exuberantly at every clack of the clapperboard.

When the commercial aired, it spread all over the web. Friends emailed me and shared pictures from the Rimmel commercial online. I had made it. This was what it had all been for—all the hiding, all the secrets. Right? It had been a little over two years since I landed at JFK, and not only had I become a model, I was in a major ad campaign. It should have felt exhilarating, like a payoff for all that sacrifice and subterfuge.

One day when I climbed into a yellow cab and took a seat, I saw my face on the TV screen embedded in the seat in front of me, the one that blares nonstop commercials. I had become one of the people on that unavoidable screen. The TV was oddly placed below my eyeline on the seat back; it was closer to my knees, which blocked the crucial shot of my illuminated lips. I was *everywhere* now, which had been my long-term goal. My face was all over New York City, but would *I* be over, too? Was this the end?

Every time my phone rang after that Rimmel commercial came out, it might as well have been an alarm going off in the middle of the night—a shrill sound that shakes you awake, leaving you wondering for a sweaty, panicked moment whether you're still trapped in a nightmare. Except that in my case, I was afraid I was waking up to the nightmare.

I dreaded my agent saying, *Hey, this* New York Post *story says you're a boy—is that true?*

I had replayed those hypothetical words in my head so many times, I could almost hear them out loud, clear as day, my agent's voice cresting downward, sinking from concern into defeat. I had imagined my blank stare as I sat up straight, dumbfounded, while he waited on the other end of the line for my response. He would hear only my breathing, silently begging him for acceptance. He would wait for me to say something, but I would be too busy worrying that

I might somehow have to pay back all the money I had made from swimsuit and lingerie ads. They would say I was a fraud. They would say I had fooled them—that I owed them their money back.

Even on the night Ericka and I were supposed to be celebrating my Rimmel commercial with champagne, I couldn't stop imagining my nightmares coming true.

The *what ifs* were obscuring the here and now to the point that reality itself didn't feel real anymore. Ericka's small studio, once so comfortable and warm, was closing in on me, pushing me down into a black hole, deeper into the inevitable. I wanted to get it over with already.

I had achieved something big. Something monumental. But that only meant I had more to lose.

I was supposed to be refilling our champagne flutes—but lost in my loopy paranoia, I realized with a jolt that I was gripping mine as tight as a cliff's edge. Two seconds longer, and I would have snapped the stem between my fingers, spilling sweet, sticky wine all over Ericka's hardwood floor.

This was supposed to be my moment of victory. I had done it. I had moved to New York with nothing but a dream, and now I was on billboards, in magazines, and on TV.

But instead I felt empty. Defeated. I had thought I could make my double life work by fleeing to New Jersey. But if I kept going like this, I wasn't sure either of my lives would be worth living anymore.

17

JANI

BEING STEALTH HAD EXACTED A TERRIBLE MENTAL COST. GONE was the thrill of being *wa buking* on the streets of San Francisco. I was a shell of my old self. And then, for the first time, I fell in love.

I met Lorenzo at Cain. He was the CEO of a luxury car company, and he looked the part: Picture Jude Law, but taller and with darker hair. We loved to play clay court tennis together and sneak into late-night showings of foreign films. He took me to Fifth Avenue private clubs and treated me to luxurious weekends away. Before long, we were sickly sweet on each other, calling each other by pet names—he was Mimo and I was Jani—and cuddling late into the night. Only six months after our first date, we were serious enough that he invited me to visit his family in Italy.

By that point, in August 2007, modeling jobs were starting to dry up as corporate marketing budgets thinned out. I would later realize this trend was a precursor to the global financial crisis—the canary in the coal mine—but at the time, all I knew was that my work was becoming sporadic and I had a sexy Italian man eager to whisk me away to a seaside village for the rest of the summer.

There was only one problem: I hadn't told Lorenzo. Whenever I was with him, I carried my transness like an invisible millstone around my neck. At first when we met, I didn't want to jeopardize our connection by saying something. And then before I knew it, I was in uncharted territory. I had never been with someone for so long without telling them, and my feelings had grown too deep for me to want to risk the entire relationship. All those beautiful months we shared would be tainted if he stopped seeing me as the woman that I was. Society already considered me to be less than, attaching an asterisk—or worse—to my womanhood. I would be crushed if Lorenzo reacted in a way that would only intensify the shame I was struggling to keep at bay.

That's why, on the car ride from the airport to his family home, I almost had a panic attack—because of course I said yes to his offer of an Italian getaway. At first, as we drove through endless rows of sun-drenched vineyards and fields of windblown rosemary, I held his hand, ready for a relaxing summer ahead. Then I thought about getting to know Lorenzo's family before he fully knew me. I was hurtling myself headlong into an uncertain future, unable to stop or change course.

We drove uphill to the medieval town, and through the passenger window, I could see the tumbling white-capped waves of the vast Adriatic Sea, beautiful but almost threatening in their insistent movement—a reminder that all secrets inevitably come to shore.

We slowly passed through the gate of a fifteenth-century fortress, the cobblestone streets growing narrower as we pulled into the town. I tried to relax. We were going to be here for a whole month, so I needed to breathe easy and let my hair down like Diane Lane in *Under the Tuscan Sun*. I needed to eat, pray, love, but mostly pray that this month would go well.

Lorenzo's family home, with its high ceilings and medieval hallways, helped me calm down. The sheer weight of its familial history was grounding. The smell of *parmigiano* cheese greeted us as we walked into the foyer. A family emblem hung over the staircase.

Lorenzo set down our bags, calling out, "Mima!"

Mima appeared—an Italian mama in her seventies with silver hair down to her shoulders, wearing a knee-length cotton summer dress with a white apron draped over it. She rushed toward us with a hug, wrapping us both in her arms.

"*Come estai? Mi chiamo Mima,*" she said. I really was living in a movie now.

Lorenzo translated, and I decided to try out some of the phrases I had picked up from my freshly bought copy of *Italian for Dummies*.

"*Mi chiamo Geena en Jani,*" I replied, using my name and the Italian nickname that Lorenzo had given me. As the words awkwardly stumbled out of my mouth, I realized it had been a mistake to trust that all the Spanish in Tagalog would give me a leg up on my Italian.

Mima looked me up and down, openly surveying and judging me with all the boldness of her years. Who was this woman that her son had brought home?

But instead of delivering her verdict right then and there, she pulled us into the kitchen. The tangy scent of cheese mingled with the salty brine of an ocean breeze pouring in from the balcony.

"*Mangiare?*" she asked us, and the invitation couldn't have come soon enough. We were both starving after our long flight.

Mima put together two simple servings of spaghetti with basil and fresh tomato sauce. Everything but the pasta was sourced from her patio garden overlooking the rolling vineyards.

"*Grazie,*" I said, nailing that simple word at least.

After lunch, we went upstairs to our bedrooms—plural. Our luggage had been placed in front of two separate doors. I looked at Lorenzo, confused. We were adults who had been dating for half a year by then. Were we really going to sleep apart for an entire month? But

I didn't have the energy to argue. Between the jet lag and all the spaghetti in my belly, I was ready for a nap.

When I woke up, I was a woman with a mission. I had to find some way to convince Mima to let me sleep in the same bedroom as Lorenzo. She was downstairs, and from the smell of it, she was cooking again. I will admit she was intimidating. She carried herself like the queen of the house—and she was. But I hadn't spent years undercover for nothing. I was determined to complete my mission. Maybe I could speak to her in a language she would understand.

I went straight down to the kitchen, where Lorenzo and his mom were catching up. I was ready to execute my plan, but first I wanted to remind myself why I was doing this.

I stepped out onto the balcony with Lorenzo, smelling the fresh, spicy aroma from the garden below, looking out past the drying white bedsheets billowing in the breeze at the countryside in the distance. It was like a scene from a postcard—but it wouldn't be picture perfect if I couldn't be in bed with my boyfriend.

When we went back inside, I asked Mima in my broken Italian, *"Io posso cucinare per cena?"*

Lorenzo translated, explaining that I wanted to cook dinner tonight.

Mima tersely replied, *"Certo,"* almost daring me to cook something worthy of her kitchen. But I was up for the challenge.

I got to work on chicken *afritada,* a simple tomato-based stew with potato, bell pepper, and bay leaf. I intentionally chose a Filipino dish that represented my heritage but used familiar Italian ingredients. Lorenzo gathered the ingredients as I prepared the chicken. When I was finished working my own magic in the kitchen, we all sat down for dinner, Lorenzo's older sister and her daughter, both of whom lived on the property, joining us around the table.

Mima looked down at her bowl suspiciously. But then a half smile curved around her lips as she took in the rich aroma. I knew then that my chicken *afritada* was a hit. Soon the wine was flowing, people were going back for seconds, and my attempts to translate Tagalog into Italian had everybody laughing along with me.

"*En casa e molto paradiso, mi piace,*" I said, trying to say that their home was my paradise, and the message came through clearly even if the words were muddled.

Lorenzo's sister, who spoke English, asked me about my modeling experience since her daughter was curious to try it, too. But then Lorenzo must have said in Italian that he was opposed to his niece getting into modeling, because after he spoke, everyone started arguing with one another, their passionate expressive hand gestures fighting for space in the middle of the table as their *r*'s rolled indignantly off their tongues. I tensed up. It seemed like the conversation would go to blows at any moment.

Lorenzo just looked at me, noticed my wide eyes, and laughed. "Jani, you see, we're being Italian."

And then finally, Mima cleared her throat, ready to deliver her verdict—ostensibly on the food, but as she locked eyes with me, I knew she was really presenting her assessment of me.

"*Che buono, Jani!*" she said.

I breathed out, then replied, smiling, "*Un piacere.*"

Of course, it was my pleasure to cook for his mom—but she and I both knew what my offer to make dinner was all about. I had proved myself to her with tomatoes and herbs.

That night I slept in Lorenzo's bedroom.

The following day Lorenzo's older brother invited us to have sunset drinks in his garden. On the way there, as we navigated the maze of marble passageways, Lorenzo pulled me aside for an *appassionata* makeout session at the bell tower that was connected to their house.

Ducking and running through the halls, we finally arrived at the small medieval bridge that connected the main house to his brother's. From the middle of the span, we had a perfect view of the vineyards. Both of us were visibly tousled from our sexy time in the bell tower—his pants were wrinkled, and my flowing floral dress was stuck in my underwear—so we tidied up and strolled into the garden, bearing a bottle of white wine.

Lorenzo's brother, a tall tanned handsome man in his forties, greeted us with arms open wide. *"Lorenzo, che bellissima la donna!"*

These charming Italians were always flattering me by declaring how beautiful I was the second they saw me—and it worked. I smiled broadly, as the two brothers picked up their childlike teasing right where it left off, tussling with each other and trapping each other in headlocks.

When they finally let up, I told Lorenzo's brother how excited I was to spend the summer in Italy.

"Be careful what you wish for," he joked, giving his brother another nudge in the ribs, and his humor felt so familiar. We were a long way from the Philippines, but he welcomed me with the same warmth and openness that we used to welcome strangers with into our own tiny space.

Maybe this could be my home, I thought, as I nibbled on the prosciutto di San Daniele that had been laid out on the table. Maybe Lorenzo could be home. Everything here flowed as easily as the wine.

For the next two weeks, we followed the rhythm of *la dolce vita*. We would wake up around nine for a breakfast of sliced grapefruit, yogurt with granola and honey, and fresh ciabatta with Nutella and jam. We'd sip espresso under the morning sun until we were ready to take the ten-minute drive downhill to the beach.

Around noon we'd get a phone call from Mima for *colazione*, usually a serving of arugula salad or tomato penne, after which we'd take an afternoon nap. Then it was back to the beach until dinner, which usually stretched languorously into the night, often as late as eleven o'clock.

But one night, instead of preparing for the family dinner, Lorenzo whispered to me, "I'm taking you somewhere tonight, Jani."

Later that night, dressed to the nines, he drove me through back-country roads, winding through the hills, until we reached a nearby town that was holding its annual opera festival. He was wearing a relaxed, light wool summer suit, looking as dapper as Jude Law in *The Talented Mr. Ripley*. I had on a high-waisted white cotton *palazzo* and a fitted black top. We were so chic and so in love.

As we approached the fifteenth-century open-air theater, I squeezed Lorenzo's hand tight, trying to etch this romantic moment into my memory forever. At the same time, I was looking into his eyes, searching for the acceptance I hoped would be there if my secret were to come out. I didn't want to lose this man.

As we entered, the orchestra swelled, the music echoing and bouncing between the neoclassical columns. We were sitting right up front, a crowd of almost four thousand packed in around us. That night we were treated to a performance of *La Traviata*, or *The Fallen Woman*—a tragic love story about a Parisian courtesan named Violetta who tries to leave her old life behind to find true love. Like me, she takes a chance on something new. Like me, she is trying to bury her past.

As the strings ascended into tremulous waves of high-pitched tension, the full gravity of the story played out in front of us. I didn't need to speak Italian to experience the emotion. My chest expanded. Blurry tears formed curtains around my vision. The looping violins and the cascading vibrato of the arias weren't coming from the stage anymore—they were coming from inside me.

So many chance encounters—from my first meeting with Tigerlily to the night I met Lorenzo at Cain—had led me to this beautiful moment. But now that I was here, I was drowning in a real-life operatic predicament, torn between my desperation for the love that Lorenzo and I had and my desire for a romance where I could truly be all of me. Life imitates art, they say, and here I was, a Violetta confronting the possibility of a tragic ending.

I looked over at Lorenzo. He might not have known what exactly was in my heart, but he could tell that it was full.

"*Amore mio,*" he said, his eyes flicking intimately between my eyes and my lips.

"*Amore mio,*" I replied, trying to hold back tears.

I meant it. He was my love. But the truth was, shame was creeping up within me, a dark shadow that only I could see.

One Sunday, Lorenzo and I attended mass at a church on top of a hill in a nearby town where some devout Catholics believed the Virgin Mary had once lived.

As the service got under way, I noticed a handful of Filipinos were in the congregation around me. Warmth traveled up my back as I started to sweat, and my forehead started to drip. I knew that it would take only one dedicated stare for them to notice. Then it happened. One Filipina lady whispered to another Filipina. The woman who had received the whisper turned and faced me, pretending to acknowledge a fellow Pinay, but I knew the real reason was to get a closer look at me. I had one minute, tops, before they would start murmuring *bakla* to one another, congratulating one another on clocking me.

Before it was too late, I turned to Lorenzo. "I'm not feeling well," I told him. "Can we get some air?"

He took me outside to safety, not knowing that I had just narrowly escaped being outed in a church. My heart was pounding after that close call, but I strolled casually alongside him, pretending I was feeling better.

Toward the end of our month together in Italy, we wanted to get away for a long weekend in Rome. For the first time, I could say

"When in Rome . . ." and mean it literally, enjoying life-altering plates of *cacio e pepe* and feasting our eyes on all the ancient culture and architecture. Every day our feet swelled up like water balloons as we made marathon walks to the Pantheon, the Trevi Fountain, the Forum, and the Vatican.

We spent our nights at a modern hotel, dripped in red decor designed by Philippe Starck, tucked away in a neighborhood far from all the tourist traps. It was there that Lorenzo took my Maserati out for *frequent* rides, if you know what I mean.

As the sun set on our last day in Rome, we walked to the Piazza del Campidoglio. After scaling the ornate staircase designed by Michelangelo, we turned around to look at the ancient city below us basking in the golden light, umbrella pines jutting out of the ruins around us, framing our view like a work of art.

Lorenzo leaned over and whispered in my ear, "Jani, turn back around."

I did, and he pointed out a stunning bronze statue of a Roman emperor on his horse.

"Remember that book I gave you?" he asked.

I nodded. *Meditations* by Marcus Aurelius—a classic work of philosophy that we had read together, and since spent hours discussing, before sex, after dinner, and during countless afternoon coffees. I found one of its teachings helpful whenever anxiety crept in: "To love only what happens, what was destined. No greater harmony."

Wrapped up in Lorenzo's arms, feeling a love as warm as the sun on our skin, we were the picture of harmony—but all I could feel was its absence.

When we returned to New York at the end of the summer, I was wracked with guilt. Lorenzo and I were deeply in love. I had gone on to form a special bond with Mima after I cooked that first dinner for her. I couldn't carry the burden any longer. I decided I needed to tell Lorenzo.

One morning after brushing my teeth at his place, I asked him, "Mimo, let's have dinner here tonight, okay?"

He agreed, not thinking anything of it, and left for work. The moment he shut the door behind him, I felt dizzy, sitting down on the toilet to search for my courage. I tried to focus on the feeling of my feet pressed firm against the floor. When I could trust my legs again, I got up and called Ericka.

"Flaka! I've decided to tell Lorenzo tonight," I told her.

I could tell from the half second of silence on the other end of the line how concerned she was about my decision. But then she offered her full support.

"Oh my god, do you want me to be there with you?" she asked. "I can wait around his neighborhood just in case anything happens."

"I'll be fine, Flaka, but I'll definitely keep you posted," I said. "I love you."

"Please do. I love you, G."

Only trans sisters know that kind of assurance because only they know how daunting it is to face danger simply for saying who you are. But not even Ericka could make me feel safe.

After I hung up, I started to panic. My breathing got shallow. My vision went blurry, then blacked out altogether, the bathroom disappearing. I told my muscles to move, but they didn't listen. I gave in and crumpled to the floor, where I lost consciousness. I woke up curled up in a ball on the cold marble tile, with no idea how many minutes had gone by since I passed out. I wanted to scream.

The agony of speaking my shame into existence would be excruciating. As long as I was silent, it was like it wasn't real, but after I told Lorenzo, he would never see me the same way again. Those words couldn't be unsaid. Would this man, who had welcomed me into his home and his family, still accept me? I felt like a hurricane was crawl-

ing toward me from across an ocean, and I was unable to flee. Lorenzo was so beautiful and so tender. If anyone would take me as I
was, it would be him, I thought. But I had been hurt before.

I stayed there on the bathroom floor, letting my panic attack work
itself through my body until it reached its own conclusion. As my
breath settled back into a regular rhythm, a sense of clarity rose inside me. No more hiding. In that moment, I felt a sudden stillness.
Peace. I never wanted to hide again, no matter what. I was ready to
receive Lorenzo's reaction. I would do what Aurelius advised and
love only what happened.

After work, Lorenzo walked into the apartment, right on time. I
took a cold Pellegrino out of the fridge, and we sat down at the dinner table. While he was commuting home, I had prepared his favorite
penne with tuna, olives, and capers—the first dish he had ever cooked
for me. I tried to stay away from mundane topics like "How was your
day?" and instead let my mind wander to the beautiful vacation we
had just enjoyed together, and what it had meant to both of us.

I needed those memories to carry me through what I had to do
next.

After dinner, we sat on the couch. He turned off all the lights, except for one lamp in the corner. My back was against the light, and he
sat facing me. I was worried that he wouldn't see my lips clearly
enough as I spoke, and that he might be confused if he misheard me.
But it was now or never.

"Mimo," I said. "I hope that you know that I love you. So much."

I took a breath, my voice shaking. I could feel my eyes well up
with tears already. I gulped and looked him straight in the eye.

"I want—" I said, then stopped to breathe. "I'm so—" I gulped and
started again. "I'm afraid and ashamed to tell you this, but I want you
to know that I'm trans."

Relief. Sadness. Freedom. As I let go of those words, my fear went
with them.

To my immense relief, Lorenzo hugged me, and we both started sobbing. "Jani," he said, "I'm so sorry that you had to hide this from me. I can only imagine your suffering all this time."

He went to the kitchen and took out a bottle of Grey Goose vodka from the freezer. We each took a generous shot. Gently, he asked about my childhood. Did I have support growing up? How did Papa treat me? He was curious but not disapproving. He had a lot to learn.

That night in bed, right before we were about to close our eyes, he sprang from the covers and disappeared into the living room. When he came back, he was holding a red leather-bound notebook in his hands: his diary.

"Look, Jani," he said. "I want to show you something."

He sat on the end of the bed and flipped to the words he had written on the night of our first date. I read them aloud: "There's really something special about this girl." I cried. He had known there was something different about me from the moment we met. He hadn't been able to put a finger on it at the time, but he told me, "Now everything makes sense."

We stayed together for another month—the first whole month I had spent with a man who knew my truth. That feeling of freedom, anchored by total honesty, was unparalleled. But when Lorenzo got a new career opportunity in Milan, he wanted to pursue it, and I didn't want to move. As much as I loved him, and as much as I worried that I would never find someone who accepted me as he did, I couldn't uproot my life and move across the world. Not again. Not so soon.

I was devastated letting Lorenzo go, but I promised myself that I wouldn't let our love end in vain—that when I fell in love again someday, I would not put myself through that shame again.

18
BUSINESSWOMAN

I SURE PICKED A HELL OF A TIME TO WORK ON MYSELF.

In January 2008 the Federal Reserve tried to save the housing market to keep the economy from collapsing, real estate prices went into free fall anyway, and then millions of jobs vanished practically overnight, including most of my modeling work. The fashion clients I still had took way longer to send out checks.

Since breaking up with Lorenzo, I had spent much of my time reading self-help books by authors like Napoleon Hill and Don Miguel Ruiz, ready to launch myself into the quintessential New York–independent–woman chapter of my life. And then, right on cue, there wasn't anywhere I could make money. I had all this new-found self-confidence and no place to put it.

Mama, as always, thought the answer was obvious.

"You should come home," she told me over the phone when I confided in her about my financial struggles. "It's never too late to start nursing school."

It should tell you something about how desperate I was that I considered it. For years, I had scoffed at the idea of moving back to San Francisco, but the safety and security of going back home was undeniably tempting. I came this close to packing my bags and flying back to California.

But then I remembered another piece of advice Mama had given me long ago, during her own working years in the Philippines. Back when she was going door to door, restaurant to restaurant, selling Kikkoman soy sauce in bulk while I waited for her in an idling taxi, Mama was dealt rejection after rejection. Still, she never gave up.

"No right now means possibly yes tomorrow," she'd always say when she got back in the cab. She was sure the little sample bottles of Kikkoman she left behind would make the owners change their minds. I first learned tenacity in the back of those taxis.

So instead of moving home, I did what so many Americans did in 2008: I pivoted. I had always been curious about technology and business, so I applied to positions at every single business magazine you can think of: *CNN Money, Fortune, The Economist*. None of them responded.

Finally, there was only one magazine left that I hadn't yet tried— and clearly, I needed to change up my tactics if I had any hope of working there. I needed some way to bypass the HR department; it wasn't exactly a mystery why I wasn't getting called back, as the only lines on my résumé were modeling and cosmetic retail sales. That's where the tenacity came in handy.

With the gumption of Elle Woods in *Legally Blonde,* I decided to apply for a job at *Inc.* magazine in person. This was how I used to do business in the modeling world, after all: I'd show up for casting calls in person before anyone rejected me. Maybe the media world needed a good old-fashioned go-see.

Through online research, I determined that Megan Burns, the business manager at *Inc.,* would be the best person for me to approach. I just needed to figure out how to get through security at 7 World Trade Center, onto the *Inc.* floor, and then into Megan's office, all without making an appointment.

On the morning of February 6, 2008, I approached lobby security in a halter-fitted black knee-length Calvin Klein dress, carrying a small brown Marc Jacobs bag and walking with an attitude like I owned the building. I held my chest up high, and my soft wavy hair fell perfectly onto my shoulders. I was serving Angelina Jolie in *Salt:* cool, confident, and in complete command of my cover story.

"Good afternoon, sir," I said, greeting security as I reached the front desk. "I'm here to see Megan Burns of Mansueto Ventures."

I figured talking fast and using the name of the parent company would make me seem even more legitimate.

"Do you have an appoint—" the guard asked.

"I don't, but we're business associates," I interjected before he could finish, sliding my ID onto the counter, hoping he'd give me a pass anyway.

Sensing his hesitation, I added some power-flirting to the equation, too. I looked at him with a calculated you-know-you-want-me stare and said, "Really appreciate it," as if he had already said yes. Hypnotized, he printed the pass and pointed me to the elevators. But when the doors slid open on the twenty-ninth floor, I had another desk to get past: *Inc.* reception.

A white guy with a slight beard and a reserved demeanor looked up at me from the front desk, introducing himself as Mark.

"Hi, I'm here to see Megan Burns," I said casually, as if I knew her.

"Do you have an appointment?"

"Uh, I don't—"

Before I could make an excuse, Mark stood up and said, "How did you even walk in here with no appointment? I'm sorry, but you have to leave."

I turned around to push open the glass door that led back to the elevators, defeated, but I paused, midstep, as I caught my reflection. I knew exactly how I'd walked in there with no appointment: because of my Horse Barbie spirit. I turned back toward Mark, flipping my long mane of hair, and decided I had one last tactic in my arsenal: begging.

"Listen, Mark," I said, making my voice sound as pitiable as possible, "it's really cold outside, and to be honest with you, I really need a job. My rent money is running out. I just need a few minutes with Ms. Burns." I held his gaze.

He looked back at me. Finally, he inhaled deeply, visibly annoyed but also worn down. "You know what? Okay. Fill out this form and wait over there by the window."

After I finished the paperwork, a bespectacled man in his fifties walked over to me, his voice soft but firm as he spoke. "Hi, I'm Dave Murphy," he said, reaching out to shake my hand. "I heard you're ballsy. Come into my office."

At first Dave seemed mostly curious about how I had wormed my way up to the twenty-ninth floor. But as we sat in his office, he asked about me and my story. He wanted to know how my parents had raised a child like me.

"We're an entrepreneurial magazine, and what you just did is what this magazine is about," he said, which made it sound like my odds were improving.

As he got up from his desk, he continued, "In my many years of working here, no one has ever walked in asking for a job without an appointment."

Finally, he walked to the door, looked over his shoulder at me, and added, "Give me a few minutes. I'll be right back."

A dark-haired woman with piercing green eyes appeared at the door a few moments later. "Hi, I'm Megan Burns."

I was speechless. Truth be told, for all my confidence, I hadn't really expected my plan to work. This was Megan Burns—not just a

Google result but a real-life person with the power to give me the job I needed. She asked me to deliver a presentation two days later to be considered for an online marketing position—which I did, and which I nailed, because I had to or else I would have ended up in nursing school.

The first words out of Megan's mouth when she called me afterward were "When can you start?"

"Tomorrow?" I asked.

"See you then."

Just so we're clear: I walked into 7 World Trade on a Wednesday with no appointment, gave a presentation on Friday, and when I walked back into the office on Tuesday morning, it was because I had a job.

It seemed like such an impossible trajectory that Mark, the receptionist who had begrudgingly let me into *Inc.* the previous week, stopped me at the door and said, "I'm sorry, but I could only give you one chance. I can't let you in again."

Oh, how I relished telling him I was actually there for my first day of work.

I liked my new job. At *Inc.*, I didn't need to be in front of the camera. I didn't need to be visible. It was nice to be anonymous, to blend in and lose myself in a routinized corporate culture. I could just type away at my desk instead of spending every waking minute paranoid about being found out. Compared to the threat of being outed, spending all day in a cubicle was downright thrilling. I even felt comfortable moving back to Manhattan, into an Upper East Side apartment.

I was in business now, and I took full advantage of the resources my new job offered me. I read all the industry magazines after my co-workers were finished with their copies. I took home books from the office library, like *Purple Cow* and *Never Eat Alone,* absorbing career advice like a thirsty sponge.

I wasn't at *Inc.* long before Bear Stearns collapsed, triggering industrywide layoffs, myself among them. But thanks to the now-relevant job experience on my résumé, I found another job, at a biodegradable trash bag company, and soon I was back in the nine-to-five office girl rhythm, rushing to the office in Midtown East in the morning, losing myself in the buzzing of the lunchtime crowd, and rushing out the door with the rush-hour throngs at the end of the day. I basically lived in sheath dresses of every color.

This was so far away from the modeling future I had envisioned for myself, but I told myself that the business world was just a pit stop. The economy was still in shambles, but modeling would pick up again one day, and maybe then I could go back. Every day, sometimes in the same hour, I'd lurch between defeat and excitement, between feeling lost and feeling excited by the novelty of my new life.

At the biodegradable trash bag company, I immersed myself in all things "green," studying up on LEED certification, the official designation for buildings that had adopted or were built with environmentally friendly designs. The packaging for our bags was green, my business card was green, and hell, I was metaphorically green at commercial sales, but I leaned into it.

Sadly, the men I interacted with in the industry weren't quite as enthusiastic about my work ethic. At work conferences, so many guys found convenient excuses to try to sit down next to me. They'd ask who I was with, trying to find out if I was somebody's wife or girlfriend, but then I'd ask substantive work-related questions in return.

Even then, they'd usually end the conversation by saying something gross like "You look too hot to be at an investment conference."

It was experiences like those that motivated me to speak up more and use my voice for good. I hadn't clawed my way into this world just to be treated like an object. In the modeling world, everyone had been afraid to criticize our working conditions because the powers that be could capriciously tank our careers at any moment. I knew there was plenty of retaliation in the business world, too, but I had a secure job, a supportive boss, and some fire in my belly.

I wasn't going to let sexist assholes keep me from networking. I went to all the entrepreneur and venture tech meetups I could, staying in the thick of the hustlers and refusing to take any guff.

Once at a New York tech meetup group event that was being held at the World Stage, I found myself watching yet another all-male panel. During the Q&A afterward, I raised my hand for the microphone.

When it was passed to me, I gathered my courage and said, "Where are the female panelists? What a limited perspective we've heard here today."

The moderator stammered, ultimately offering a cop-out response: "We will do better."

There was murmuring in the room—*chismis,* my old friend, was swirling around me again. Everyone seemed surprised that I had asked the question, but I was just as surprised that no one else seemed to notice the absence of women on the panel.

I had been scared to try to lead a life outside the worlds of modeling and stage performance. They were all I knew—who would I be without them? But as a businesswoman, I learned that you could take me out of a wedding dress, put me in a blazer, and I'd still have the spunk I got from Mama.

19

NATURE GIRL

THE MOST EXCITING THING I HAD EXPECTED TO FIND IN THE Hamptons was organic produce.

It was Fourth of July weekend in 2009, and Ericka and I were headed to Sag Harbor with our girlfriends Ilka, Valencia, and Eva to share a rented four-bedroom house with a group. Except for Ericka, none of them knew I was trans, because even though modeling had been in my rearview mirror for a while, I hoped to go back—and besides, by then I had gotten used to living in the shadows. When you keep parts of yourself hidden away for long enough, it's so much easier to just leave them there.

I was hoping for a mindless weekend filled with polo games and pool parties. Maybe I'd meet a handsome stranger, but even hookups no longer seemed all that exciting. They were fun, don't get me wrong, but their novelty was wearing thin. In the year since Lorenzo and I broke up, I'd developed a stronger sense of myself, and the validation of being desired no longer scratched the same itch.

Basically, I just wanted to enjoy myself and eat some grilled corn.

After we arrived at the house, we had a barbecue lunch, and then

I headed out with Ilka and Eva. Because we couldn't all fit in one car, Ericka and Val volunteered to stay behind.

Before we left, I slipped on my favorite summer dress, which I had bought for three dollars when I was sixteen years old at an outdoor market by the Baclaran Church in the Philippines. I have been dressed in haute couture bridal gowns, and it is still the finest garment I've ever worn—a short, fire-red, body-hugging little number with a ruffle-edged hem, almost magically resistant to wear and tear. It still fits me as well as it did that Saturday afternoon.

Our friend Ari drove us out to Amagansett, and Ilka, who had visited the Hamptons a few times prior, suggested we go to Cyril's Fish House, an iconic seafood shack on Napeague Stretch, right by the ocean. On summer weekends, the place was packed with people having a drink or two or six on their way from the beach to dinner.

Ilka raved about the Bailey's Banana Colada, Cyril's famous blended drink. They called it the BBC for short—not to be confused with the British Broadcasting Corporation—and I got thirsty just thinking about it. I could almost taste the sweet, icy slush hitting the back of my throat.

A question from Bob Marley greeted us over the loudspeaker as we walked into the restaurant. "Could you be loved and be loved?" he crooned over the sound of guitar and clavinet—and it was something I had been asking myself a lot. I had spent so many years in a muck of shame, feeling sorry for myself, believing all the bad things society said about me. But finally I was starting to love myself—a feeling that was as powerful as it was brand new. For the first time in my life, I was focusing on my own happiness, not on the next big accomplishment, and trying to appreciate the fullness of who I was: a survivor, a daughter, a performer, a sister, a friend. I was almost ready to love me. But could *I* be loved?

It felt like an almost cosmic coincidence that I saw him right then. As my friends and I squeezed our bodies through the crowd toward the bar, I locked eyes with a man who looked like George Clooney wearing a fitted black-cotton shirt. His eyebrows were thick, prominent, and sexy as hell. He had a slight air of mystery about him, but there was also an undeniable warmth in his gaze and in his unguarded smile. The connection was instant and deep. Even then, I could sense he was interested not just in my looks but in all of me, body and soul.

The music seemed to fade into the background as I drank in his hazel eyes for a second longer, wondering which of us would look away first, but he just kept staring, his willful attention sending goosebumps skittering across my skin.

And then Ilka's hand pulled me forward through the crowd, toward the bar. As I stumbled forward, the music came roaring back to full volume. When I looked back, my Clooney was gone. Lightning had struck, fast and fleeting, and now that man would be nothing more than a memory.

Ilka and I brought a round of freshly made BBCs back from the bar to our friends. The four of us, caught up in the warm summertime ease, clinked our glasses and toasted "living the dream."

But we'd barely finished our first sip when Ilka cried, "Wait! We forgot the floaters!"

There were four extra shots of Bailey's back at the bar that we had forgotten to take with us. We couldn't leave good liquor behind. We all grabbed our drinks and squeezed our way back toward the bar, the crowd growing larger by the minute.

That's when I saw him again: my Clooney, making a beeline in my direction, moving with almost surgical precision through the crowd. I tried to sip my drink as seductively as possible, hoping to capture his attention. The thumping music went quiet again. He slowed down, not because his pace was slackening but because time itself seemed to stretch out to infinity. There was no mistaking it: He was trying to get to me.

Intrigue and familiarity were wrapped up in a single expression on his face. He was looking at me as if he wanted to get to know me, but also as if he had known me for years—as though he were an old friend who just wanted to catch up. I didn't know why I already felt so comfortable returning his gaze, but I did.

And then I realized: I wasn't thinking about modeling or trans-ness or my dwindling savings account. I was entirely in the moment. With him. Finally, he reached me, the masculine gravel of his voice starting the world back into motion.

"Hey, how are you?" he said. "I'm Norman. What's your name?"

"Hey," I purred—look, a girl's gotta have game—and then remem-bered I had to have a *name,* too. "I'm Geena. I'm here with my friends."

I turned to introduce Norman to Ilka, Eva, and Ari, but my focus stayed on him—this mystery man who had apparently made it his mission to find me again. After enthusiastic hellos, he invited us, al-most too eagerly, to join him at his table. He carried himself with focus and intention, like a panther poised to pounce, but not in a way that made me afraid. In fact, his whole being seemed to emanate warmth, offering silent reassurance that I would be safe with him. When he blinked, still awaiting our answer, he revealed black eye-lashes so thick I swear they fanned me—and I needed to be cooled down. I was getting hotter by the second just looking at him.

"Yes, we'd love to join you," I told him, and our eyes locked in a silent, and much more explicit, conversation.

I wanted him. He wanted me back.

I sat on the wooden railing, my legs tightly crossed. Norman and I weren't touching, but it felt as if we were, that palpable energy puls-ing like a frisson between our bodies. The hem of my short red dress kept sliding up from my lotioned, sweaty legs.

"Have you eaten?" Norman asked us once we'd all settled in, his voice as clear and deep as a tropical lagoon.

Even though we had just had lunch, I said, "I'm starved," and he ordered some calamari for the table. While we waited for the food, I talked about my travels—first about a trip I had taken to Sweden, then about the Philippines—and Norman wanted to hear more about my home.

I raised an eyebrow. "Sure. We have seven thousand islands. Which one do you want to hear more about?" I wanted to add a little edge to my flirtation, and judging by the surprised but pleased expression on Norman's face, I'd succeeded.

Every time Norman mentioned somewhere he had been, I pictured what it would be like to travel alongside him. I didn't care whether it was in a hotel suite or a backcountry tent, I just wanted to share a pillow. As he regaled us with stories about building a hut on a Moroccan beach and watching whales breach by the shore, I tried to focus, but I didn't really care about the whales. I was picturing us together in that hut.

After about an hour of flirting, calamari, and some strong BBCs, Ilka signaled it was time to head out for our next stop. I hesitated, remembering the time I found a hundred-dollar bill in a random pile of sand in the Philippines. How crazy it would have been to just leave it there! Still, my friends were my ride, so I told Norman he could find me later at Surf Lodge in Montauk, where we'd be dancing and watching the sunset.

I didn't have a glass slipper, but I left him with my cell number—and I saved his, too.

We beat the crowd to Surf Lodge, securing a prime spot at a fire pit near the dance floor to watch the sunset. No part of me wanted to play hard to get, so I texted Norman right away to ask if he was coming—but he didn't respond. Maybe he was back at Cyril's, talking to someone else by then. Maybe he had had his fill of flirting with me.

We all had a couple of drinks, and I was feeling good, dancing barefoot on the sand as it cooled. The sun dipped deeper toward the horizon, and a chill ocean breeze blew in from shore. If Norman didn't come—if all we had shared was that look and nothing more—I told myself it would be okay. That moment had been enough.

But then, sensing movement behind me, I whipped around.

Norman.

He was here.

"Hey," I said, my face close to his.

"Hey."

The deep boom of his voice was now a soft, breathy whisper, barely audible over the live music. No one had ever said "hey" to me in quite that way before—not like a greeting but like an absolute recognition of everything I was and could be. Even at twenty-six, I had lived so much life. I had been a pageant queen and a Macy's girl and a New York model, a Filipina and an American and an aspiring citizen of the world. Yet I also had so many possibilities still ahead of me that my future felt difficult to articulate. I often felt untranslatable, even to people in my inner circle, as if no one could possibly encompass all of me at once. Norman did it with a word.

We didn't have to say anything else. Touching became our new language. I held him tight as we danced, our bodies swaying with the rhythm. Our embrace felt urgent, as if we were meeting again after eons apart, distant planets finding each other after a long, strange orbit. I wanted the song to last forever.

But much too soon, the final note rang out. My friends encircled us, greeting Norman, and we fell back into the pitter-patter of conversation.

Norman, it turned out, was a Hamptonite. He told us about some of his favorite hidden spots and offered to show us around if we were staying for a while. I winked at Ilka. He was already showing off, trying to impress my friends. It was cute.

The fire was roaring by now, and the crowd gathered around it for warmth. But Norman and I kept dancing by the water, totally absorbed in each other.

Just as I was pointing out the rise of the nearly full moon against the dusk-blue sky, our wonderment was cut short by some bad news, courtesy of Ilka: Surf Lodge had a three-hour wait for a table, so if we wanted to eat dinner, we'd have to go to a nearby Italian restaurant. Why hadn't we thought to put our names in when we arrived? My friends gathered their things, but I didn't want any damn pasta. I wanted Norman—and I wasn't leaving him behind again.

I squeezed Norman's hand and smiled at him, my stomach turning over as if I were on a precipice—but my Horse Barbie spirit was telling me to leap off it. I told Ilka to pick me up after dinner, and then as my friends departed, I returned to Norman's side. I had made my choice and was comfortable with it—with *him*—but my heart was still beating hard and fast. Even though Norman made me feel safe on a soul level, that inner doubting voice was back in my head again, no longer a whisper but a shout: *Norman doesn't know!*

I couldn't forget all the times I'd been rejected for being trans— but I also couldn't forget the promise I'd made to myself after Lorenzo. If I fell in love again, I wanted to be loved as *me*. My whole self, with nothing to hide.

Norman and I went to the wooden dance floor by the fire pit. Our lips touched, slowly at first, as if he were asking for permission, and then finally he kissed me. Soon we weren't just dancing but enveloping each other, two bodies becoming one. Intertwined beneath the moonlight, our hips ground together as I wrapped my legs around his thigh, swaying to the beat. I wasn't wearing any underwear, and I think Norman realized it.

"Hey, hey, hey," he said, his voice breathy, a little shaky. He liked what I was doing but wanted to take it slow—something he clearly wouldn't be able to do if I kept grinding on him. I liked that. I liked the power it gave me. But I had mercy on him—if mercy looks like making out for another half hour.

Eventually we sat down, away from the dance floor. The ocean breeze sent my long black hair fluttering around my shoulders, dry-ing some of the sweat I had built up. Together we looked out at the glimmering silver shimmers of moonlight rippling across the water in front of us. Only a few yards away, hundreds of people were danc-ing and partying. But right then there was no one else on earth but us.

Our total absorption in each other was interrupted by a text from my friends. Dinner was over, and they were here to pick me up. We walked out front to meet Ilka, Eva, and Ari, who were waiting in the car with the windows rolled down. I leaned over on the passenger side where Ilka was sitting.

"Hey, love?" I said, blushing. "I think I'm going to go with him."

In a flash, Ilka was out the door, pulling me aside, her face hard with concern. "Are you sure, love?" she whispered under her breath. She might not have known the additional layer of potential danger for me that Ericka knew, but she was speaking the sacred language of sisterhood. "Geena, look me in the eye and tell me you're not on drugs."

I nodded and said, "I'm not," hoping Norman wouldn't overhear our conversation. "I can give you his cellphone number if you want."

"Text it to me now," Ilka insisted.

After her phone buzzed, she turned and strutted over to Norman, staring him down. "Take care of her, okay?" she instructed, speaking louder now.

It wasn't a request; it was a threat, but even then I could sense it was unnecessary.

There was something freeing about getting in Norman's car and feeling the night stretch out before us, as empty and full of possibility as the Montauk Highway at midnight. His black two-door 1992 Mercedes-Benz 560 SEC had soft, coffee-colored leather that almost perfectly matched my skin tone. It was handsome. Vintage. Just like him. I belonged in this car.

But I also needed something to eat.

"Is there a Burger King nearby?" I asked.

Norman's face lit up. "I can make us ham sandwiches at home?"

I grinned, gently bit my lower lip, and winked. We both knew what his invitation meant—and I loved the thrill it sent through my body. But something about the way he said those last two words—"at home"—also felt familiar, as if it were already my home, too.

Norman's house was beautifully lit, the entire floor plan open and airy with posters of vintage French wine and his own macro flower photography on the walls. He pulled deli-wrapped packets of ham and cheese out of the fridge, along with a jar of mayo, then toasted the bread.

Before we even finished our sandwiches, we were back to making out, mustard and ketchup smeared on our lips. We stumbled toward the bedroom, still kissing. Norman lit a candle, its dim yellow light projecting our silhouettes across the room. We fell together onto the bed, a whole drama of shadow and light playing out on the wall as we moved into and with each other. Our breath was like music beyond melody.

Gently, he shifted me to be on top of him. My movements were intuitive. With every thrust upward, I felt an explosion of power. With every grunt came a soaring release. I was in a state of perfect flow.

I couldn't see his hands, but I could feel his fingers as they moved across and up my body. He tucked my hair behind my ears, as if he were trying to find my face in the shadows. He wanted to see me in the light.

Afterward, brushing my teeth with my finger in his bathroom, I noticed a small black-nylon pouch with several small syringes lined up next to it. A flicker of doubt took hold in my heart. Clearly, he was taking some kind of drug, but I didn't want to ask him about it yet. The sex was too good.

Instead, I went back to bed, wrapped his arm around my waist, and went to sleep.

I woke up six hours later to the sound of chirping birds. I rolled over in bed and gazed past Norman, through the large sliding-glass door, to a backyard so green and lush it looked almost like a rainforest. The last drifting remains of morning fog mixed with the steam coming off the heated pool, casting the whole scene in a dreamlike glow, like a perfume commercial. I untied the white cotton robe I had worn to bed, walked out the door, and jumped into the pool naked.

Before long, Norman was standing above me, a big smile on his face.

"Good morning, beautiful," he said.

"I feel like I'm in paradise!" I spread both of my arms, basking in the brilliance of the morning sky.

Norman undressed and approached the edge of the pool. I couldn't believe this was real. I half-expected the man to walk on water, or at least for it to part around him like the Red Sea, but soon he was wading over to me. The water reflected the blue sky back at itself, shimmery and mirrorlike.

This was a true Bond girl–style morning after.

"Last night," Norman said with his boyish grin and deep voice, "you weren't wearing underwear."

That's the first thing he thought about the morning after? The guilt-tripping Catholic deep inside me should have wagged her finger, but this morning I felt no shame.

"Why are you still thinking about last night," I asked, matching the mischief in his tone, "when I'm naked here *now*?"

The flirting was fun. We fell back effortlessly into witty repartee. But this time I didn't have the benefit of tequila to blunt my insecurities. I worried about how I would make my feet look smaller when I got out of the pool. My feet—larger than usual—were not my favorite feature. I still believed in the traditional beauty standard that big, wide feet were manly, which was why I'd never tried modeling for any shoe ads.

But when we climbed out of the pool, Norman didn't seem to notice. Maybe the early-morning light bouncing off the water distracted him. Or maybe he saw and thought nothing of it. I breathed a sigh of relief either way.

When we got inside, Norman proved he could do more in the kitchen than spread mayo on bread. As I watched in awe, he toasted and buttered English muffins, then topped them with fresh Citarella Parmesan cheese and thin slices of jalapeño. Two eggs, fried over easy, went on top, melting the cheese below it. The finishing touch? A sprinkle of black pepper that perfectly matched his salt-and-pepper hair. All the while we chatted idly about cooking, our travels, and even the different types of trees in his backyard.

After breakfast, I didn't want to leave. Norman's place already felt like home. But I knew my friends were worrying about me. Like a true gentleman, he pulled the shiny black car around to the front of the house while I gathered my things, and I slipped back into the leather passenger seat.

As we came closer to Sag Harbor, chatting the whole time, I noticed a slight lag in Norman's response times. I watched with growing concern that sweat was dripping down his face, even with the windows down and the wind in our hair. Calmly but urgently, Norman pulled the car in front of the Golden Pear Café, parked it, and got out, telling me he needed to get something to eat. I waited in the car, wondering what was happening.

He reemerged with two cinnamon rolls, handing one to me. Were we having some morning dessert? I was confused and alarmed, my mind flashing back to the paraphernalia I'd seen in his bathroom the previous night, but after finishing his cinnamon roll, Norman acted like himself again.

"Sorry about that," he explained. "I have type 1 diabetes, and my sugar was low."

Relief and tenderness flooded my body as I realized he had been so engrossed in our conversation that he hadn't even had a chance to explain. He popped open the middle front seat compartment and pulled out a black pouch, which I recognized as the one I had seen on his bathroom counter with all the syringes the night before. He pulled out a small device that looked like a kitchen timer with a pointy nub on it, placed his index finger on the pricker, then pressed the blood on the meter.

"We're good," Norman said. "Eighty-five to 115 is a normal blood sugar range." As he suspected, the cinnamon roll had been enough to correct the dip.

"Did that hurt?" I asked.

"Not at all," he replied, winking at me.

As we sat in the car, my fingers greasy from tearing off pieces of cinnamon roll, I marveled at how forthright Norman was about his condition, thinking nothing of testing his blood sugar in front of me. Of course, he had no choice—this was a life-or-death decision for him. But wasn't my own "secret" life or death, too? What would it be like for me to share my transness as casually as Norman shared about his diabetes?

If I were going to keep seeing Norman, I couldn't hide who I was from him. He could see through me in a way that felt exhilarating, and he didn't put up any walls around himself either. Choosing him would mean choosing the same openness he shared with me—and that both thrilled and scared me. Was I ready? I hoped so. But I knew one thing I *wasn't* ready for: to say goodbye.

When I stepped out of the car in front of the house I was sharing with my friends, I turned back to look at him. "See you later," I said, and it felt like a sacred oath.

Back in the city later that week, I wrote to Norman on Google Talk all day. We spoke over the phone, too, but there was something deliciously clandestine about seeing his name pop up on my computer screen and hearing that dinging notification sound. It felt like he was sitting at my desk with me. There was nothing more exciting than seeing those three blinking dots in the chat box, knowing that he was about to send me more pieces of him—more facts from his life, more updates on his garden, more stories. Every ellipsis was a new chapter.

We were still feeling each other out, sketching portraits in the darkness.

Norman had gone to Berklee College of Music in Boston, then moved to New York to start his career. For a while he played guitar in a funk band called Ocean to Ocean. Then he did independent producing and ultimately was asked to join an independent record label. His company had made soundtracks for shows on HBO and for documentaries. I loved music—and I wanted to sing for him.

Maybe it's because we were only typing to each other, but in those chats, I felt free to be vulnerable. I was just being *me*—and weirdly, that's exactly what Norman seemed to want. Norman wanted me *for* me.

Still, I was selectively editing my life, careful not to share anything that might give me away. When he talked about camping, I told him stories about my time in *Girl* Scouts, not Boy Scouts.

Inevitably, our chats ended with Norman asking me when I could come visit. Luckily for him, the biodegradable trash bag company let me go, and the first thing I wanted to do with my newfound free time was visit him. Two weeks after we met, on a Friday afternoon, I took the Jitney bus out to the Hamptons.

Everything about that first weekend at Norman's was as heavenly as our first night together. His longtime friends from Texas came over, and they taught me how to make guacamole. We had our first "official" date renting kayaks at a deli with a Jackson Pollock hanging on the wall—*very* Hamptons. Norman, always full of facts, told me that before Pollock became famous, he used to trade his paintings for groceries there. I came up with my first nickname for him—"Nature Boy"—because of how much he loved being outside. He filmed me in his kitchen after I told him my dreams of hosting a cooking show. Together, we were playful. We improvised. And we laughed about everything.

I didn't leave after the weekend ended, and Norman didn't ask me to go. It felt natural for us to just stay together. A week passed. I kept expecting the other shoe to drop. Something was supposed to go wrong, wasn't it? But deep down, I knew that I was the one holding the other shoe. There was no way to get rid of my dread until I showed Norman all of me—not just me naked in his pool, but the entirety of my personhood.

I wanted to honor the honesty that had defined our connection from that very first night at Cyril's. The promise I had made to myself after Lorenzo.

So less than a month after we met, I decided it was time to share my transness with him. I was determined to think of it as "sharing" because, until then, my moments of disclosure had come from a place of shame. I had always started those past conversations by saying, "I need to tell you something," which implied that those men had a right to my history—that they were owed something, and it was my duty to offer it up.

I didn't want to *tell* Norman I was trans. I wanted to share it with him.

For the first time, I felt happy with myself and confident in my decision to come out to someone.

One afternoon we were lying together on the couch, our faces close together. I was wearing one of his red plaid shirts with no pants, and he was wearing the same shirt, but in blue. I looked him in the eye, as intently as I had at Cyril's.

"Hey, Norm? I wanna share something with you."

I had thought maybe that when I got to this point, I would still feel some residual fear. But now that the moment was here, I felt only freedom. The shame was gone. My usually shaky voice was calm and steady. He held me closer as I took a deep breath, and I felt assured, emboldened even, to keep going.

To be honest, Norman might have had some idea what I was about to say. He sometimes looked at me knowingly, in moments like when we brushed our teeth together. Once, with toothpaste lathered over his lips, he seemed to start to say something, then chose not to. Instead, he looked at me in the mirror with a quiet assurance that he knew me, that he saw me.

But I still needed to say it out loud.

"It's something about me, that made me who I am today, but I think you kind of already have a feeling what I'm about to tell you," I went on. "I'm trans."

He smiled at me, his expression blissful and serene. Men had said so many wrong words to me in moments like this. Curses. Insults. Ugly slurs. But when Norman opened his mouth, only the right words came out.

"Thank you for sharing," he said. "You're right, I did have an idea. This is my first time dating a trans woman, and I'm so grateful you trusted me enough to share this with me. I know how I feel about you, and that's what's important."

Relief flooded my heart. I sank my head into Norman's shoulder, holding him close, reassured by the steadiness of his heartbeat. He had seen me, all of me, and he wanted me, not despite who I was but because of who I was.

"Now," he asked me, "can we keep loving each other?"

We spent our first year together exploring new layers of intimacy and unlocking deeper levels of trust. I kept my apartment for a while, and we split our time between the city and the Hamptons, until it didn't make sense for me to pay rent anymore and I officially moved into Norman's place. Together, he and I made that house our own little world, Nature Boy and his girl carving out their own patch of earth. It was my first time fully experiencing the changing of the seasons in an intimate way, watching summer turn to fall, the foliage going from green to copper.

Norman was always showing me that I was more confident and capable than I allowed myself to believe. By sharing with him, I had peeled away that first layer of internalized shame, allowing authenticity and truth to flow out of me like water through a burst dam. I realized there was a vastness I could explore now that I had gotten to the other side of this obstacle—a realm of possibilities I had never anticipated being able to access. Norman opened my heart. He opened my life.

He told me later that July 4, 2009—the day he approached me at Cyril's—had been his first time out of the house in three months. He had been in a near-fatal car accident in which his Bronco truck was flattened and the airbags didn't go off. The Fourth had been the first day he felt like he could get out of bed, and he didn't want to just sit around at home. That Independence Day, he had gone out to celebrate his own freedom. I found mine with him.

To this day, my iPhone contact for him has the note "Met at Cyril's" after his name—a pin I've placed in the map of my memories. After all these years, that detail reminds me to cherish serendipity—to love the little unforeseen moments that seem to happen when you're least expecting them but you need them the most.

A three-dollar dress, a banana cocktail, and a little courage can change everything.

PART IV

THE WORLD

20

INDIANA JONES

FOR TWO YEARS, THE STEADINESS OF NORMAN'S LOVE ALLOWED me to reach further into myself. He was like a touch tree I could always return to as I made deeper and deeper forays into my own consciousness. He was a supportive partner and lover—and by far the coolest man I had ever met—but part of what made our life together so incredible was that he understood I was on a personal quest. He honored my insatiable curiosity and my desire to find my own path. I had resumed modeling in 2011, carefully and on my own terms, accepting some catalog bookings. But it was clear that being a model could never define all of me. I had so much more to explore.

So when our cardiologist friend, Miguel, invited me to go to Burning Man on only three days' notice, Norman encouraged me to take the opportunity. I thought I would have a fun new experience— and yes, I'm talking about LSD. What I didn't know is that it would play a pivotal role in my own journey toward self-acceptance.

Miguel took me from the Reno airport straight to the festival in a chartered single-engine plane. Below us, the late-morning light cast the desolate mountains in a golden hue. Only forty minutes later the plane decelerated and dipped slightly toward the earth, revealing a giant clock-shaped pattern laid out on the ground below us. It was a makeshift city, with a central hub and dirt roads shooting off in each direction, forming circular grids that came into sharper focus as we flew closer. It looked like we were landing on the set of *Mad Max*.

But instead of finding myself in a postapocalyptic nightmare, I was greeted by friendly campmates who immediately made me feel welcome, wrapping me in warm hugs. As I walked through the massive art installations that day, I felt the music in my bones, awakened my innate curiosity, my love of adventure and discovery. After dinner, I took my very first tab of LSD, letting it dissolve slowly on my tongue. I had no reference point for how it was going to feel, but if there was any place to try acid for the first time, it was Burning Man.

That night two of our campmates brought out their Candy Car, a tricked-out, peppermint-colored four-seat off-road vehicle that had been custom-made with red and white lights, a surround sound system, and a cushy bed in the back that could carry ten people. We piled in and rode to a party where we found ourselves surrounded by dozens of other colorful art cars. It felt like the beautiful, bizarre, high-octane future of my science fiction dreams. Forget *Mad Max;* I was full-on in *The Fifth Element* now.

We got out of our Candy Car and blended into the dancing throng all around us, throwing our hands into the air. As thousands of bodies moved together like one single throbbing organism, we kicked up a cloud of dust that filled the air around us like a smoke machine, adding to the night's surreal flow. I don't even know how long I danced, but I do know how it felt. It felt like joy. And that joy wasn't emanating from me, it was Joy itself with a capital J—the principle given physical shape, turned into sand that covered every inch of me, flooding my body with euphoria.

Time collapsed in on itself. Hours passed like seconds. The green

couches back at our camp—wait, when did we go back to camp?—
had grown arms and legs and were now furry mascots cheering just
for me.

As dawn approached, a few of my campmates and I got up and
rode our bikes back to the party, but we ended up watching the sunrise instead. My eyes welled with tears of gratitude for the day and for
the life I had lived so far. Joy, gratitude—these were still relatively
new feelings for me in an adulthood spent living under the shadow
of fear.

What was so exhausting about chasing my modeling dream was
that nothing was ever enough. There had always been another milestone to achieve, another high bar to leap over. I couldn't help being
ambitious, but when had I last stopped to feel pleasure? When would
I feel like I'd had enough?

Through my tears, I looked at the Temple of Transition, a wooden
structure that was meant to be a sacred space for rituals and offerings. The whole thing was massive: five wooden outer temples ar-
rayed in a circle around a central inner temple, all connected by
sixty-foot-long walkways. The central structure stood over one hundred feet tall, while the outer temples still managed to tower five stories overhead.

Yesterday, throngs of people had been pouring in and out of its
entrances, dust swirling around it like a desert fairy tale. But now that
it was slightly less crowded, the splendor of its presence was speaking
to me, beckoning me to make my own pilgrimage.

Rows of pictures, letters, flowers, and all types of offerings covered the interior walls. At first I was quiet, absorbing the somber
meditative energy surrounding me. The rhythmic harmonies of Hi-
malayan singing bowls and chimes infused the temple with an ethereal peace.

Then the thought of Papa suddenly entered my mind. Inside that
temple, all aspects of my transition were coming back to me, floating

calmly to the surface of my mind. I could see the pattern now: Because Papa had allowed me to be my femme boy self at home, I had been gifted an early glimpse of my own womanhood. He had shown me a future he didn't live to see.

Emotion rose inside me. I wanted to apologize to Papa for not remembering him as often as I could have. I wanted to thank him for not punishing my femininity as a child. A domineering man like him could have traumatized me, but instead he accepted me and never said one discouraging word about what I wore or how I carried myself. It took acid and a night of psychedelic dancing to realize it, but standing inside that temple, I finally made the connection between Papa and my life journey so far. He met my early femininity with a masculine love that set me free. He was the reason I was standing there.

Psychedelics can make you hear and see things that aren't real, but sometimes we need fiction to tell us the truth. And as I stood looking out over the railing, watching the dust swirl in the morning light, listening to the pulsating house music beats from afar, I heard Papa say to me, *"Your femme boyhood was enough. You are more than enough, my Bojojoy."*

And I cried as Papa used to cry in our bedroom at night, my tears watering the parched earth below.

A few nights later, at the Man Burn, as I felt the heat of the flaming effigy on my face, I made a promise to stop rushing to the next milepost before I had the energy to move forward. Taking psychedelics with a community like Burning Man, one committed to radical inclusion, made me realize there is a world out there ready to accept me for who I am.

I wasn't just where I was supposed to be; I was *who* I was supposed to be.

· · ·

Four months later, in January 2012, in the middle of a two-month-long trip across Southeast Asia, I learned that fires don't have to be huge to change your life.

Sometimes all it takes is a single match.

Norman and I were enjoying our last night on the remote island of Koh Lipe in Thailand, a tiny speck of land in the far southwest of the country, just offshore of the Malaysian border, caught in the currents between the Andaman Sea and the Strait of Malacca.

Though small, this island was rich with history. The sun dipped below the horizon, turning the water shades of purple, red, and orange. I felt deeply at peace in this place in ways I didn't quite understand, and I didn't want to leave.

But the next morning found us packed onto an old forty-foot wooden cargo boat headed back to the mainland. We needed to catch our plane to Bali, the final stop on our vacation.

The seats inside the boat smelled moldy, and Norman and I felt claustrophobic, so we decided to go sit upstairs with the locals on the open deck. The water views were so stunning we didn't mind squeezing between cages of live chickens and big crates of vegetables. We made ourselves comfortable, nestling amid the cargo.

"Excuse me, do you have a lighter?" I heard someone ask me.

I turned to find a bald man with inquisitive eyes, wearing a white shirt and denim shorts. He had come up on deck to smoke a cigarette. We had only matches, though, so he, Norman, and I had to huddle together to prevent the wind from blowing out the flame. With this simple ritual, we formed a momentary bond.

"I'm Lucio," he said, taking his first drag. From his accent, we could tell he was Italian.

"I'm Norman, and this is Geena."

Lucio looked at me pointedly and asked, "Where you from?"

"Um, we live in New York, but I was born in the Philippines," I said, wondering where this line of questioning was going.

His eyes lit up as if I were the missing piece to a puzzle he had spent his whole life waiting to solve. "You know you're cousins with the Chao Leh, right?"

He pointed back at the island and motioned to the dark-skinned locals on the deck with us. I still wasn't following.

"You're Austronesian!" he said, as if that explained everything.

"Austro what?" I asked.

It sounded like a mash-up of Australian and Polynesian, but I had never heard the term before. Luckily, my question was all the prompting Lucio needed to launch into the most informative lecture I had ever heard.

"The Chao Leh are an indigenous seafaring tribe on Koh Lipe," he told us, explaining that they belong to the same Austronesian language family as Filipinos. Around five thousand years ago, tribal groups from the Philippines sailed and followed the south wind, migrating to Indonesia. Then they developed long-distance sailing canoes and went east to Melanesia, the Polynesian islands, New Zealand, Rapa Nui, and Hawaii—and west from Indonesia all the way to Madagascar. "Your ancestors carried their language and culture with them across oceans," Lucio said. "If you went to Madagascar right now, you'd find an indigenous tribe there that looks like you and speaks a similar language."

My mind was blown. This was not the conversation I was expecting to have with a random guy who just needed a light. Norman and I exchanged awed glances.

"How do you know all this?" I asked Lucio.

"I'm an anthropologist specializing in Austronesian languages," he explained.

We talked for the next couple of hours as the cargo boat steadily churned toward the mainland, then had to say goodbye to Lucio just as quickly as we had met. In exchange for a match, he had given me knowledge that changed my perspective on my history forever.

Norman and I shared an interest in anthropology. But for me, find-ing out about the Austronesian language family was deeply personal. I felt like a real-life Indiana Jones ready to go searching for more artifacts from my past. For the last few years, I had been on a quest of continuing self-discovery: decolonizing my mind outside the confines of Catholi-cism, appreciating my dark brown skin, having a spiritual awakening at Burning Man. I had come a long way in embracing myself and my his-tory. But this felt like the missing link, the key to unlocking everything.

The information Lucio gave me about my ancestral lineage filled a space that had been intentionally left blank. While I was growing up in the Philippines, our school curricula were still taught from the perspective of our Catholic and American colonizers. As a result, I found out more about my origins from a stranger on a cargo ship than I ever did at school.

In Bali, my odyssey continued. We landed at the airport and took a taxi to the mountain town of Ubud, an arts and culture hub perched amid terraced rice paddies. When we stepped out of the car, the kids playing on the street spoke Balinese to me. I smiled. This usually hap-pened whenever I traveled in Southeast Asia—another testament to our common origins that had taken on new meaning after what Lucio had told me. Whenever someone in Thailand, Indonesia, or Malaysia tried to speak to me in the local language, I'd just politely say, "Me no Thai," "Me no Indonesian," or "Me no Malaysian." I still couldn't speak those languages, but now I knew our words were de-scended from the same roots.

Norman and I walked to our Airbnb on a trail that led us through the paddies and beneath a lush towering canopy of coconut, banyan, and bamboo trees. Greenery exploded from every available surface, nourished by the mineral-rich volcanic soil. If I had been taken to this place blindfolded, I could have easily mistaken it for the rice ter-races in the Philippine province of Ifugao. Even though this was our first time in Ubud, everything felt familiar.

Our rental was inside a traditional Balinese walled compound with four pavilions and a complex of family temples. As we entered, we were greeted by women in colorful lace *kebayas* and printed sarongs. They were hanging out in the center pavilion, some of them making flower offerings, others lighting incense. The scene reminded me of our *barangays* in the Philippines, indigenous communities where central gathering spaces serve as a hub for daily activities and organizing.

Our small house was near the back of the compound, facing the rice paddies with a majestic view of the 5,600-foot active volcano Mount Batur in the distance. The living room and bedroom were made of intricately hand-carved teak, the lacquered brown sheen of the wood giving the space a comforting warmth. This was where we would stay for the next three weeks—our last before we'd have to go back to our New York routines.

One morning while Norman was at the gym, I was sitting outside a neighborhood coffee shop when a short-haired petite Balinese woman in her forties walked past me. Trailing behind her were whiffs of a soft, gardenia-like scent with hints of cream and pineapple, the air seasoned with herbs and flowers. Mesmerized by her perfume, I followed her inside the café.

She spoke to me in Balinese. When I said, "Me no Bali," she let out a big, loud, welcoming laugh.

"Me Indah," she said by way of introduction.

"Me Geena."

We were like sisters who had been separated at birth—members of one Austronesian family that had been divided by colonization. Merely finding a way to talk to each other felt like we were writing new history in our own small but significant way.

We settled on English as the best way to communicate, combined with a fair amount of pointing and gesturing. Indah was at the café dropping off soaps, oils, and shampoos she was selling. That's why she smelled so good. In fact, she was making some products in her kitchen right now, she told me.

"Come, come," she said, gesturing for me to leave the café with her and head down the road.

A couple of doors down from the café, Indah led me along a walking path that ended in her lush garden. The yellow and white flowers of frangipani trees glowed like garden lights overhead. Clumps of yellow ylang-ylang flowers were draped around the sides like an octopus escaping its aquarium tank. Amid it all, bright red hibiscus flowers shined like stunning rubies, providing pops of color against the subtler hues.

"Come, come," Indah said, inviting me inside to the kitchen, and again I followed.

She was already dipping a spatula into a pot on her stove that was simmering with a fragrant red substance. In her free hand was a red bar of soap. Indah pointed at the pot, then at the bar, trying to tell me that they were the same thing. Indah then lifted the reddened spatula out of the pot and gestured for me to try it—like, *literally* try it.

"Soap organic," she said. "Eat it."

I had never eaten soap before, and I had met Indah only minutes beforehand, but I trusted her implicitly. I took the spatula and licked some of the liquid. It tasted like hibiscus with a hint of tart. Soap had never tasted so soothing.

Indah was watching my reaction, and when she saw my smile, she said, "We have Ogoh-Ogoh Festival this afternoon. Come?"

I had heard about the yearly festival in Ubud, which happens just before their Balinese New Year, Nyepi. In *Lonely Planet* guidebooks, I had looked at the towering papier-mâché statues of demonic cannibals, vampires, and witches rooted in Balinese and Hindu mythology, all of them rendered in vivid colors. The noisy processions were meant to ward off evil spirits, and men would bang gongs to scare them away.

I had wanted to see the festival but would never have dreamed of participating in it. It felt like a local custom that belonged to Indah, not to me. But this stranger-turned-friend was insistent that I accompany her.

I ended up walking in the middle of a street procession, next to a twelve-foot-tall papier-mâché Hindu demon with a blue, green, and red train held up like peacock feathers by rows of bamboo. The children around me wore elaborate gold and silk clothes with floral headdresses, the women in white long-sleeve lace and printed sarongs. The men, wearing black-and-white-check sarongs over their shirts, were banging those gongs as hard as they could. I didn't recognize every custom, but I didn't feel like a tourist, either. All of it felt culturally and spiritually familiar to me.

The Philippines' precolonial animist culture had practiced similar festivals that three hundred years of Spanish colonization had co-opted into honoring Catholic saints and patrons instead. As I walked and waved to the crowd, I thought of our Ati-Atihan festival, the pagan animist festival honoring our indigenous Aetas. Our Pahiyas and Kadaywan festivals were our way of giving thanks for a bountiful harvest and asking for the blessing of abundance. Even the gongs echoing through the streets around me looked and sounded like the ones we used in the Philippines.

The next morning Norman and I took a five-minute scooter ride to the Ubud market. Flowers were laid out in round rattan baskets, overflowing circles of purple, orange, red, pink, green, and blue petals waiting to be sold as temple offerings to the early risers. As we walked through the rows of stalls, I glanced at a display of colorful sunglasses, then did a double-take. What I saw was simultaneously the most bizarre and the most expected thing in the world: the word *mata* next to a pair of glasses that was listed for 30,000 rupees, about three dollars.

In Tagalog, *mata* meant "eyes." It was the same word.

I grabbed Norman's shirt and pointed, "Look, love! Look at the sunglasses!"

"What is it?" he asked.

At first, Norman didn't get why I was so transfixed by a pair of shades, but I couldn't explain just yet. I was still mesmerized. I walked closer to the sunglasses and stared at the word *mata*. Here—in the middle of a crowded local market, on a mountaintop on the lush island of Bali, one of more than fifteen thousand in Indonesia, an archipelago bridging the gap between the vast Pacific and the Indian Ocean—I should have felt totally lost, a lone traveler awash in newness. But everywhere I looked, I was seeing comforting reminders of home. Before I met Lucio, I had never heard the word *Austronesian*, and now my inherited Austronesian lineage was hitting me like a wrecking ball everywhere I turned. It all made sense. My words, my language, was *everywhere*. I was part of something almost incomprehensibly vast.

"This is so crazy!" I whispered to myself, still staring at the sunglasses. All the lenses were reflecting my face back at me, but the spiritual reflection happening inside me felt just as kaleidoscopic.

I thought about what Lucio had told me about my lineage, mentally transporting myself back to a precolonial world where my seafaring ancestors had carried the word *mata* from the Philippines to Madagascar to Hawaii, keeping the same meaning with every shore they reached. This felt like the next clue on my treasure map.

But as we continued through the market, other clues sparkled around us in the gentle morning light. The written Indonesian names for the fruits we were purchasing were, more often than not, the same as they were in Tagalog.

The milky white fleshy pods of mangosteen went by the same name. So did rambutan, the small red round fruit with soft spines and lychee-like insides. Durian was the same, and nangka, and langka, too. I couldn't believe it. To understand the Philippines—to truly know myself—I had to go halfway around the world and back again.

After leaving my motherland, I had worked hard to create a sense of home in San Francisco and New York, but I'd never expected to find it in a remote Indonesian market. Every shared word felt like a whisper from my ancestors: *You belong here, Geena.* My identity felt more expansive and more rooted than it ever had before. Yet I couldn't ignore the small pang in my heart that asked, *How much longer can I go on hiding who I am?*

When I got back to New York, I was a changed woman. Eager to build on the knowledge Lucio had given me, I spent hours furiously googling Austronesian language families, my keyboard an instrument to acquire even more self-knowledge.

Sitting in the kitchen of our home in the Hamptons, I was transported back to the Ubud market, the fruits and sunglasses calling to me in my own language. I discovered that there were more than twelve hundred Austronesian language families, each with its own diverse vocabulary, but the numbers one through ten are almost exactly the same, especially the numbers five, *lima,* and eight, *walu.* The word *pulo,* meaning "island," is spread across most of them. So are *tao,* meaning "people"; *ama,* meaning "father"; and *ina,* meaning "mother."

But of all the words I discovered, the most powerful revelation was the ubiquitous Tagalog gender-neutral pronoun *siya.* We don't have "he" or "she" in our language. Instead, the pronouns in almost all the Austronesian language families, spoken by close to 400 million people—the fifth-largest language group—are gender-neutral. We have no word for "husband" or "wife." We have the word *asawa,* which means "partner." Our precolonial culture was an egalitarian society, where gender didn't dictate your social status—until Catholicism forced us into a destructive patriarchal binary.

Stunned by this revelation, I recalled that when I first came to America, I felt ashamed of how often I would mix up *he* and *she,* constantly apologizing for my failure to assimilate to a binary English language. I realize now that growing up with gender-neutral *siya* was my ancestors' way of telling me that there was life beyond the binary. They always knew I was one of them.

Remember it, they were whispering to me. *Be proud.*

Our gender-fluid precolonial *babaylans* were shamans, healers, and respected leaders. They were spiritual healers who were believed to have access to the divine, intermediaries between the visible and invisible worlds. Studying the history of my language was teaching me so much about this mythology, each word like a tour guide through a forgotten underworld. I wanted to bring it all to the surface and look at it and find my place in it. I wanted to reclaim that history.

I was finding new connections everywhere, but how could I honor them if I was still disconnected from myself? Didn't I owe it to Papa, and to all my ancestors, to bring my full self into the future they had envisioned? If I belonged, all of me belonged.

21

SEA TURTLE

ON THE SURFACE, MY LIFE SEEMED TO BE GOING WELL. BETWEEN Burning Man and Thailand, I was unlocking new depths to myself, feeling more confident than ever in claiming the fullness of who I was. I had a wonderful man by my side who loved me unconditionally, in a way that inspired me to love myself more. Even my modeling work, which had once driven me to the brink, made me feel powerful and in control.

But even though I thought I was on the right track, my body begged to differ.

It started with an itch between my fingers.

Then I noticed a big red rash above my right elbow and over both knees. Bumpy welts formed around my navel, seemingly overnight. The itch spread everywhere, beginning with my feet and slowly creeping upward, as if I were pulling on a scratchy bodysuit, inch by excruciating inch. I went to a doctor, who thought I might have scabies, but the cream she gave me did nothing. The itch kept spreading, eventually reaching my scalp.

What the fuck was happening to me?

Desperate for answers, I wondered what Mama would do. Back home, when Western medicine couldn't offer us answers, we put our faith in *albularyos,* animistic healers who could reverse illnesses caused by the *taong-lupa* surrounding all of us. When I played hide-and-seek at night, I would say, *"Tabi-tabi po"* as I crept through the old trees or crouched in the corner of the neighbor's laundry room, politely asking the *taong-lupa* to move aside so I wouldn't bump into them.

The first time I had an issue with my skin, Mama had taken me to see an *albularyo*. When I was eight years old, big patchy bruises appeared all over my body—giant blue-black circles that were totally painless. How they got there was a mystery. After puzzling over them for a few days, Mama took me a few towns over to see the local healer.

A lanky, bandanna-wearing middle-aged man greeted us, then led us into his small wooden home. There were only about two inches of clearance between the top of his head and the six-foot ceiling, making him look larger than life, like Gandalf in Frodo's hobbit hut. His long rock-star-style hair, his bare feet, and the lit cigarette that dangled from his mouth, obscuring his face in plumes of smoke, only added to his mystique.

He gestured for me to sit on a small metal-backed chair that was positioned inside a large shallow basin of water on the floor. I did, placing my feet on a footrest sticking up out of the water. Then the *albularyo* started chanting.

The whole situation was so new and strange to me. I couldn't hide the funny look on my face, but I hoped Mama wouldn't notice. I didn't want her to see my doubt.

The *albularyo* asked me where I'd been playing lately and whether I'd been in any dark places. Then he lit some paper on fire and moved it around my body, holding the flames beneath the seat of my chair so the smoke billowed up and around me. He was inviting the spirits to answer us.

Next, he procured a metal spoon and melted candles onto it, pouring the drippings into the basin at my feet. A shape began to form on the surface of the water as the hot wax cooled and solidified. It looked like . . . yes, a small boy. A flash of recognition went across the *albularyo*'s face. This was the answer he was looking for.

He told me that there was a *duende* residing in our bathroom and that I needed to pay respect to that gnomelike spirit for my bruises to go away. He fished the solidified candle wax out of the pail, crushed it, wrapped it in notebook paper and a rope, and presented it to me. To appease the *duende,* I was to place the bundle under my pillow for the next ten days.

Sure enough, by the eighth day, the black and blue patches began to fade. Maybe it was the placebo effect, maybe it was magic, but Mama and I did what we had to do, and those damn bruises disappeared.

Years later, dealing with another skin mystery, I needed answers again. I was just about ready to go looking for an *albularyo* in the Filipino-town in Queens.

First, though, I saw a dermatologist. She inspected my arms and elbow, explaining that she was checking for scabies, even though we had already ruled that out. Between all her poking and prodding, she asked what treatments I had tried so far. I was ashamed to be seen like this. My whole body was covered in rashes. I felt as if I had somehow failed my body. I was totally helpless.

Finally, she stood up and met my eyes. "This looks like eczema to me." Her voice was calm yet firm.

Her certainty was a relief. Now that we knew what it was, she could give me some drugs, and we'd end this nightmare once and for all! I was ready to bolt out of there with a prescription, rush to the nearest pharmacy, and fix it. I wouldn't have to put anything under my pillow—no, medicine was going to solve this problem!

To my surprise, though, she didn't reach for her notepad. "What is going on with you emotionally?" she asked.

I started, taken aback. What did my emotions have to do with my eczema? "What do you mean?" I asked.

She didn't speak right away, but the kindness in her expression surprised me. She was asking out of genuine concern, as a sister or a friend might. I felt cared for. Seen. Somehow she could tell that underneath my raw and painful skin was a heart crying for help so quietly that even I hadn't heard it. Before she could speak, I burst into tears.

Coming out to Norman—showing the entirety of myself to him— had been a major step. But there were still so many people I was keeping in the dark, so much of myself that I was editing out anytime I opened my mouth to speak. My life had been one long transformative, transpacific, transcontinental, transgender journey, and I was showing only one tiny sliver of it to everyone else.

This ugly rash all over my skin was trying to tell me something. The message was etched all over my body; my insides were crying out to be heard. These angry red patches were the external manifestation of ugly forces eating away at my spirit: fear, doubt, self-hatred.

It was time to put a stop to them.

"I need to honor my eczema!" I blurted out between sobs, right in the middle of the exam room, as jubilantly as a soldier declaring victory atop a hill. I knew what I needed to do; all I had to figure out was the timing and the method.

"Take care of yourself," my dermatologist told me as I left her office that day, after giving me a prescription for steroids and some instructions for lowering my stress level while managing the pain. I didn't even stop at the pharmacy—my newfound clarity filled me with such elation that I hardly felt a single itch.

Walking up Church Street after the appointment, I had a clear view of the Manhattan skyline, stretching all the way uptown. There was a skip in my step, as all the city's possibilities spread out in front of me. Usually I hated being seen with my rash, but that afternoon I felt like the woman on the street in one of those Maybelline commercials: *"Maybe she's born with it, maybe it's stress!"*

When I got home to the Upper West Side apartment I shared with Norman, I was tempted to tell him everything I'd realized. He and I shared everything with each other. But I wanted to keep it to myself for now. To let the idea marinate. This was a step in my journey I wanted to figure out myself first.

I jumped into the shower to prevent myself from breaking my resolve and found myself belting out "Unwritten" by Natasha Bedingfield at the top of my lungs as the soothing water poured down on me. The echo boosted my voice, but it still wasn't enough for me to match the full power of her husky alto. Still, I sang, "I'm just beginning," and meant it more than ever.

"The pen's in my hand / Ending unplanned."

"Your birthday's coming up," Norman said over dinner a few weeks later. "What do you want to do?"

"Tulum!" I told him a little too quickly. It was obvious I had been waiting for him to ask.

The rash had subsided by then—not all the way, but enough to give me some relief—through a combination of medicine, yoga, and meditation, although the true healing was coming from deep within my soul. If stress had caused my eczema, I needed to get my feet in the sand and an umbrella in my drink, pronto.

Back in 2013, Tulum was a sleepy, laid-back beach town that wasn't on the tourist radar the way it is today. Instagrammers hadn't discovered it yet, mostly because Instagram was still full of blurry selfies and food photos taken with the flash on. Everything I knew about Tulum I had learned from my own research as I'd thought about how I wanted to celebrate my upcoming thirtieth birthday. It had pristine white sand beaches, thirteenth-century Mayan archaeological ruins, and crystal-clear cenotes, underwater sinkholes that could be hundreds of feet deep.

It sounded perfect. Norman agreed.

I was going to honor my eczema.

The property we stayed at—Residencia Gorila—was gorgeously appointed. In the middle of the lush courtyard was a small, five-foot-deep dipping pool, and the shared outdoor kitchen was kitted out with a stove, a refrigerator, and a blender. Maybe I could whip us up some BBCs for old times' sake.

Every morning I woke up at five to watch the sunrise on the beach, admiring the way the light arced over the ocean, painting the massive, billowing clouds in tropical shades of orange, purple, and pink.

As Norman and I acclimated to Tulum, measuring time in sunrises and siestas, we got invited to local activities, away from the tourist traps. We went to one of the tallest houses in the middle of the forest, made from local wood, with a rooftop that looked out over an endless expanse of trees. We floated in our life vests at Sian Ka'an, a marine biosphere that fed the ancient winding Mayan canals.

I spent one afternoon embroidering IN LAK'ESH across a red handloom fabric Norman and I had picked up at the Tulum market. The phrase was a traditional Mayan greeting that could mean either "I am you; you are me" or the more modern interpretation, "I am another yourself." It was a gift to express our gratitude for our host's hospitality, but after everything I had been through, the saying felt deeper and more significant: We can cling to our individualism all we want, but in truth we are all deeply connected to each other because on some level, we *are* each other.

As I handed the fabric to our host near the end of our visit, I felt a desperate yearning to be recognized in that way and to deepen the new global connections I was forming. I wanted community, to be around and among people, so a Sunday salsa dance on the beach seemed like the perfect send-off.

When we arrived that night, we found the dance floor—really just a spot on the beach—crowded with people swinging back and forth, their bodies fully surrendered to the beat of the drum. The singer sounded like a leader rallying his troops, except instead of marching us to the battlefield, all he wanted us to do was have fun.

Knowing a little Spanish didn't mean I could dance salsa, but that didn't stop me from pulling Norman onto the dance floor and ordering two margaritas to help us find the rhythm. The truth is, I'll dance to my own rhythm as long as I can feel the music in my bones.

We were barefoot in the sand, the enticing smells from the restaurant mingling with the aroma of the salty sea breeze as it blew in from the shore. We were in heaven. I let myself go completely, stomping my feet harder and harder, grinning from ear to ear. My margarita was sloshing out of my glass onto the sand, but I didn't care. Not one bit. I felt free. Liberated. New.

Norman must have noticed. He turned to me during a break in the music, caught my gaze, and asked, "Gee . . . what does turning thirty mean to you?"

There was something so open and guileless about the way he asked. My Nature Boy, always sincere, wanted to find out what was in my heart. But those seven words pierced me: *What does turning thirty mean to you?* My answer would encompass everything I had been holding in emotionally—all the worries, fears, and self-imposed limitations. Turning thirty meant leaving all that behind.

It was time to make my plan real.

I looked him in the eye, then leaned in to whisper in his ear, "Love, I'm ready to come out. I'm ready to tell my story."

For a moment, I felt suspended in time. I'd spoken aloud the truth that had been burning in my heart since my appointment with the dermatologist. I'm not sure I had ever actually said the words *come out* aloud before. For many years, they had bubbled up to the front of my mind, only for me to shove them back down into the darkness. The truth wasn't just something I could let out and leave behind; the truth would ask things of me, pulling me into a future where I would have to be open, transparent, and bold. I was afraid of my truth. I was afraid of how pure it was. Before I knew the world saw people like me as an abomination, I had been a child who just wanted to express her femme self, who couldn't help but walk with a *kembot* sway down the street. Being as honest as that child again would be a challenge indeed.

In the second after I spoke, I thought about taking back what I had said to Norman. Could I really be the person the truth would require me to be? Could I stand, exposed, without the protective walls I had built around myself?

But I held Norman's gaze, digging my toes into the sand as the salsa music continued to play in the background, and realized I was finished letting my life be dictated by fear.

I had thought I was afraid of other people—the models, the photographers, the agents. But the whole time I was most afraid of myself.

It had been so easy to hide behind the curtain of being stealth; if people didn't like me, well, I wasn't showing them the real me anyway. I had buried myself beneath layers of internalized transphobia and self-loathing. Coming out would mean having nothing left to hide behind. But for the first time, as I stood with the man I love on that beach, that idea felt thrilling.

Suddenly, as if on cue, the band stopped playing, diverting Norman's and my attention. The vibrating echo from the drums lingered for a second more, and then the only sound we heard was the gentle blowing of the sea breeze.

The singer leaned into the microphone. *"Amigos! Amigas!"*

We were confused. Had there been an accident?

But then the crowd shifted as one, turning to the north. Following their gaze, we saw hundreds of newly hatched sea turtles crawling toward us, emerging from the darkened bushes into the moonlight. My mouth fell open in disbelief as they scooted toward us, their tiny flippers pushing their bodies along the sand. I had never felt such overpowering awe. An entire drama of birth and survival was playing out before our very eyes.

The singer said something in Spanish, issuing instructions to the crowd. Apparently, the vibrations from the live music and dancing had disoriented the baby sea turtles, and they needed to be redirected to the water. People began kneeling down and picking them up, cradling them in their hands as they carried them to the ocean one by one.

When in Tulum . . .

Norman and I followed suit.

As I reached for my first turtle, a man called out to me, *"Amiga! Amiga!"* He pointed at my drink. *Oops.* I was clutching my margarita in one hand and the precious animal in the other. I had never before double-fisted a drink and a turtle. I set down my glass. I needed to direct all my attention to this solemn duty.

Norman and I made at least ten trips between the dance floor and the sea before all the babies had been returned to their home. It was exhilarating. When we were finished, he and I walked to the sea to wash away the sand.

As I rinsed off, I cried as I realized what had just happened. When I had told Norman *"I'm ready to come out,"* nature had responded.

Out of all the thousands of moments when those sea turtles could have hatched, they hatched then. Coincidences don't get any more cosmic than that. I could follow their example. I, too, could be reborn. All I had to do was step into the light.

I woke up the next day feeling as if I had just gone on a cold swim, my body refreshed and clean, my muscles limber. The night before felt like a revelation, as if a splinter had been pulled from my soul.

That morning, as we watched the Tulum sunrise reach our rooftop, I held Norman's hand—reassuring, knowing, loving—and thought of the word *transgender* again, expecting to feel the usual shame I associated with it. But the shame was gone. Gone, as my fear was gone. Instead, pride swelled in my heart.

I looked at the scars all over my body from the eczema. What had once made me scream in pain now left me feeling grateful. I knew now why it had happened. What had begun at the dermatologist's office, with me proclaiming "I need to honor my eczema!" ended with me saying out loud, "I'm ready to tell my story."

The story was written on my skin, crying out to be told.

22

STORYTELLER

AFTER TULUM, I FELT LIMITLESS. ALL THE RESIDUAL SHAME AND fear I used to feel evaporated, dissipating like fog in the daylight, freeing me to see more clearly than I had ever thought possible. Maybe I was making up for all those years I had allowed negative thoughts to govern my life, but I suddenly swung hard in the opposite direction, setting what seemed at the time like genuinely batshit goals.

At the start of 2014, less than three months after my thirtieth birthday, my New Year's resolutions were to give a TED Talk and to speak before the United Nations High Commission for Human Rights. Totally normal goals for a person whose only public speaking experience was in pageants!

But I felt as if a power had been unleashed within me that couldn't be stopped. I wanted to tell my coming-out story in the most courageous way possible. What could be scarier or bolder than sharing it at the annual TED Conference, the most influential public speaking platform in the world? Go big or go home, right? An undeniable inner drive was guiding my actions, telling me I could do things that seemed unlikely or even impossible.

Hell, I had dominated beauty pageants, become a fashion model in New York City, and talked my way into a magazine job I wasn't even remotely qualified for. I had done incredible things in my life, but I was finally starting to *believe* I could do them—and that unlocked a whole new tier of possibilities in my mind. Between Norman, the discoveries about my ancestors, and the sea turtles, I had been shown a path forward, a whole constellation of surreal circumstances nudging me in the right direction, telling me to fully come into myself. All I had to do now was take the first step.

My friend Cameron Sinclair, who I met through the entrepreneurial group Summit Series while I was working for the biodegradable trash bag company, had won the prestigious TED Prize in 2006, so I decided to ask him if he'd make an introduction with the organizers, explaining that I wanted to come out as transgender in my talk. On January 20 I got an email back: "TED says maybe. They will be in contact."

The next day I took a call with TED director Kelly Stoetzel, who explained that the main stage was almost totally full because this year's conference was only two months away. But I walked her through my story anyway. I talked about growing up in Asia and moving to America, and about the trans models who had come before me. I told her how their stories had been cruelly taken from them, and how I wanted to finally take control over my own, live onstage.

When I was finished speaking, Kelly told me that if I were accepted, I would be the first transgender person to speak about trans identity on the TED main stage.

Bear in mind that this was January 2014, five months before *Time* magazine declared "The Transgender Tipping Point" on its cover, and one month before Janet Mock released her groundbreaking memoir *Redefining Realness*. A movement for trans visibility was emerging and gaining rapid momentum, but to do something like TED was still a bold step forward at the time. Kelly wanted to know if I was willing to be that standard bearer.

I told her I was—and despite my nervousness, I actually meant it. I wanted to make the kind of statement that couldn't be ignored. I would do it for myself, for Tula, and for every trans person out there who felt alone and unseen.

Kelly ended the call by telling me, "We'll be in touch," and a few days later, an official email appeared in my inbox: "Invitation to Speak at TED 2014."

It was happening. Now I just needed a speech.

A month later, with my first draft in hand, I went to the TED headquarters in SoHo for my first rehearsal in front of Kelly and a few other curators. It was partly for me to practice but also partly a test—speeches could still be canceled, and this rehearsal was one way for the TED team to make their final decisions. I walked into a small, darkened room, with a spotlight trained on the center of a circular stage that was surrounded by rows of seating. It was a terrifying space to debut my talk, like something out of *Eyes Wide Shut*.

But I stepped into the spotlight and started anyway.

I wasn't good. I trembled. The intimate space, the twenty-odd people judging my every word, their eyes trained on me—it all felt like a stimulus overload. People don't usually walk into dark rooms and tell strangers their life story. I was so nervous that I opened with the statement "I'm a proud trans woman," cutting right to the chase. That didn't get the reaction I was hoping for. Without any context, the big reveal just left my small test audience looking confused. Again, this was 2014, and not everyone even knew what being a "trans woman" meant.

I could tell that I was losing them before I was halfway finished. I struggled to find the flow of my words, and my body kept shaking. Accustomed as I was to dominating pageants, it was scary to feel my powers waning, like Supergirl exposed to kryptonite.

Afterward the TED organizers asked me to repeat the speech, but this time at a slower pace. I barely made it through, and I was glad when it was over. I knew I'd blown it, with the same certainty—but the exact opposite feeling—as when I'd stepped onto pageant stages with all my Horse Barbie spirit, knowing I would take the crown.

Kelly came up to me and delivered a polite compliment, but I could hear a telling tinge of disappointment in her voice. Even worse, I had to take a seat in the audience and watch the rest of the speakers rehearse their talks. They were all so polished compared to me. I was embarrassed, I was jealous, and I was furious at myself for ever believing I deserved a spot alongside them.

After the rehearsal was over, I felt a tap on my shoulder. "Hey! Geena?"

I turned. The voice belonged to a petite woman with her hair cut in a short black bob, a proud gray streak running through it. She looked like a miniature Cruella De Vil, but a whole lot friendlier.

"My name's Gina Barnett," she said. "I'm one of the TED speech coaches. I believe you have an important story, and I think I can help you tell it. We have the same name, after all, so I think it's meant to be."

This was one of those magical coincidences in life that I had learned not to ignore. What are the chances that someone with my name would be there to help me come out? She spelled her name G-I-N-A, but not everyone had my mama to help them change the vowels.

Gina Barnett changed everything about my approach to the talk. Instead of coming out in the first sentence, she told me to tease the audience instead. "Make them beg for it," she advised. "You want to have them wrapped around your finger."

In weekly meetings at her Rockefeller Center office, Gina told me to think not about the points I wanted to convey but about the experiences that had been important to me. Some of the stories I shared with her were about feeling empowered; others were about my inability to share my full self with friends, colleagues, and lovers. All the stories were like puzzle pieces strewn across Gina's desk, and now all we had to do was assemble them.

It had never occurred to me that these stories were valuable in and of themselves. All quarters of society tell trans people that our lives are worthless. I thought my TED Talk had to be a passionate plea for equality to win over a skeptical audience.

But Gina told me, "They're already on your side. You don't need to convince them. You just need to tell your story like you're telling it to one person."

Those words were like a lightning bolt. *I just need to tell my story.*

I didn't need to *make* it powerful. My story was powerful already, and if I talked around it or tried to dress it up too ornately, it wouldn't shine through brightly enough. People didn't want to hear me spout statistics—"just share one," Gina advised—they wanted to know who I was, where I came from, and how I had been shaped by a world that didn't seem to have space for me until I carved it out myself.

That's when the opening sentence of the speech crystallized. "The world makes you something that you're not," we wrote, "but you know inside what you are."

The rest of the talk would just be my story, simple and unadorned.

I was so busy preparing for my TED Talk that I almost forgot to let people know I was doing it. By this point, I had been modeling again full time for three years, and I realized my agent might like to know that I was just about to come out as transgender on one of the world's biggest stages.

I was so worried about how he would react that I overthought it. *Should I send him flowers with a note? Maybe a handwritten letter?* But then I thought, *Fuck it, I'll just pick up the phone and call him.*

After a few minutes of catching up, I eased into it. "By the way, Ron, I wanted to let you know I'm doing a TED Talk."

I couldn't bring myself to say it all at once.

"Oh, great!" he said. "I love TED! What are you talking about?"

I took a breath.

"I'm coming out," I told him.

"Oh, Geena! I'm so proud of you! Coming out as a lesbian—that's so big, that's so powerful."

There was no circling around it anymore. I had to say it.

"Actually, no, Ron, I'm coming out as a trans woman."

The next three seconds were some of the longest in my life. He had been working with me for four years. Together we had worked with Hanes, Nordstrom, and all my major catalog clients. He wasn't just my business partner; he was my friend, too, and he had never known this about me—hadn't even expected it. I'm surprised he didn't take a full minute to let it sink in, but it felt like one anyway.

"You know what, Geena?" he said, breaking the silence at last. "You are such a great model for us. I honor you. I respect you. I commend your bravery. Do it. If you feel like this is what you need to do, do it. We'll figure out the rest later."

I was so relieved. It was rare to get so perfect a response in the moment. Usually, people stammered or asked questions. Never once did my agent make me feel guilty for hiding it from him. Nor did he oversimplify the situation and pretend it didn't matter.

In fact, he was upbeat about my prospects. "We'll find out what the market will say," he said, adding with a laugh, "You may not work in the southern catalog markets anymore, but we'll see. Who knows? You might even gain some clients!"

I called Tigerlily, too, to let her know my plans.

At first, she was anxious. "I trust your decision but whatever happens after it, be ready," she cautioned. She didn't need to say it out loud, but I knew she was thinking about Tula.

Then after a pregnant pause, she pivoted to the excitement of everyone in the Philippines seeing me speak at TED. "Your entire trans pageant family has been waiting for this moment! Their long-lost sister Assunta reclaiming her stage! Horse Barbie making her comeback!"

I felt her love all the way from Manila.

"Also," she continued, "I can't wait to finally boast about your modeling success to anyone and everyone! All your magazines can't stay in my closet forever!"

Mama wasn't as optimistic. When I told her I was going to Vancouver to come out to the whole world in a TED Talk, she worried what people would say about me. She was scared I would lose my career. For years, I had felt guilty about making her and my family maintain my cover story, but now that I was finally giving Mama the chance to drop it, she doubted it was a good idea.

I understood Mama's concern. She just wanted to keep her baby safe. She wasn't Ma'am Rocero anymore. She couldn't protect me from the bullies forever. But what could bullies do to me if I took their power away from them and claimed it for myself? I would be coming out before any tabloid could out me. The industry could blacklist me if it wanted to, but no one could accuse me of being a coward.

People used to throw stones at me in the Philippines, so let them throw words if they wanted. I knew what I had to do. I wasn't going to wait any longer for the world to accept me; I was ready, at long last, to be free.

. . .

Everything became real during my final rehearsal onstage in Vancouver.

Standing inside that iconic red circle on the stage, facing an empty audience in a huge auditorium that would soon hold thousands, I launched into it: "The world makes you something that you're not . . ."

I was given the option to have my speech displayed on a "music stand" in front of me, but I declined. I wanted to be like the Diva in *The Fifth Element*, effortlessly commanding the stage with almost operatic inflection, channeling the cosmic power of the story I was about to tell, with no barriers between myself and the audience. Even with thousands of eyes on me, I wanted to create a sense of intimacy. I could hear Gina Barnett whispering in my mind, *"Make sure you breathe. Take . . . your . . . time."*

I knew my speech backward and forward by this point. Gina had told me to rehearse it every day in preparation, first out loud in a silent room, then out loud with noise in the background, and then in my head with the noise still going.

"Memorize it in your muscles," she had instructed, and that work paid off, because during my final rehearsal, I wasn't even thinking about the words in my head. I was fully in my body. My pageant training kicked in. Everything clicked into place. I was Horse Barbie again, commanding the stage, projecting with ease, my movements refined and purposeful. I nailed it.

The night before the conference, TED held a massive dinner for the attendees. Being around everyone there was still surreal. One minute I was talking with the mayor of Vancouver, the next I was talking with brain scientist Jill Bolte, who in turn stopped our conversation midsentence to point out Will Smith walking by. It wasn't lost on me that I might be the only trans person in that room. Hopefully my talk could change that.

But because I needed to save the reveal for the next day, when people asked what my talk was going to be about, I said, a little slyly, "It's different. You'll just have to see for yourself."

On the morning of the speech, I woke up at five, having barely slept, and started doing my obligatory three run-throughs. The first went well. For the second, I got in the shower and turned on "Unwritten," my hype song and personal anthem ever since my bout of eczema. The fog from the shower must have gotten in my brain because as the music played, I got confused, forgot the order of my paragraphs, and tripped over the words.

The third run-through was even harder: Saying it in my mind with the shower going and the song competing for my attention felt all but impossible.

I would have to trust my gut. I knew the speech. It was just nerves.

Looking at my reflection as I put my makeup on, I couldn't help but think of the young trans girl who grew up poor in that *eskinita* in the Philippines. Here I was, standing in front of a hotel mirror, about to share my story with CEOs, scientists, and movie stars—and with millions of complete strangers, when it was posted online. I had no way to wrap my head around how I had gotten from there to here. It was mind-boggling to think back on all the choices and chance events that had put me in this privileged position.

I found it so impossible to comprehend that I almost felt like I had teleported straight from that alley to the TED main stage. One day I was a child with a T-shirt around my head, and the next I was a grown woman in a Zara dress and YSL stilettos, getting ready to speak my truth to the world.

Walking out of the hotel to the TED stage across the street early that morning, I held my coffee in one hand and my printed speech in the other, squeezing in one last rehearsal. The spring air was crisp and clarifying.

Breathe, Geena, I told myself. *Breathe*.

I arrived backstage at around eight-thirty and went straight to the private area designated for speakers. It was cold, dark, and quiet. The radio communications were crackling, and someone whispered into their headset, "Geena Rocero just arrived backstage."

Gina Barnett came to my rescue, giving me a tight hug. "I'm proud of you," she said, her voice thick with emotion. "You've got this."

"Don't make me cry! I don't want to ruin my makeup!" I said, squeezing her back.

Before she left, she did one last bit of coaching: "Just remember, rehearse the first sentence of your talk before you go on. Do it over and over."

It was a tactic she used to help speakers avoid the infamous blank-out that sometimes happens when they step onto the stage. If I already had the opening line in my head, I could ease into the rest of the talk instead of starting cold.

Shortly before my talk was scheduled to begin, a sound guy came over with a thin beige headset microphone for me. He took one look at my body-hugging dress and asked as delicately as possible if there was anywhere inside that we could clip the microphone battery. "Of course," I said, unzipping my dress, but then I stopped.

"Sir, uh . . . I don't know how to say this, but there's nowhere to clip it. I'm not wearing a bra."

I guess I thought going commando would make me feel confident, but now I was about to give the most important speech of my life and had nowhere to clip the microphone!

But the sound guy was a total pro about it. "No worries—we'll make something work."

He walked away and returned a few minutes later with a thin Velcro belt that I could wrap around my waist inside my dress. We clipped the battery onto the back of it, and then I zipped my dress back up. It was so minimal that you could barely see it through the fabric.

With the sound figured out, I remembered Gina's parting words to me and began repeating the opening line of my talk, reciting it like the catechism: "The world makes you something that you're not, but you know inside what you are."

After about twenty repetitions, the sound director's voice crackled into my earpiece: "Uh, Geena? I think you got it."

I burst out laughing. The whole sound department must have thought I'd lost my mind! "Thanks," I said, "and sorry." The embarrassment actually helped calm my nerves, keeping me grounded and distracting me from what I was about to do.

And then it came: "Please welcome to the stage . . . Geena Rocero!"

The loud applause and bright lights very quickly brought me into the present. I was really doing this. I felt somehow as if Tigerlily were standing there with me, cinching my hips with that crackly tape, making me stand up even straighter. As I walked toward the center of the stage, my demeanor shifted. My gait felt more intentional. With every gliding step I took, I felt my Horse Barbie power take over my body. It didn't feel strange to be there anymore. It felt like home.

I reached my mark and began my speech, holding the PowerPoint clicker loosely in my right hand, my voice calm but powerful. As I moved from paragraph to paragraph, I felt like a dominatrix, wrapping the audience in my whip, in command of their attention. Every bit of inflection in my voice, every hand gesture, came straight from my soul. The nervousness vanished, and only I remained. It was all me.

Toward the middle of my speech, when I revealed a picture of myself as a young boy, the audience reacted with both jaw-dropping shock and smiles of affirmation. To maintain my composure in that moment, I picked a woman to my left wearing a yellow jacket and eyeglasses and kept my focus on her, watching her smile back at me through the remainder of the speech. She was my beacon. It was as if she recognized the courage it took to be on that stage.

I ended my nine-minute speech with a question to the audience, but the truth was that my TED Talk was the last step in my own self-acceptance. "My deepest truth allowed me to accept who I am. Will you?"

Close confidantes had warned me before I gave the talk that people would label me as "trans" afterward. Even Gina Barnett had told me, "The moment you open up this box, you cannot close it again," wanting to make sure I understood the weight of my decision. I would be called a "trans model" in headlines—maybe for the rest of my life. But I didn't care.

After so many women like Tula had been driven out of the industry simply because of their gender identity, the phrase *trans model* had a revolutionary power all its own. The industry wanted those two words to remain forever apart, like magnets repelling each other. I embraced the idea of holding them together in the face of that pressure. I didn't see the word *trans* as a qualifier or disclaimer anymore; I saw transness as power.

It was that power I felt as the audience gave me a standing ovation, responding to my closing question with fervent applause. I floated off that stage on a high, glowing from within. I had hoped to feel unburdened, but nothing could've prepared me for the absolute elation that followed.

Backstage, Gina rushed toward me and wrapped me in a tight hug. "Honey!" she cried into my shoulder. "You were so *you*. You're so precious. You've shared a powerful gift with the world."

On that stage, I didn't just let go of my fear—I discovered my own voice.

Or rather I *rediscovered* it, my pageant panache and pizzazz bubbling back up from beneath layers of self-doubt. Back in the Philippines, I had been just a girl, the goofy jokester of the Garcia clan, but the second I stepped onstage, I was an untouchable queen. That was my superpower—being able to transform a mischievous *makulit* into the renowned Assunta de Rossi.

At TED, I performed that magic trick once again. Everyone out there in the audience had seen the perfectly polished and poised presenter, an elegant and articulate woman in total control of herself; they hadn't seen me muttering the first line to myself a thousand times as if I had a screw loose. But that ability to switch on was a gift—and I realized now how much good I could do with it.

After the applause died down, a production assistant took me to a long meet-and-greet line filled with people who wanted to talk to me. There weren't many trans people in that group—although that would certainly change in TED Conferences to come—but the universal themes in my speech had resonated powerfully. *Eat, Pray, Love* author Elizabeth Gilbert came up to me and thanked me for sharing my story, telling me how courageous I had been. Others opened up to me about how they were going to free themselves from the limiting expectations society had placed on them. They were vulnerable with me because I had been vulnerable with them, and together we were strong.

I knew from that outpouring of love that my TED Talk wasn't the end of a journey, but the beginning of a new one. Suddenly my second New Year's resolution, speaking at the UN, didn't seem so farfetched. I could use my story, and a dash of my magic Horse Barbie charisma, to help others feel like they didn't have to hide anymore. I didn't have to be the most knowledgeable advocate, although I certainly did my homework, and I didn't have to preach, even though I was passionate about trans equality.

I just needed to do what Gina told me to do.

I had to go out there and tell my story.

.   .   .

One of the first phone calls I made when I got back to my hotel was to Mama. I thanked her for all her support and unconditional love through the years, for everything from her acceptance of my femininity as a child to our unforgettable vagina road trip in Thailand. She cried during the whole conversation.

Mama's earlier reserve seemed to melt away. She was excited to flaunt the magazines I was in, which she had been hoarding, waiting for the day she could show them to guests. She told me with pride that she could put my modeling pictures on display now instead of hiding them every time a visitor came over.

My older sister Glenda later reminded me that my TED Talk was a coming-out moment for my family, too. For years, they had kept my secret, telling lies about what I was doing in New York so that no one could out me in the modeling world. Their stories had had to match mine to protect me.

"Geena," she told me, "now that you're free, we're free, too."

I had never thought about it that way before. Freedom was contagious. If I could share it more widely, maybe I could help others shake off their own fears.

I spent the days between my TED Talk and its online posting thinking about how to do just that. My friend Allie Hoffman and I had already been brainstorming an advocacy campaign and media production company called Gender Proud, and we spent that time building a website for it, fine-tuning the branding so we'd have an online presence by the time my talk went live.

I flew to Chicago for a trans event, staying at the home of Angelica Ross and Jen Richard, two trans writers and actors who had become supportive sisters when I told them about my TED Talk. They knew I was about to face a full-on media spotlight. A model who had been stealth for years? The story was irresistible.

"We're here for you," they told me. "For whatever comes next."

The next day, on March 31, the International Trans Day of Visibility, my talk went live—and it instantly went viral. That morning I flew to New York for a media bonanza, doing interviews with *The Huffington Post*, CNN, MSNBC, and more. I told my story to anyone who would listen.

But amid all that attention, and as my advocacy began, I tried not to lose sight of who I now knew myself to be: a daughter, a partner, and a jokester, someone who values the silly as much as the sublime. Public speaking could be something I did because I cared about it. But offstage, away from the bright lights, I was still just me—the silly, goofy girl who liked to *gigil* cuddle and travel to far-off islands with Norman or talk on the phone for hours with Mama.

Today my talk has had close to five million views, from various platforms, and has been translated into thirty-two languages.

I'm proud of those five million views—but at the end of the day, the most meaningful are the hundred thousand that Mama jokes are hers.

23

LUCKY KID

AFTER I SHARED MY TRUTH AT THE TED CONFERENCE, MY RELA-
tionship with Mama grew deeper. Mama saw me as a woman who
wanted, for the first time, to take control of her own narrative. Perhaps that was what finally prompted her to share how my story really
began.

One night in the summer of 2015 while I was visiting her in San
Francisco, she sat me down on the couch and told me about a night
in February 1983 when she was six weeks pregnant with me. She'd
come home late from a full day's work as an elementary school
teacher, followed by her side hustle selling Kikkoman soy sauce. Her
voice was hoarse, her feet were aching, and she still had a pile of stu-
dent homework to grade.

Exhausted, she worried about what her life would look like with a
fourth child running around underfoot. The family had barely
enough money to feed everyone as it was. Having another baby
seemed like an impossibility, in that nine-by-twelve-foot wooden
sublevel home.

After dinner that night, Mama and Papa, my two sisters, and my brother gathered in front of the black-and-white TV to watch a movie. A 1981 film called *High School Scandal* was playing. Directed by Gil Portes, it tells the story of two high school senior girls, Roselle and Lynette, as they navigate prom and puberty. After being dumped by her date, Roselle has sex with one of her guy friends to validate her bruised ego. She winds up pregnant and decides to get an abortion, but the doctor is a quack. The following day, due to complications from the procedure, Roselle dies.

On its face, the movie was a morality play—the kind of story that conservatives would love to use as a counterargument to those who call for reproductive rights today. But however it might be co-opted now, back then the movie had a major impact on Mama.

The very next morning, Mama had been scheduled to have an abortion with the exact same kind of neighborhood quack doctor that Roselle had gone to in the movie.

"I had already borrowed the abortion money from the teacher's cooperative," Mama told me. "I was ready to go. Everything was set."

But after watching *High School Scandal,* Mama told me, she felt traumatized. "I was shaking when I went to bed," she said. "I tossed and turned thinking about Roselle's death. I didn't want to die."

Early the next day she canceled her appointment and decided to put the abortion money toward food and daily survival expenses. She still didn't know how she was going to feed four kids, but she would try.

For a long time, I wondered why Mama always called me her *maswerteng bata,* her "lucky kid." That night in San Francisco, I learned why.

"I'm lucky that you were born," she told me, and after so many years together—after our entire journey from the Philippines to San Francisco to Thailand and beyond—I felt the full weight of those words. I felt lucky, too. I felt lucky that she was Mama and that we had shared so many adventures together.

Right as I was tearing up, Mama broke into an almost impish grin, as if she were about to blow my mind with whatever she said next. Her story had one final twist.

"You know which actress played Roselle?"

"Which one *po*?" I asked.

"Gina Alajar," she said in a reverent whisper, her eyes wide, as if she herself couldn't believe it.

I was speechless. Gina Alajar, one of the Philippines' most respected actresses—a woman who literally shared my name—was the reason I was born.

I paused for a few seconds, taking in the story. Then I blurted out, "Mama, that's so crazy! Can you imagine? One Gina has to die for another Geena to live!"

In a way, my whole life has been shaped by Ginas, in a series of wild coincidences, each Gina teaching me something unique about the power of storytelling. Gina Alajar, the actress who played Roselle, essentially gave birth to me—she was a message to my mama. As a child growing up in the 1990s, I had named myself after Gina, the lead character in our popular teen TV drama *Gimik*. She represented possibility. Gina Pu-keh was the first trans woman I saw who I knew had received gender confirmation surgery. She allowed me to dream. And Gina Barnett, my TED Talk coach, helped me share my own story—to learn the power of telling the truth.

When I was seven years old, Ate Christie, our only neighbor who had a Betamax player, yelled into our alley, calling in the children, *"Mga bata manonood na tayo!"*

She was inviting everyone to watch the new Betamax tape she had rented. It was about to start. Their living room was our own private screening space. All of us squished together like *lumpia* spring rolls, just as I would later do with my Garcia clan in Tigerlily's house, to watch the film. That night I had squeezed past the children spilling out onto the street to claim my own patch of floor.

Peeking through the gaps in the crowd, I caught a vision of an animated mermaid with long, flowing red hair and a resplendent green tail. As she looked up through the ocean toward the light filtering down from above, she sang, "Up where they walk, up where they run . . . Wanderin' free, wish I could be part of that world."

I was transfixed. I somehow felt alone but not lonely. It was as if Ariel were singing only to me—or maybe as if I were singing through her, my seven-year-old femme spirit wishing to be part of a world I didn't know how to access yet. Her song was a twinkle of possibility in a dark room. Even as a kid, I wanted to be somewhere I could feel seen, somewhere I could use my voice. I wanted light. I wanted freedom. I wanted the world.

24

HOMECOMING QUEEN

MY PAGEANT TRAINING CAME IN HANDY AS MY ADVOCACY WORK took off. After my TED Talk went viral, I was flooded with public speaking invitations. My story hit on so many different topics— gender, immigration, race, AAPI identities, LGBTQ equality—and suddenly I was being asked to share it far and wide, from Washington, D.C., to Bogotá, Colombia. But even as I launched into a full-on speechmaking bonanza, I was still the same scrappy beauty queen who did quick changes on bumpy boat rides between islands.

Nowhere was that more evident than at the White House, where I went to speak in July 2014. The nonprofit group Lesbians Who Tech and the White House Office of Public Engagement had invited me to speak at an LGBT innovation summit, in a conference room at the Eisenhower Executive Office Building. I took the Acela from New York in a comfortable travel outfit: gym leggings, a sweatshirt, my trusty Converse, and a denim tote. I was perfectly incognito, just rushing in for a quick engagement at the nation's capital like a spy who wanted to escape notice. Before I left, I had given my eyebrows a basic shape, put my curled hair in a bun, and powdered my face, but that was it; I looked like I was going to yoga class, not like I was about to walk through the halls of power.

When the train pulled into Union Station, I ducked into the nearest bar and emerged from the bathroom ten minutes later, looking like a totally different person, with a defined smoky eye, nude lipstick, some light contouring, and my hair pulled back into a sleek middle part. I wore diamond-shaped hoop earrings and a tight-fitting black halter dress from Zara with a slight peplum hem. Thanks to the wrinkle-resistant fabric, it had survived the train trip in my tote unscathed. I took off for the White House like Olivia Pope ready to defuse a hot-button situation.

These weren't skills I learned from modeling; this was entirely due to all those nights I wriggled out of an evening gown in the back of a bus as it careened through mountain switchbacks.

But I wasn't just rediscovering my ability to put on makeup in the terrible lighting of an Irish pub bathroom. The full power and confidence of my Horse Barbie days were returning in full force. I was a sleeper agent, suddenly reactivated. The TED Talk had brought me back, shaking off the remaining rust. Right away I was performing at my peak again—but this time more authentically, and in the service of something bigger than myself.

At the White House that day, I walked up to the podium with pride and began: "Being LGBT is innovative in and of itself. In a cis heteronormative world, we've managed to be here—I mean here in this room—collectively sharing our resources, our struggles, and our vision for a more just and compassionate world."

This was all second nature to me now. I didn't have to repeat the first line of my speech anymore to psych myself up; I could just stand and deliver. I wasn't winning crowns or posing for magazines, but I hoped I was helping, in some small way, to change things.

· · ·

Right after my TED Talk, Allie Hoffman and I got to work doing advocacy around gender recognition policies through our new organization Gender Proud. Allie, a petite blond woman with short hair, was a powerhouse who shared my passion for media as a form of advocacy. Her background in documentary filmmaking was a perfect fit for my work, and her friendship made the hard work rewarding.

I wanted to focus on one specific issue—something that mattered to me, something that connected to my story, and something that would make a material difference in the lives of trans people worldwide. And I knew exactly what that issue was.

When I had first accepted Mama's invitation to move to the United States, I was motivated by California's gender recognition policy, which allowed me to get an F on my ID if I received gender confirmation surgery. I didn't know then that California's policy, which has since changed, was actually more restrictive than what other states and countries offered their trans residents.

I gave myself a crash course on the full range of gender recognition laws and policies as Allie and I worked on Gender Proud, partnering with organizations like OutRight Action International. I learned from experts like Zach Hudson at Fordham Law School's Leitner Center for International Law and Justice. I became a bona-fide policy geek, learning the ins and outs of how each country did—or didn't—allow transgender people to change their identity documents.

On one hand, the Philippines has no gender recognition policy. Anatomy is destiny there; what's printed on your birth certificate is what you're stuck with forever. In the middle of the range, various countries and localities allow trans people to change their gender markers if they can prove that they've undergone surgery, taken hormones, or otherwise received treatment from a doctor. These policies are an improvement, but they still exclude many members of the trans community and place unnecessary obstacles in the path of self-actualization.

Imagine trying to get a job as a trans person living in poverty if your ID has the wrong gender marker on it. Imagine getting pulled over by police and having a driver's license that shows someone who doesn't look like you. Imagine trying to travel abroad and not having your passport reflect who you are.

As Gender Proud got off the ground, I talked about these issues at any venue I could—from UN events to State Department conferences to USAID engagements—personally testifying to the real human impact of making gender recognition policies more progressive. I traveled to South America, India, Thailand, and beyond. In a way, I felt it was my patriotic duty to give back. I spoke about how I had moved to California all those years ago because I had heard the state would recognize me as a woman. I talked about how much it meant to see that F on my license.

But I also talked about the pain of giving up my Filipino citizenship when I became a U.S. citizen in July 2006. Although I had the option to retain it, I couldn't bear the thought of having a male gender marker in my Filipino passport. There was guilt and shame in that complicated choice. At first, I felt like I was letting go of my heritage. But then I realized it was my home country that was trying to erase its own heritage, suppressing knowledge of my gender-fluid ancestors, and trying to keep trans people locked into rigid boxes for their entire lives. That kind of gender policing was not something I could cosign.

My hope for the future of the Philippines could be found in Argentina. In 2012 that deeply Catholic South American nation had passed one of the most progressive gender recognition laws in the world, allowing trans people to essentially fill out a form and get new ID without any medical requirements—a policy known as self-identification. Whenever people told me they weren't optimistic about seeing trans rights advance in a country as religious as the Philippines, I would say, "The pope is from Argentina, and they've got the model law!"

I heard from friends and family that my TED Talk had made a big splash back in the Philippines. It was widely covered in the media, in large part because all those years earlier, after rising to the top of the pageant scene and appearing on TV, I had suddenly disappeared—I was nowhere to be found. Only Tigerlily knew what had happened to me. And now I had reappeared, as if I were back from the dead.

Whenever Filipino media outlets reached out for an interview, I was savvy about how I responded. I knew they wanted my story, so before I agreed to speak with them, I'd say, "You have to describe me as a 'transgender woman.' You can't call me *bakla*." Though that word had an important and complex indigenous history, it was mostly used in a derogatory way to insult trans women, and I wasn't going to be a party to that denigration. That word had been shouted at me too many times on the street.

Tigerlily, who was now the production manager at a trans cabaret tourist attraction known as the Amazing Show, told me that she had shown my TED Talk to new girls almost like an orientation video. "Use the word *transgender*," she told them. "There's power in it."

It brought me joy to hear that I helped introduce that more humanizing and globally recognizable term into the mainstream. Filipino news outlets started covering violence against trans people differently, no longer reporting quite so sensationally about *baklas*. Many of the pageants even changed their names to reflect a changing cultural reality in which trans people were demanding more respect and more accurate language. Now instead of being called "Miss Gay This" or "Miss Gay That," they'll be called "Miss Queen This" or "Miss Trans That."

But changing the conversation was only one part of the equation.

The laws needed to change too—and I believed that they could. If Argentina had done it, so could the Philippines.

Those first months after my TED Talk were filled with relentless optimism.

For the first time, with the help of technology and global travel, LGBTQ people all around the word were connecting with one another, comparing their struggles, and learning that they were part of a broader community. And in the latter years of Barack Obama's presidential administration, the United States was making rapid advances on trans rights via executive order. I felt like we were on the cusp of a big leap forward.

So, when I was invited to speak at the Democratic National Committee's LGBT Gala in the summer of 2014, I happily accepted. And yes, I did also want to meet President Obama. I spent about as much time imagining what I'd say to him as I had working on my speech with Gina Barnett.

What seemed at first like a straightforward assignment got progressively more difficult, because the Obama administration was implementing new trans rights policies faster than I could update my speech. On May 30, 2014, only two weeks before I was to deliver it, the Department of Health and Human Services reversed a rule that barred Medicare from covering gender confirmation surgery, a major win worthy of celebration. But pragmatically speaking, it meant I had to go revise my talk again, which was complicated because every time I updated it, I had to get the new text approved by the DNC. Still, I jumped through all the bureaucratic hoops I needed to and got the Health and Human Services policy change added to my remarks.

And then, I kid you not, the *literal* night before the gala, the news broke that the Obama administration was going to require all federal contractors to have antidiscrimination policies in place that covered LGBTQ people.

I wish I could say my first thought was for all the people whose lives would be improved by this new policy—and I promise that would sink in for me later—but at the time, I just thought to myself, *Shit! Now I have to revise my speech again!*

I rushed to get the text cleared again—just in time.

The gala was held inside New York's glamorous Gotham Hall. The historic nine-thousand-square-foot venue, with its spectacularly ornate stained-glass skylight, was giving Gilded Age opulence. Bruce Wayne would have fit right in. Surrounded by Democratic Party power brokers, I kept my eye out for President Obama. But I didn't run into him; nor was he backstage after I delivered my speech, even though he spoke directly after me.

Eventually, after all the speeches were over and everyone was mingling, an aide found me and took me up to meet him. "Mr. President, this is Geena Rocero. She spoke before you tonight."

In the flesh, Obama had an otherworldly, almost mythical charisma. He greeted me warmly with that big beaming smile of his. I had decided long ago what to say to him, but I wanted to make it seem natural. I didn't want to fangirl; I wanted him to remember the interaction. So I told him I knew the White House chef, Cristeta Comerford, and asked, "So, Mr. President, what's your favorite Filipino food?"

"I love chicken adobo," he said—and few words are more entertaining to hear Obama say in his distinct cadence than *ad-o-bo.*

I gushed about *lumpia* and *pancit,* prompting him to say, "Geena, you speak about transgender rights and Filipino food with equal expertise."

What impressed me so much about him was that even in the middle of meeting so many people, none of his responses seemed rote or wooden. He was completely in the moment with me, cool and col-

lected. Before I said goodbye, I had one last trick up my sleeve. I
pretended to be mad at him for updating his policies so fast that I had
had to keep revising my speech.

"Two new policies in two weeks? Really?" I said. "You're like a
nonstop Twitter feed!"

He threw his head back and laughed, and luckily, at that exact
moment someone snapped a picture of him. And now I have photo-
graphic proof that I made the president of the United States laugh.

In late 2014, nearly a year after I gave my TED Talk, I was invited
back to the Philippines—back to where it all started.

For years, an antidiscrimination bill had advanced in the Philippines' House of Representatives, but it had never made it through the
Senate, blocked by lawmakers who wanted to keep the country's
Catholic culture frozen in time. In light of the publicity my TED Talk
had gotten, Filipino LGBTQ organizations wanted me to speak about
trans rights to the legislature—along with other leaders, congressio-
nal representatives, and even Catholic bishops—so we could try to
move the needle on this key legislation.

It didn't matter to me if the bill wound up getting blocked again.
In the same way that I felt a patriotic duty to the United States to
speak about gender recognition policies around the world, I felt I
owed it to my home country to try to make it a better place for people
like me.

On the morning of December 2, 2014, I found myself in a Manila
hotel room, putting on a royal blue V-neck fitted sheath dress that
had been custom-made by one of my trans Filipina sisters. Tigerlily
was standing next to me, giving me a pep talk, just as she had when I
was about to step onto a pageant stage for the very first time all those
years ago.

"My Horse Barbie is back," she said, her voice full of that familiar pride, but I also heard a note of longing.

In a way, we had been on this journey together the entire time, even when we were an ocean apart. Geographically, our lives had taken different paths, but spiritually, we were both trying to make futures for the next trans generation.

By this time, I had spent months traveling the world speaking about trans rights, being recognized and addressed as a woman everywhere I went. But going back to the Philippines would be different. My *wa buking* powers were all but worthless there.

Still, I carried myself with pride as I walked toward the House of Representatives Building in Quezon City alongside Tigerlily and a few members of my old entourage. Years ago we had spent long nights goofing around at 24/7 eateries after pageants, and now here we were about to advocate for human rights legislation. It felt incredible to bring my pageant family into this space.

But as I approached the security gate to enter the building, a guard singled me out, suddenly crying out in a stern tone, *"Oy Oy dito po kayo pumasok sa pang lalaki!"*

He was trying to tell me to go through the men's section of the gender-segregated security entrance. Even though I looked like a Filipina Angelina Jolie that day, even though all my documents said "female," and even though I was literally there to speak about anti-trans discrimination, he wanted me to erase my identity by walking through the wrong section.

Time stood still. Here I was walking in, head held high, when one ignorant person tried to cut me down. In the humidity, my sweat felt like it was baking my brain. I had a choice: either quickly walk through the men's section to get it over with and be sure to enter, or stand my ground and risk being turned away. I was already stressed, so I chose the path of least resistance and walked toward the men's section. And then a few feet from the gate, I stopped. How would I be able to give my speech a few minutes after passively accepting discrimination, when I had the power and privilege to do something about it?

I turned on my heel and walked up to the guard. "Listen," I said. "I know it's your job, but . . . *look at me.*"

He tried to ignore me, but I wouldn't let him.

"The next time you see someone dress like a woman, who looks like a woman . . . *she is a woman!*" I said, then turned on my heel and walked through the women's entrance without a backward glance.

The bill didn't pass that year—and it still hasn't to this day. But I am enormously proud that I went back and spoke—and I continue to share a kinship with the trans people in the Philippines who are still fighting for a future where young girls like me don't have to fly away to be recognized for who they are.

I kept doing public speaking after 2014—and still do it now—but not at such a breakneck pace. That first year was absolutely exhausting.

I loved the work, but it was tiring. Progress was hard-won and easily reversed. But I knew I had a limited window to make an impact. I wasn't interested in running for office or working for a larger advocacy group. My strength lay in storytelling, so I needed to share mine where it could make a difference for as long as people wanted to hear it.

The following year, as I was preparing to leave a speaking event in Australia, I realized with a shock that my passport would expire in less than six months, which meant I wouldn't be able to board the first leg of my flight home. I sent a panicked email to my contacts at the State Department, who helped me secure a temporary passport a mere three hours later, but I'd already missed my flight.

The following day was my birthday, and I'd been looking forward to spending it back in the United States with Norman. But having once won a bridal pageant with toilet paper, I'd picked up a few skills—I was nothing if not adaptable.

My new flight itinerary had a long layover in Fiji, so I reached out to my friend Resitara, a Samoan *fa'afafine* goddess I had met through my advocacy work, to see if I could do any socializing while I was there. Resitara knew everyone; her network was fittingly oceanic in its vastness.

"Don't worry," she assured me. "I've got the girls for you."

When I landed, my new Fijian trans friends were waiting for me. Together, we took a two-hour taxi ride around the island to the quiet, white-sand Natadola beach near the Intercontinental Resort—a five-star experience without the five-star price. We laid down our sarongs and had a mini picnic, complete with tequila. Some tourists rode by on horseback and offered us rides, which we gladly accepted. Only hours before, I'd been stressed out of my mind about my travel plans, and now I was riding horses with fellow trans girls in Fiji on my birthday—a beautiful balm for a tired soul.

I've held on to experiences like these as ethnonationalism resurges worldwide, and as the Trump administration undid many of the gains made by the Obama administration. Perfect memories like my unexpected Fiji birthday remind me that trans people are a global family who can never be erased. Countries can try to suppress us. They can refuse to recognize us. But we are increasingly recognizing the light in ourselves—and realizing that we are powerful together. We have tasted too much freedom to ever go back to a life in the shadows.

25

PLAYMATE

HOW DO YOU TELL YOUR MOM YOU'RE GOING TO BE IN *PLAYBOY*?

Well, let me back up. First, you have to get into *Playboy*.

Near the end of 2018, I was nearing the end of my full-time modeling career. I had stopped going to castings and was doing only selective work that conveyed who I was and what I wanted to say.

In the initial aftermath of my TED Talk, I'd done a beauty campaign for a major department store. There had been an interview attached to the shoot, so I asked if we could discuss trans rights during my conversation. I had recently made international news, after all. "Maybe let's just focus on the skin care product," the interviewer told me. After that, I didn't like to model unless I could also spread my message. If you were booking me, you were also booking my story. There's only so much you can say about face lotion.

As my modeling career was winding down, I had one last major goal I wanted to cross off my list: posing in the iconic *Sports Illustrated* swimsuit issue. At the time, no trans model had ever appeared on the cover, but that didn't intimidate me. I was still riding that limitless post-TED high. I thought I would get to set a precedent and feel damn sexy doing it. Booking the swimsuit issue could be a career-defining capstone achievement.

My agent, Ron, emailed an editor he knew at *Sports Illustrated* signaling my interest but didn't hear back. The next week he followed up, and there was still no response. Using the same enterprising spirit that got me the job at *Inc.* magazine, I emailed them myself the following week. We heard nothing for a month, not even a polite rejection.

By December, I was disappointed. But when 2019 arrived, and we still hadn't gotten so much as an acknowledgment, I felt disrespected. This isn't me being full of myself; I had the kind of résumé that should at least have warranted a response.

At least tell me no, I thought.

One day Norman and I talked it out, and he told me that while it wasn't right, and he knew how important it was to me, it would help me move on if I accepted that it wasn't happening rather than clinging to the last shred of hope. I was sad, but he was right: I had done everything I could. Besides, I had done so many amazing things in my career. Did I really need this? I took a breath, made peace with my unrealized vision, and moved on.

Literally the next day I opened my Instagram and saw a direct message from *Playboy*. I thought for a moment that it wasn't real, but then I saw the blue checkmark next to the account name. I opened it. The message was from a woman named Kristi Beck who asked me point-blank if I wanted to be a Playmate, no audition necessary.

"I believe you have an important perspective to share and am eager to lend you our platform," she wrote. "I would love to hear your perspective and to include your point of view."

They wanted me. They wanted my story. I had been rejected by one brand only to be offered a platform with an even more iconic one.

Apparently when God closes a door, He opens a *Playboy*.

On a video call, Kristi told me more about the summer issue she wanted me to pose in, which would coincide with the fiftieth anniversary of the Stonewall Riots and the accompanying World Pride Celebration.

"It's going to be all about gender fluidity and sexuality," she explained. "We think you'd be perfect to represent the brand."

I would also set a precedent for *Playboy* as the brand's first transgender Asian Pacific Islander Playmate—and only the second trans Playmate in history. Two years earlier a French model named Ines Rau had become the magazine's first out trans Playmate. When asked in an interview if anyone had inspired her to come out, she said, "Yes, the one and only Tula." Tula had influenced so many of us.

A few weeks later, at a global *Playboy* conference in New York, I took Kristi and her team—Anna Kerns-Wilson, Shane Michael Singh, and Anna Ondaatje—to the Filipino restaurant Jeepney in the East Village. If I was going to get naked around these people, I wanted to see how comfortable they'd be on my home turf. We shared big servings of the coconut-braised pork belly dish Bicol Express, barbecued shrimp, roasted chicken, vegetables, and garlic fried rice. I acted like my silly self, joking that they didn't know who they had invited into their family. But they kept up with me—and weren't put off by my mischievous ways. I felt welcome with this crew. I could work with them.

So after plenty of negotiating about what I would do and how my images could be used, I said yes. Everyone—but especially Playmates—needed to read the fine print.

My first thought after transmitting the signed contract was *Oh, shit. How am I going to explain this to Mama?* The answer was simple: I wouldn't. Not yet. A tinge of that old Catholic guilt was resurfacing, even though I thought I had vanquished it forever. I had months before Mama would see the shoot. There would be time to tell her later.

Instead, I lost myself in the details. For the photography, we settled on the Miami-based husband-and-wife duo Wiissa. They shot almost exclusively on film, both still and video, relying on natural light and Super 8 cameras. The vibe of their work was a chic 1970s throwback inspired by music videos. I loved it.

Originally, we planned to shoot in the Philippines, but we had only a five-day window, so we needed to figure out how to re-create the environment in a limited time frame. Costa Rica was the best substitute we could find, so *Playboy* rented a two-story, three-bedroom indigenous-style home that had been handcrafted out of hardwood. The house, called the Beautiful Mermaid, was tucked away in the middle of a beachside forest in the Manzanillo, Limon, area on the Caribbean side of the country. The surrounding jungle spilled right onto a pristine beach, totally untouched, with no bars or tourists to be found. It was the perfect place to run around in the buff.

But I wasn't just thinking about logistics. I was also processing the precedent I was about to set. I felt proud, and absolutely sexy, to be featured in *Playboy*. Yes, a lot of it was about looking good—find me a model who *doesn't* take pride in that—but it was also about the opportunity to put my full trans self at the center of pop culture, where *Playboy* had been since the 1950s.

Marilyn Monroe had been on the magazine's first cover. In the 1960s, the magazine was at the forefront of the sexual revolution, advocating for reproductive rights, for global freedom of the press, for pleasure and agency. *Playboy* even published a letter to the editor about the dangers of antigay conversion therapy in March 1969.

All the major literary writers of the twentieth century had a *Playboy* byline. "The Playboy Interview," its iconic editorial sit-down, had featured everyone from Malcolm X to Martin Luther King, Jr., to Steve Jobs. Feminists like Betty Friedan, filmmakers like Stanley Kubrick, and musicians like Miles Davis had all been showcased in the pages of the magazine. I wanted to be a part of that cultural and intellectual legacy. When they asked me to write my own Playmate feature to accompany the photo shoot, I jumped at the chance to write myself into that history—especially because I knew I would be pushing *Playboy*'s trans representation forward once again.

Even though Tula was outed in a tabloid after appearing in a *Playboy* spread, the magazine invited her back in 1991, making her the first openly trans model to be photographed in its pages.

I thought about Tula, and of those gorgeous shots of her standing in a waterfall, wearing only high-waisted leopard-print bikini bottoms, looking at the lens with a sultry gaze. When Tigerlily showed those photos to me at age seventeen, they had expanded my vision of what would be possible for me as a trans woman. Now here I was, about to fly to Costa Rica and follow in Tula's footsteps. Moments don't get any more full circle than that.

An intimate team—only six of us—flew to the location in April 2019. We shot in two places: one was the beach by our rental, which was virtually deserted. The other was a gorgeous rocky area in a popular tourist spot, so we could shoot there only at off-hours when it was empty. I felt totally comfortable with my team, knowing that in the end the photographs would look chic and classy, with tropical backdrops and the kind of gorgeous detail only real film can render.

And even though I looked sexy as hell, what I'm proudest of is that I stayed true to myself. During our lunch break on the second day, while I finished eating, I made two bunny ears out of palm leaves using thin wires that I had brought with me, and then they shot me wearing them. It felt like they really wanted to capture my essence, not just my body.

The whole experience was such a far cry from when I first started modeling—back when I was still hiding, projecting whatever persona the photographer wanted to see, be it a bride or a boom-box-carrying babe. *Playboy* wanted to see everything I was about. I didn't have to explain myself. They knew what I represented, and they wanted all of me: quirky but sexy, funny but serious when the occasion called for it, equally comfortable speaking to politicians and prancing around fully nude on the sand. I wasn't a walking contradiction; I wasn't one or the other. I was an amalgamation of so many things, all of them bound up in the beautiful trans Filipina body I had come to embrace. Being in *Playboy* was personal. Being in *Playboy* was political. Being in *Playboy* was powerful.

When I was asked, for the accompanying article, who my role model was, I of course responded, "Tula." I said that when I first saw her, I thought, "Wow, if she could do it, maybe I can as well," adding that "I wanted to be as sexy, beautiful, and confident as she was."

I'm not sure anyone can live up to the incomparable Tula.

But on that Costa Rican beach, I gave it my all.

When I got back from the shoot, I decided I had to tell Mama.

There was no way to stop her from seeing the pictures now. On a video call, feeling more nervous than I had been in front of her in years, I told her, then watched apprehension wash over my Catholic mother's face in real time. "The shoot was beautiful," I assured her. "Very tasteful."

Still, there was a long pause. Finally, she said, "I trust you," which was the best response I could hope for.

I was grateful. But look, I also love making trouble.

The next time I saw Mama in person at a family gathering in San Francisco, I pulled out my phone. "Mama," I said. "I was waiting to tell you this in person. What I'm about to show you aren't my own photos, but I did want to show you some examples of the kind of poses I did at my *Playboy* shoot."

I held up my phone and watched her face turn as red as a stop sign. I showed her Photoshopped pictures I'd got online of celebrities she'd recognize, where they were fully spread-eagled in lewd poses.

"I wanted you to see that real celebrities have done this, too," I went on. "It's not just me."

"Glenda!" Mama stammered. "I need some water, Glenda."

My sister ran over, panicked, as Mama repeated "Oh my god. Oh my god," in a dazed voice.

Glenda looked at the phone, then turned to me. "Geena, please," she said sternly. "You have to tell her."

Mama *did* look like she was near to passing out. "Mom, I'm just joking," I said, and she started to breathe, her face returning to its normal color. And that's how you tell your mom you're going to be in *Playboy*.

In July 2019, shortly before my issue came out, I went to New York to speak about trans and nonbinary identities at the United Nations' first-ever high-level meeting on the subject. You might think I'd be self-conscious about having just done *Playboy* before speaking in front of ambassadors, but instead I called the UN and asked if *Playboy* could come and document my talk.

"We've never had *Playboy* at the UN before," my contact said. "Let's bring them in."

I was finished splitting up my life and putting each piece in a silo, even if it meant building some new bridges.

After the issue came out in August, I did a flurry of interviews. The precedent I'd set generated huge media attention, and I loved the platform it gave me to talk about trans rights and gender recognition. The article I wrote to accompany my Playmate shoot was even nominated for a GLAAD Media Award. *Playboy* had afforded me the opportunity to model as my full self, and I was taking full advantage of it.

But even as I felt celebratory about my shoot, I knew that the U.S.

Supreme Court was set to decide in a few short months whether Americans could be fired just for being transgender.

On October 8, as my *Playboy* publicity was winding down, the American Civil Liberties Union invited me to speak at a rally in front of the Supreme Court to support Aimee Stephens, the transgender plaintiff in the pending case who had been fired from her job at a funeral home after she began transitioning. I had already signed an amicus curiae, or friend of the court brief, on her behalf, but I wanted to lend my voice to her as well. I met Aimee briefly and, after I gave my remarks, watched her speak a few feet in front of me.

The scene on the steps was surreal. On one side were all the LGBTQ people gathered to support Aimee, flying trans and rainbow Pride flags high, holding protest signs aloft, their hearts full of hope for a future in which we could be who we are without retribution. And then, directly next to us, were loud far-right protesters trying to drown us out with their bigotry. They didn't care about constitutional originalism or anything like that—they just wanted us to suffer. They wanted us to be unemployable, afraid, and alone.

I wasn't new to being screamed at by haters, but this time it hit differently. When I got back home to New York, I entered a deep depression. Nothing made sense to me anymore. I didn't see any reason to look forward to the future if this was the kind of cruel opposition we were facing. I felt surrounded by cliffs on all sides, hemming me in, cutting me off from any sense of time or purpose. My mind grasped for some jolt of energy that could motivate me again—something that could launch me forward to the next chapter—but instead I just got even more entrenched in a rut.

I stayed in bed all day, every day, for weeks. Part of it was the crash that comes after a high. I had spent the last few years accomplishing major career milestones, and now they were behind me. But it was mostly the whiplash: One moment I was doing *Playboy* press, celebrated the world over for who I am, and the next, I was standing in front of a columned building in D.C., begging for the most basic rights. That disparity was so extreme I couldn't make sense of it.

It had been almost thirty years since Tula first appeared in *Playboy* as an out trans woman. Would it be another thirty before things finally changed for good?

I felt lost. I kept the blinds down so I could sleep through the days as well as the nights. Norman would check on me, sit next to me, caress my unwashed hair, hug me, lie down next to me, and tell me stories to remind me that I was loved. But apart from his visits, the only other interruption to my monotonous routine was the dinging of the microwave, letting me know my food was ready. I was in a dark place—maybe the worst since my panic attacks over being stealth.

Weeks passed. I canceled the birthday dinner we had planned in late October. November came. I was still stuck in bed. It wasn't until I realized that Mama's seventieth birthday was coming up that I started to climb out of my depression. Glenda, Rhomalyn, and I had planned a four-day Mexican cruise for her, and I knew I needed to be there. I couldn't bring my gloom onto that boat with me, not when Mama had given us all so much.

Seeing Mama in person again, being hugged by her, helped continue the healing process. I was reminded that the people closest to me were the ones who mattered most. As much as outside forces— like validation from *Playboy* and condemnation from protesters— affected me, the reality was that I still had family, both chosen and biological. I had Norman and Mama and my sisters and so many other people in my corner. Their love mattered. And allowing myself to feel their love mattered.

I would still have to fight for my rights and for others'—for what I believed in. I'm not the kind of person who lies down and gives up. But I realized on that cruise with Mama that I didn't have to fight all the time.

"Our rights movement is like a relay race," the late trans activist Monica Roberts once said. "The torch got handed to me at a certain point, and when it's time for me to pass it on, I'm just going to turn around and hand that torch back to the next generation."

Tula broke barriers for me so I could break barriers for someone else—and when the time comes, someone else can inherit my palm-leaf bunny ears.

Epilogue

ALL OF THE ABOVE

WHEN I GO BACK AND WATCH THE MUSIC VIDEO FOR JOHN LEG-
end's "Number One" today, I barely recognize the woman dancing in
silhouette behind the curtain.

Each move she makes is painstakingly deliberate and overly precise, a double meaning laced through every gesture. She knows that
she can't be uninhibited, can't truly let herself go, and so each sway of
her hips is slow, deliberate, and over-rehearsed. She looks like she's
trying to solve a math equation to figure out how to be sexy instead
of simply *being* sexy. I can tell this is a job to her, nothing more.

But there's another place you might have seen me dance, if only
for a split second.

The June after I delivered my TED Talk, I was asked to be the key-
note speaker at the Trans March during San Francisco Pride. For me,
it was a homecoming. Thirteen years before, I had flown from the
Philippines into SFO with no idea where life would take me, and now
I was coming back to a city where I had found my Filipino trans community, deepened my relationship with Mama, and made lifelong
friends.

But I was also coming back changed. I was coming back free.

The experience of sharing my transness with the world had taught me not that my dreams were wrong but that they came with costs. The paranoia and heartbreak of my stealth years had reduced me from a vibrant, proud, and unapologetic Filipina trans woman to a stranger. I wasn't Horse Barbie anymore; I was the sexy girl in the background of a music video. I almost lost myself, but then I found my way back to me.

The goofy girl who just liked to clown around with her friends, the young woman who sang along to Christina Aguilera with Danmark between puffs of a joint, the pageant queen and the baby of the family—she came back after TED.

That's the thing about trans joy: It can never be fully extinguished. People can try to narrow the possibilities for our lives, even end them, but our spirits will always expand to fill whatever space we are given. We will find the power in us.

The sun was beaming over Dolores Park on the Friday afternoon I spoke to the attendees of the Trans March, thousands of people stretched out across the gently sloped lawn, the grass rippling beneath a gentle breeze. Among the crowd were Mama, both my sisters, and my nieces and nephews, all of whom were watching me speak in public for the first time. It took so much self-control to stop from laughing through my remarks because my little niece Makaela was jumping up and down the entire time, agog at the sight of her silly auntie doing something so serious.

Only a few years ago, talking openly about being trans in front of thousands of people would have been a stress nightmare. Now it just felt beautifully surreal in the best way.

When I was finished, I hugged everyone I could find: Tita Aida from the Asia Pacific Wellness Center, march organizer Tracy Garza, and all my friends. My family came backstage to celebrate me, showering me with affection. My soul was already bursting with joy when music began to play, the happy chatter of thousands of trans people filling the space between beats, wrapping me up in a glorious wall of sound.

And I danced. I danced with the kind of joy I did when I performed "Pearly Shells" for my family, or when I was hanging out with Danmark, or when I totally let go with Norman, dancing under the moonlight on the night we met, and in Tulum, where baby sea turtles guided my rebirth. My smile wide, my hands flowing, my hair tousled, I was lost between sunbeams, blissful as the summer breeze.

Looking higher up the hill, I spotted a small camera crew approaching. I was confused for a moment until I saw Lana Wachowski and her wife, Karin Winslow Wachowski, directing the team.

"Geena, hi!" Karin said, introducing herself. They were filming the Netflix series *Sense8*. "Your dancing just looks so full of freedom. I was wondering if we could shoot a couple of minutes? I want to capture this joy that's emanating out of you."

For maybe the first time in my life, I wasn't worried about what the camera would see. I just agreed, looked at the lens, and kept dancing, my movements flowing as freely as they had before. It was like they weren't even there; I was still enveloped in the warmth, the joy, the music. And then the crew was gone, and I was still dancing, still surrounded by love. Aside from signing a release at some point, I didn't hear anything else about it.

The following year, when *Sense8* premiered, my phone started buzzing. People were tagging me on Instagram. Friends from Brooklyn all the way to Berlin were texting me: *"Oh my God, is this you?"* and *"Of course they got a shot of you dancing."*

I pulled up the opening credits and there I was at the one-minute-forty-nine-second mark, amid a montage of people experiencing moments of connection all over the world. It's a split-second shot of me dancing, sunshine glowing on my skin, my eyes crinkled up in a big openhearted grin. I looked happy—a complete 180-degree turn from how I danced in that cold, smoke-filled set when John Legend sang, "Now who is she?"

I was happy because I had finally answered that question.

For so much of my life, I threw myself headlong into one pursuit right after the next, trying on different identities and sometimes maintaining a dual one. I had been Assunta de Rossi and Horse Barbie, a Macy's girl and a Divas legend, a high-fashion model and a nine-to-five corporate climber. I had been Gina, Jani, and finally Geena with two e's, Mama's lucky kid and Papa's late-night confidante.

All those different personas were like suits of armor I put on to get through life's challenges. So many times I had to forge a path that was not laid out for me in a world that didn't want a trans Filipina immigrant to succeed. At the time, the fight felt desperate, frenzied, almost manic, as I sprang from one thing to the other. Maybe while reading this book, you've gotten whiplash from how often my life changed overnight, so imagine how confusing it was to live it! Often it took most of my mental energy just to make sense of my ever-shifting circumstances.

But now I look back at the turbulent, twisting river that was my life and realize that it healed me, too. I was healed through all of it. In the face of pain and rejection, no matter how much shame I felt or how many times my love was rejected, I kept growing. Each tumultuous chapter of my life taught me something new about myself, piece by piece, until I felt whole. Maybe there are less stressful ways to find yourself, but if there are, I don't know them—and perhaps that's what it means to be human: trying and striving until something sticks, then sloughing that off when it no longer suits you.

We are all of us works in progress, every draft of ourselves that has ever been written and all the versions of ourselves that haven't been sketched out yet.

So who am I? I'm all of the above. I am the "sun kid" selling *kala-*

may on the streets of Makati. I am little Bojojoy holding Papa's hand as he weeps on my bedroom floor. I am a pageant superstar, unbeatable when my magic horsey powers reach their peak. I am a fashion model and a public speaker, and I make the best damn chicken adobo you've ever tasted. I'm a partner, a daughter, a best friend; a spy, a Playmate, and an explorer. None of it has left me. All of it has accrued like sediment in the delta of that river, each memory a pebble that I can pick up between my fingers.

I think I spent so long thinking I had to be one version of myself, working and building toward some illusory ultimate *me,* because I was afraid to embrace my wholeness—until the risk of losing myself altogether was too great.

Writing this story has been a kind of therapy. At each juncture of my life, part of me wanted to erase what came before so I could survive my new surroundings. But when I went back and chronicled all of it, start to finish, I realized I wanted to keep every word. As I traced how I went from the femme child in the church choir to the stealth model riding the PATH train to the unapologetic advocate for trans rights, bridging the gaps between each era, I was finally able to acknowledge how much hurt I endured along the way, and to be more compassionate with myself. I went through it—but I *got* through it. And I'm not finished yet.

A lot has changed since that day I danced in Dolores Park. What felt like a heady, optimistic moment for trans people in America gave way to a presidential administration that seemed to delight in attacking us, then to years of discriminatory legislation aimed at the youngest and most vulnerable members of our community. The door that was opening in 2014—that moment of opportunity to center trans stories—now feels like it is being slammed back shut. It makes me angry, but above all it makes me want to care for those who come after me.

My favorite work these days is speaking at colleges and universities. It's more than just a job to me; it's a spiritual journey. I go onstage and tell my story, yes, but what I really cherish is the one-on-one time I spend with small groups of LGBTQ students, letting them ask me questions, joking around with them, and listening to them talk about their own dreams. Here they are, ages eighteen through twenty-one, seeing a proud immigrant trans woman of color from the Philippines speaking proudly about her journey, unafraid to share what she's experienced.

Many students ask me how I keep my drive and my optimism, because I'm still very much an optimist. I answer by telling them about growing up in the Philippines, where trans people have mainstream visibility but no political recognition. In a way, that's the reality many on the right are trying to bring about in the United States—a future where people like me are on TV and in magazines but not teaching in schools or using public bathrooms. I tell them that visibility is not the one and only answer, that we need equity and justice, too, and that the only way to survive while we push for change is to lean on one another.

Because what enabled me to survive in the Philippines—and not just survive but imagine bigger things—was the support I had from Tigerlily and my pageant family, who nurtured me and cheered me on for so long even after I moved away. To this day, they all still call me Horse Barbie. Their stories—the stories of my trans ancestors— are always there in my mind, whispers passed down through generations. It's these whispers that I carried with me across an ocean, then a country, and ultimately around the world: advice from Tigerlily, the story of Tula, and the legacy of the beautiful *babaylans,* my precolonial predecessors. They all live with me now.

Our stories can soothe with an almost meditative gentleness. And if we can just hang on long enough, they will one day reshape our reality. There is power in queer people recognizing and amplifying and documenting one another's voices, finding happiness among one another, and celebrating ourselves.

That's why, when young queer and trans people ask me about our nightmarish present, I don't tell them your problems will go away. I tell them that there is healing to be found in searching for joy, in processing your resentment for a world that rejects you, in accepting that *all* of being alive—the good, the bad, and the hateful—is part of a journey you don't get to do over. It will be difficult. It will be sad. I have the scars to prove it. But we will have one another—and you will have you.

Because no matter how scared you might feel—whether you're a trans kid or a ninety-year-old grandma—you have one of the most powerful things a person can wield: a story. A story worth sharing; a story worth living. You have a place in this vast tapestry of interconnected experience. Ecstasy and pain and romance and dream-making all belong to you just as much as they do anyone else. Find your place among these feelings. Dig deeper. Get hurt and keep going.

I am chapters that are still unwritten, and so are you.

Acknowledgments

THIS MEMOIR WOULD NOT HAVE BEEN POSSIBLE WITHOUT THE BE-lief, dedication, and hard work of so many people. In Filipino, we call this virtue *Kapwa:* an inner self shared with others. I have deep grat-itude to Jon Michael Darga, my book agent. Week after week, he sup-ported me in this journey from writing the book proposal to finding our best publishing partner. He really fought for me. And he likes my cooking. Thank you to David Kuhn for inviting me to be a part of the Aevitas Creative family. To Allison Warren, who never once thought that my ideas were too big or too wild, thank you for all your support and guidance.

To Katy Nishimoto, my editor at The Dial Press, cosmic coinci-dences brought us together, for real full circle, and when things like that happen, the ancestors are saying, go for it! Your guidance, humor, wit, and love made *Horse Barbie* the book that it is. Huge thank-you for creating a space for my story. Samantha Allen, you're the best col-laborator one could wish for. Thank you for helping me hone my writing, voice, and tone. I've learned so much from you. In moments when I wrote through tears, you allowed me to be, and when humor, particularly specific trans humor, flowed onto the page, I will always remember our nonstop laughter as if we'd just taken over the world with our wit.

Thank you to Whitney Frick, VP and editor in chief at The Dial Press, and Avideh Bashirrad, SVP and deputy publisher. Thank you to everyone on the publicity and marketing team: Maria Braeckel, Carla Bruce-Eddings, Debbie Aroff, and Jordan Forney Hill.

Rachel Ake Kuech, your book cover design captured my spirit. Thank you to my friend David Dougan for the cover photo and Tigerlily for handwriting my book title font.

Thank you to my managers Tara Timinsky and Matt Rosen, who see all my possibilities. America Ferrera for inviting me to contribute to her book *American Like Me,* which is how I met David Kuhn. Jennifer Rudolph Walsh, thank you, thank you for planting the seeds!

Thank you to everyone who listened month after month as I read my early drafts: Tommy McCall, Danmark Bantay, Tigerlily, Bing Morales, Grace Chang, Jose Antonio Vargas, Isabel Sandoval, Kate Stone, JP Moraga, Norman, my sisters Rhomalyn and Glenda, and my mom.

Allie Hoffman, my Gender Proud co-founder, you've been instrumental in my journey to finding my voice and purpose. Cameron Sinclair, without your trust and introduction, I wouldn't have been part of the TED Conference. Deep gratitude to the organizations that created space for me and inspired me to dig deeper and dream bigger: Summit Series, Dot2Dot, TED, Outright International, and API Wellness Center (SF).

Last but not the least, thank you to my friends who accept me for who I am. My Tao family, my Berlin crew, my San Francisco and Seattle fam, I love you.

Napakaraming salamat to my Tristar Garcia pageant family in Hulo, Mandaluyong, Philippines, for allowing this fifteen-year-old Horse Barbie to gallop further than I could ever have dreamed of. *Rampa Na! Kain Na!*

HORSE BARBIE

Geena Rocero

A BOOK CLUB GUIDE

Discussion Questions

1. How do the Philippines and the United States differ when it comes to trans rights? What about trans representation? What contradictions do you see in the ways each country treats its trans citizens?

2. "When I was growing up, Catholicism and trans beauty pageants inspired equal fanaticism," Geena writes. "No one really saw this as a paradox." What did you make of this?

3. What strengths does Geena develop from her time in the pageant world? How do they show up later in her life and career?

4. How does life change for Geena when she arrives in America? In what ways are things better? In what ways are they worse?

5. Geena is fortunate to have extremely supportive parents who accept—and even celebrate—her transness. How does her family's support bolster her?

6. Geena's language around coming out evolves as she does, from "disclosing" to "sharing." How does this linguistic shift reflect Geena's internal one?

7. Who does Geena consider the members of her chosen family and trans sisterhood? How do they support one another?

8. Discuss how Geena changes after she starts unlearning the colorism she was raised with, and learning about decolonization and the history of her ancestors?

9. Seeing the sea turtles in Tulum represents a turning point for Geena: She decides to come out publicly, once and for all. What factors into this decision? What was Geena risking by deciding to live her truth out loud?

10. How do the trans women who came before Geena inspire her to keep going?

11. Watch Geena's TED Talk, "Why I Must Come Out." What was it like to watch, knowing what you now know?

A Conversation with Geena Rocero

Originally published in *Harper's Bazaar* as
"Geena Rocero Celebrates the Multiplicity of Trans Identities,"
by Meredith Talusan, printed with permission

GEENA ROCERO HAS BEEN TELLING HER STORY AS AN OPENLY trans, Filipino-American model since giving a TED Talk in 2014 that went viral. That video turned her into a leading trans advocate and activist overnight. In her new memoir, *Horse Barbie,* Rocero takes us on a vivid journey, from the gay pageant scene in Manila, capital of the Philippines, to the New York City modeling industry, from a life of intense isolation and secrecy to one of advocacy and community.

Throughout that journey, the spirit of the "Horse Barbie" guides and buoys her. What started as a mean nickname from the pageant scene became, for Rocero, a symbol of a wild, gender-nonconforming spirit that has been part of Philippine indigenous culture for generations, even as Filipinos like us absorbed and made American culture our own through nearly half a century of Western colonization. The result is a trans woman who is unafraid of being brazen, confident, and honest about who she is and what she stands for. I had the opportunity to interview Rocero over Zoom a few weeks before *Horse Barbie*'s publication.

You wrote this about the moment you were about to take the TED stage: "It wasn't lost on me that I might be the only trans person in that room. Hopefully my talk could change that." The first article I wrote about being trans was in response to your talk, so I'm one of the living embodiments of your words. How do you feel about the fact that there are so many people who were inspired to live our lives publicly as trans because of you?

We're starting with this? (Tearing up.) You're making me all emotional here; I thought we were just going to have a kiki. It's all this crazy full circle. I literally just got back from the TED conference last week. And it was my first time back since my TED Talk. It's particularly emotional because I was so afraid of doing that talk. I knew I wanted to do it because I was suffering. It was really the mental anguish that I was feeling of having to—I was done hiding. I was done having to manage two realities in my life, this paranoia that made me sick, that made me exhausted all the time, having to carry the burden of my secret. People at TED came up to me and said things like, "Your talk in 2014 was the most memorable" or "Your talk, I've shared it to a young, trans niece that I have that's coming out." I just get really emotional. I wanted to free myself, and to hear from people like you. Knowing my story freed other people too, it makes me feel good.

How does telling your story in book form feel, after telling it at TED and in other ways?

This book is my way of processing what happened after that TED Talk, because I went from super stealth, super afraid, and then I went viral. And that launched me everywhere, right? I went from being afraid, worried, paranoid, to swinging to the other side, an unapologetic trans woman. I worked with the UN, President Obama's State Department, traveling the world, going back to the Philippines. This book was my way to process what happened in that in-between and to dig deeper. Even just giving the TED Talk—I had never given a public speech before, but I had been on pageants before. I was the diva in pageants. I remember standing on that stage, and that Horse Barbie spirit came back off that pageant scene. I borrowed elements of it, the inner desire to share something. Writing this book allowed me to go back there, trace my family, trace the relationships I've had, from my dad, from my mom, to my trans mother, Tigerlily. All of those things led me to where I am right now. Each chapter is written sort of as the different identities I've inhabited. And there's a lot of them.

You write about *babaylan,* who were priestesses and trans shamans from our indigenous traditions. Can you talk about where that spirit comes from and how it moves through you when you experience it?

I am well aware that being onstage, I carry with me this long history of precolonial trans identities, genderfluid in spirit, gender-neutral in our language—though, on top of that, the forces of Spanish colonization. That's why we have religious fiestas. On top of that, the forces of American colonization. So I carry all of those with me. All of those things are me. All those complicated forces and nuances, they're all me. Having lived in the Philippines half of my life and half here in America, I will always be on that spectrum, and in that fluidity of perspective and analysis or spirit, notions of kapwa (community). I will always have that. It's so lively, the community aspect in the book, because I don't know anything else. American individualism was such a foreign concept for me. I was born in a poor, working-class background. I was always surrounded by people. It's this notion of community as something embedded in our culture. So, moving here in America at the beginning, certainly it was so confusing for me. This thing of Puwede na iyan, bahala na iyan *("It's fine; let's leave it up to the gods") is sort of speaking to notions of "Let's just be present here." Whatever the expectations of the gathering or an event or whatever someone is going through, in that moment when you just say, you know what,* "Puwede na iyan. Bahala na iyan." *Let's just be present here. This is what we have.*

Can you talk a little bit about what it was like for you during that stealth period, being alone, having to cut yourself off from communities you had formed in San Francisco, for the sake of protecting your privacy?

I made the decision to start writing the part that was most difficult to write, which was my time when I was stealth as a fashion model, because it was the most complicated moment in my life. It was both femme-affirming as a fashion model, but also the saddest, because I was not in touch with my trans pageant family. I left my best friend, Danmark, in San Francisco, and my trans family in San Francisco that took me in, that showed me the way. I had to leave all that behind. So thank God I had Erica as my one trans best friend who knew everything. And if I didn't have that, I don't know if I would have survived. Because I had to protect everything. Every single thing in my life was all about being vigilant and being limited and being calculating and editing everything, you know? That would drive some people crazy. It almost drove me crazy. So it was sad, but also, again, this complicated thing. Maybe it's this American individualism—I really want to be at the top of the game. I really have this ambition. *So I really needed to get through it. I needed to just put that aside. But I also know how sad that was.*

And lonely.

Very lonely. When I was joining trans pageants, I was always surrounded with fans, my trans pageant family. I always had people with me. So to compartmentalize that world, it was a struggle.

    I was in an industry that is all about the power of imagery. I was so visible, literally and figuratively, in all the senses of the word, but I was also at the same time consciously invisible. That's what I did.

It was really striking to me when you wrote about being in Indonesia and finding out how our languages are related. I wanted to ask you about this word *sulit*, which in Tagalog means *worthwhile* or *worth it*. But *sulit* in Indonesian means *difficult*, which feels like a great metaphor for the paradox of being trans. You describe your life as a trans woman as something difficult, a struggle. Do you think the struggle was worth it?

The most powerful thing we have is to understand the real power of what it means to be a trans person, particularly as someone who comes from a culture that's been colonized multiple times over. To truly understand, particularly the precolonial belief system and what it is that's always been there. It's in our blood, in our culture, in our language. It's in our spirit. And that power is so innate, but all these forces—media, political realities, cultural things, shame, masculinity, all of that—try to really bury that power from us. [For trans people of other cultures, you must] find that out on your own terms, go back to your history, unpack the myths, the stories, the expectations of your own culture, how you've been raised, how you've been taught, signals and messages that you've been brainwashed to believe. Because once I've pushed through it, I love being a trans Filipina. It is really my secret power.

This interview was edited for length and clarity.

Born and raised in the Philippines, Geena Rocero is an award-winning producer, director, model, public speaker, trans rights advocate, and television host. She was named by *Time* magazine as one of the "Top 25 Transgender People Who Influenced American Culture," and her TED Talk "Why I Must Come Out" has been viewed more than five million times and translated into thirty-two languages. Geena made history in 2020 as the first trans woman Playboy Playmate of the Year, and again as the first trans woman ambassador for Miss Universe Nepal. In 2020, she was honored on Gold House's A100 List of the most impactful Asians and Pacific Islanders. In *Vanity Fair,* she was featured as one of Gold House's AAPIs who are forging a new culture alongside Marvel film director Destin Daniel Cretton, *Crazy Rich Asians* director Jon Chu, the Academy's president Janet Yang, and many other trailblazing AAPIs. Geena's directorial debut, her limited series *Caretakers,* was nominated four times at the 65th Annual New York Emmy Awards held in October 2022.

*The Dial Press, an imprint of Random House,
publishes books driven by the heart.*

Follow us on Instagram:
@THEDIALPRESS

Discover other Dial Press books and
sign up for our e-newsletter:

thedialpress.com